CHANNEL SURFING

ALSO BY HENRY A. GIROUX

Ideology, Culture and the Process of Schooling [1981]

Theory and Resistance in Education [1983]

Schooling and the Struggle for Public Life [1988]

Teachers as Intellectuals: Toward a Critical Pedagogy of Learning [1988]

Postmodern Education: Politics, Culture, and Social Criticism
    (co-authored with Stanley Aronowitz) [1991]

Border Crossings: Cultural Workers and the Politics of Education [1992]

Living Dangerously: Multiculturalism and the Politics of Culture [1993]

Education Still Under Siege (Second Edition) (co-authored with
    Stanley Aronowitz) [1994]

Disturbing Pleasures: Learning Popular Culture [1994]

Fugitive Cultures: Race, Violence, and Youth [1996]

Counternarratives (co-authored with Peter McLaren, Colin
    Lankshear, and Mike Cole) [1996]

Pedagogy and the Politics of Hope: Theory, Culture, and Schooling [1997]

CHANNEL SURFING

RACISM, THE MEDIA, AND THE DESTRUCTION OF TODAY'S YOUTH

Henry A. Giroux

St. Martin's Griffin
New York

CHANNEL SURFING: RACISM, THE MEDIA, AND THE DESTRUCTION
OF TODAY'S YOUTH
Copyright © Henry A. Giroux, 1997, 1998.

ISBN 0-312-21444-8 paperback
Library of Congress Cataloging-in-Publication Data
Giroux, Henry A.
    Channel surfing : racism, the media, and the destruction
of today's youth /
    by Henry A. Giroux.
        p.   cm.
    Includes bibliographical references and index.
    ISBN 0-312-16265-0 (cloth) 0-312-21444-8 (pbk)
    1. Youth—United States. 2. Mass media—Social aspects—United
States. 3. Racism—United States. 4. Popular culture—United
States. I. Title.
HQ799.7.G57 1997
305.235—dc21   96-48009
                                                    CIP

Book design by Acme Art, Inc.

First published in hardcover in the United States of America in 1997
First St. Martin's paperback edition: October 1998

For Susan

CONTENTS

ACKNOWLEDGMENTS

Writing is always done in collaboration with the ideas and support of others. I want to thank Carol Becker, Lawrence Grossberg, Ann Wiens, Stanley Aronowitz, David Theo Goldberg, Glenn Harper, David Trend, Jon Epstein, Valerie Janesick, Joe Kincheloe, Shirley Steinberg, Donaldo Macedo, Roger Simon, and Pat Wilson for their warmth, comments, and support. I also want to thank Ron Chennault and Ken Saltzman for their enormous help in doing the research on many of these chapters. I am deeply indebted to Michael Flamini, my editor, for supporting this project from its inception. Thanks to Alan Bradshaw who could not have been more patient and helpful as the production manager. I also want to thank my students, who are always a great source of hope and education for me. And, of course, to my three wonderful boys: Jack, Brett, and Chris. Susan Searls, in spite of the enormous demands on her time, read and edited every page of this manuscript. This book is dedicated to her.

The following essays, which have been revised for this volume, have been previously published: "Something Comes Between Kids and Their Calvins: Youthful Bodies, Pedagogy, and Commercialized Pleasures," *New Art Examiner* (February, 1996), 16-21; "Playing the Race Card: Media Politics and the O.J. Simpson Verdict," *Art Papers* 20 (January/February 1996): 14-19; "Race, Public Intellectuals, and The Bell Curve Debate: The Crisis of Democratic Vision" (with Susan Searls), in *Measured Lies: The Bell Curve Examined,* eds. Joe L. Kincheloe and Shirley R. Steinberg (New York: St. Martin's Press, 1996), 71-90.

My main problem is to try to understand what happened to me. My trajectory may be described as miraculous, I suppose—an ascension to a place where I don't belong. And so to be able to live in a world that is not mine I must try to understand . . . what it means to have an academic mind—how such is created—and at the same time what was lost in acquiring it.

—Pierre Bourdieu

RACE AND THE TRAUMA OF YOUTH

> Youth is a material problem; it is a body—the individual
> body and the social body of generations—that has to be
> properly inserted into the dominant organization of
> spaces and places, into the dominant systems of eco-
> nomic and social relationships. As a body, it has to be
> located in its own proper places and its movements have
> to be surveyed and constrained. And as a body, its
> gendered and racial identities have to be neatly defined,
> its behavior regulated and its sexuality policed.
>
> —Lawrence Grossberg[1]

HEROIN CHIC, RACISM, AND THE CRISIS OF YOUTH

The bodies of youth are sprawled across the media in a public display of social disorder, laziness, menace, and aberrant promiscuity. Youth have been projected as a social problem second only to race-bound issues such as multiculturalism, welfare reform, and immigration. They are accused of leading the country into moral decline and tearing the fabric of the nation asunder, giving credence to the truism that how American society feels about youth is partly determined by how they are represented and imagined in popular narratives. Kids emotionally and intellectually define and create themselves in the same postmodern culture that presents (in the mass media, through its representations, discourses, and educational practices) their bodies as spectacle and threat.

Unfortunately the range of possibilities open for youth in the dominant media has become enormously limited. Demonized or trivialized, young people increasingly are portrayed in Hollywood films as either a social menace or as groveling dimwits patterned after the anti-intellectual histrionics of stars such as Jim Carrey and Chris Farley. If not demonized, youth are either commodified themselves or constructed as consuming subjects. In some cases, this commodification of youth pushes ethical boundaries: for example, the world of media advertising parades prurient images of youth across high-gloss magazines, appropriating the seedy world of drug abuse to produce an aesthetic that has been termed "heroin chic." Capitalizing on the popularity of heroin use in films such as *Trainspotting,* barely dressed, emaciated youthful models with dark circles under their eyes combine the lure of fashion and addiction with an image of danger and demonization.

American society increasingly produces and spreads through the media a hyped-up rhetoric of moral panic about the state of youth culture. Releasing itself from its obligations to youth, the American public continuously enacts punishment-driven policies to regulate and contain youth within a variety of social spheres. For instance, policy initiatives have shifted from social investment in youth to legislation primarily designed to contain and discipline them. This becomes clear as jobs disappear, public services in the inner cities are abandoned, and the criminal-justice system takes the lead in regulating large numbers of working-class and black youth.

Racism feeds this attack on kids by targeting black youth as criminals while convincing working-class white youth that blacks and immigrants are responsible for the poverty, despair, and violence that have become a growing part of everyday life in American society. Racism is once again readily embraced within mainstream society. As the gap between the rich and the poor widens and racism intensifies, neo-conservatives and liberals alike enact legislation and embrace policy recommendations that undermine the traditional safety nets provided for the poor, the young, and the aged. As the realities of high unemployment, dire poverty, bad housing, poor-quality education, and dwindling social services are banished from public discourse, white and black youth are offered a future in which they will be earning less, working longer, and straining to secure the most rudimentary social services. As American society reneges on its traditional promise of social and economic mobility for the marginalized and disadvantaged, it accelerates its war on the poor, immigrants, and blacks while simultaneously scapegoating the young as a substitute for addressing the economic and political factors that undermine the possibility for a multiracial society and the formation of broad-based political coalitions.

While it is imperative to understand the rise of racism and the current attack on youth within the context of past and current historical conditions, it is also crucial to experience one's relationship to the present from the inside, as part of an ongoing dialogue between oneself, the past, and the emergence of a present that dispenses with the obligation to remember. More specifically, it is crucial to remind oneself that any discourse about youth is simultaneously a narrative about the ideologies and social practices that structure adult society. Such narratives become useful educationally and politically when used to provoke and interrogate history—especially the history of the much-maligned sixties and the emergence of the often-celebrated Reagan-Bush period beginning in the 1980s—in order to enable the past to become part of a broader dialogue in understanding the current circumstances shaping the lives of young people. Of course, kids bear the burden of such a past more directly than adults do since they generally are in a much weaker position to modify or transform the effects it leaves upon their bodies and psyches. (This is not meant to suggest that kids bear the effects of generational attacks in the same way—effects vary depending on how one is situated in the class-race-gender intersection.) But the legacy of the culture of Reaganism does not merely limit the power of agency and sour the willingness of young people to transform the conditions they inherit; it also provides the educational grounds for memory-work, that is, individual and collective inquiries into how public memory about the sixties and the Reagan-Bush eras is written and used to legitimate the oppressive policies that currently frame the regulation of schools, courts, families, and the health professions.

The starting point for this book's memory-work is twofold. First, it begins with a recognition that the category of youth is constituted across diverse languages and cultural representations as well as racial and class-based experiences. Moreover, the multiplicity and contradictions that work within and across generations are both historically specific and subject to continuous change. Youth is a fluid historical and social construction as well as a space, location, and embodiment in which the personal and social intersect and give meaning to the particularities of individual and social differences. Second, it is personal and includes the recognition that understanding youth as lived experience demands, in part, an inquiry into the formative conditions of my own youth as it was lived out within the overlapping boundaries of racial and class divisions that fueled my entry into the sixties and later into the long march through the Reagan-Bush era.

This inquiry is not meant to be confessional. Instead, I want to reconstruct how my own experience of youth differs from that of a generation of contemporary working-class youth whose experiences occur within vastly disparate political, cultural, and economic conditions. Most notably, excavating my own experiences of youth prompts me to be attentive to how youth and the interface of race and class are signified and lived out differently across various historical conjunctures. For instance, memories of growing up in the late fifties and early sixties recollect for me a period of time that seemed more open, a period when dreams of social and economic mobility did not appear out of reach, as they do for so many young people today. On the other hand, race and class divisions in my youth were rigidly defined around most cultural, social, and political fronts. Today's youth confront a different set of circumstances. Nearly all working-class white and black kids face the threat of dead-end jobs, unemployment, and diminished hopes for the future. Moreover, they are located within a culture that is more porous, fluid, and transitory. Hip-hop culture, for example, reflects this, providing a style, language, and set of values, as well as diverse modes of behavior, that cut across racial and class divisions. Young people today live in an electronically mediated culture for which channel surfing, moving quickly from one mode of communication to another, becomes the primary method through which they are educated. Such conditions not only have refigured the class and racial landscapes of today's youth, but also have redefined how adult society names and treats young people at the end of the century. For example, the attack on youth and the resurgence of a vitriolic racism in the United States is, in part, fueled by adult anxiety and fear over the emergence of a cultural landscape in which cultural mobility,

hybridity, racial mixing, and indeterminacy increasingly characterize a generation of young people who appear to have lost faith in the
old modernist narratives of cultural homogeneity, the work ethic,
repressive sublimation, and the ethos of rugged individualism.

Youth as menace symbolizes both a collective fear and the
changing face of America—a change characterized by diverse public
cultures, racial spaces, languages, media cultures, and social relations.
Young people more than any other group appear to represent the
emergence of new forms of community, national identity, and
postmodern citizenship. The changing conditions that signify youth,
especially working-class white and black youth, have not been lost on
conservatives such as Allan Bloom, Jesse Helms, William Bennett, and
Bob Dole. Youth, in this discourse, have been shaped by what is
perceived as a serious moral and intellectual decline as a result of the
student movements of the 1960s and the leveling ideology of democratic reform movements that embrace multiculturalism, political
correctness, feminism, and other "anti-Western" influences. According
to conservatives such as Robert Bork, youth have been corrupted by
"tribal loyalties," "voguish nonsense," and "anti-rationalistic enter-
prises" that threaten to usher in "a barbarous epoch."[2]

RACIALIZED MEMORIES AND CLASS IDENTITIES

> How does a reconnection with a past practice support a
> disconnection from a present practice and/or a development
> of a new one?
>
> —Hal Foster[3]

As a young kid growing up in Providence, Rhode Island, I was always
conscious of what it meant to be a white male. Whiteness was a

defining principle shaping how I both named and negotiated the boundaries that my friends and I traveled when we went to school, played basketball in gyms throughout the city, and crossed into alien neighborhoods. Whiteness and maleness were crucial markers of our individual and collective identities; yet we were also working-class, and it was largely the interface of race and class that governed how we experienced and perceived the world around us. Of course, we hadn't thought deeply about race and class in a critical way; we simply bore the burdens, terrors, and advantages such terms provided as they simultaneously named the world and produced it.

In my working-class neighborhood, race and class were performative categories defined in terms of the events, actions, and outcomes of our struggles as we engaged with kids whose histories, languages, and racial identities appeared foreign and hostile to us. Race and class were not merely nouns we used to narrate ourselves; they were verbs that governed how we interacted and performed in the midst of "others," whether they were white middle-class or black youths. Most of the interactions we had with "others" were violent, fraught with anger and hatred. We viewed kids who were black or privileged from within the spaces and enclaves of a neighborhood ethos that was nourished by a legacy of racism, a dominant culture that condoned class and racial hatred, and a popular culture that rarely allowed blacks and whites to view each other as equals. Everywhere we looked segregation was the order of the day. Community was defined within racial and class differences and functioned largely as spaces of exclusion—spaces that more often than not pitted racial and ethnic groups against one another. Solidarity was mostly based on the principles of exclusion, and race and class identities closed down the promise of difference as central to any notion of democratic community.

When college students walked through my Smith Hill neighborhood from Providence College to reach the downtown section of the city, we taunted them, mugged them on occasion, and made it clear to them that their presence violated our territorial and class boundaries. We viewed these kids as rich, spoiled, and privileged. We hated their arrogance and despised their music. Generally, we had no contact with middle-class and ruling-class kids until we went to high school. Hope High School (ironically named) in the 1960s was a mix of mostly poor black and white kids, on the one hand, and a small group of wealthy white kids on the other. The school did everything to make sure that the only space we shared was the cafeteria during lunch hour. Generally black and working-class white kids were warehoused and segregated in that school. Because we were tracked into dead-end courses, school became a form of dead-time for most of us—a place in which our bodies, thoughts, and emotions were regulated and subjected to either ridicule or swift disciplinary action if we broke any of the rules. We moved within these spaces of hierarchy and segregation deeply resentful of how we were treated, but with little understanding, and no vocabulary to connect our rage to viable forms of political resistance. We were trapped in a legacy of commonsensical understandings that made us complicitous with our own oppression. In the face of injustice, we learned to be aggressive and destructive, but we learned little about what it might mean to unlearn our prejudices and join in alliances with those diverse others who were oppressed.

Rather, the everyday practices that shaped our lives were often organized around rituals of regulation and humiliation. For instance, the working-class black and white kids from my section of town entered Hope through the back door of the building while the rich white kids entered through the main door in the front of the school. We didn't miss the point, and we did everything we could to let the teachers know how we felt about it. We were loud and unruly in classes, we shook the rich kids down and took their money after school, we cheated whenever possible, but more than anything, we stayed away from school until we were threatened with being expelled. While race was a more problematic register of difference, class registered its difference through a range of segregated spaces. Along with the black kids in the school, our bodies rather than our minds were taken up as a privileged form of cultural capital. With few exceptions, the teachers and school administrators let us know that we were not bright enough to be in college credit courses, but were talented enough to be star athletes or do well in classes that stressed manual labor. Both working-class whites and blacks resented those students who studied, used elaborate, middle-class language, and appeared to live outside of their physicality. We fought, desired, moved, and pushed our bodies to extremes, especially in those public spheres open to us. For me, as a white guy, that meant the football field, the basketball court, and the baseball diamond.

As a working-class white kid, I found myself in classes with black kids, played basketball with them, and loved black music. But we rarely socialized outside of school. Whiteness in my neighborhood was a signifier of pride, a marker of racial identity experienced through a dislike of blacks. Unlike the current generation of many working-class kids, we defined ourselves in opposition to blacks, and while we listened to their music, we did not appropriate their styles. Racism ran deep in that neighborhood, and no one was left untouched by it. But identities are always in transit: they mutate, change, and often become more complicated as a result of chance encounters, traumatic events, or unexpected collisions. The foundation of my white racist identity was shaken while I was in the ninth grade in the last year of junior high school.

I was on the junior high basketball team along with a number of other white and black kids. The coach had received some tickets to a Providence College game. Providence College's basketball team had begun to receive extensive public attention because it had won a National Invitation Basketball tournament; moreover, the team roster included a number of famous players such as Lenny Wilkens and Johnny Eagen. We loved the way in which these guys played, and we tried to incorporate their every move into our own playing styles. Getting tickets to see them play was like a dream come true for us. Having only two tickets to give away, the coach held a contest after school in the gym to decide who would go to the game. He decided to give the tickets to the two players who made the most consecutive foul shots. The air was tense as we started to compete for the tickets. I ended up with two other players in a three-way tie and we had one chance to break it. As I approached the foul line, Brother Hardy, a large black kid, started taunting me as I began to shoot. We exchanged some insults and suddenly we were on each other, fists flying. Suddenly I was on the floor, blood gushing out of my nose; the fight was over as quickly as it started. The coach made us continue the contest, and, ironically, Brother Hardy and I won the tickets, shook hands, and went to the game together. The fight bridged us together in a kind of mutual esteem we didn't quite understand but respected. Soon afterward, we started hanging out together and became friends. After graduating from junior high school, we parted and I didn't see him again until the following September when I discovered he also was attending Hope High School.

I made the varsity team my sophomore year; I never knew why but Brother Hardy never bothered to try out. We talked once in a while in the school halls but the racial boundaries in the school did not allow us to socialize much with each other. But that soon changed. The second month into the school year I noticed that every day during lunch hour a number of black kids would cut in front of white kids in the food line, shake them down, and take their lunch money. I was waiting for it to happen to me, but it never did. In fact, the same black kids who did the shaking down would often greet me with a nod or "Hey, man, how you doin?" as they walked by me in the corridors as well as the cafeteria. I later learned that Brother Hardy was considered the toughest black kid in the school and he had put out the word to his friends to leave me alone.

During the week, I played basketball at night at the Benefit Street Club, situated in the black section of the city. I was one of the few whites allowed to play in the gym. The games were fast and furious, and you had to be good to continue. I started hanging out with Brother Hardy and on weekends went to the blues clubs with him and his friends. We drank, played basketball, and rarely talked to each other about race. Soon some of my friends and myself were crossing a racial boundary by attending parties with some of our black team-mates. Few people in our old neighborhood knew that we had broken a racial taboo, and we refrained from telling them.

I couldn't articulate it in those formative years, but as I moved within and across a number of racially defined spheres it slowly became clear to me that I had to redefine my understanding of my own whiteness. I had no intention of becoming a black wannabe, even if such an option had existed in the neighborhood in which I grew up and, of course, it didn't. But at the same time, I began to hate the racism that shaped the identities of my white friends. My crossing of the racial divide was met at best with disdain, and at worst with ridicule. Crossing this border was never an option for Brother Hardy and his friends; if they had crossed the racial border to come into my neighborhood they would have been met with racial epithets and violence. Even in the early sixties, it became clear to me that such border crossings were restricted and only took place with a passport stamped with the legacy of racial privilege. My body was relearning lessons of race and identity because I was beginning to unlearn the racist ideologies that I took for granted for so long. But I had no language to question critically how I felt nor did I understand how to reject the notion that to be a working-class white kid meant one had to be a racist by default.

The language I inherited as a kid came from my family, friends, school, and the larger popular culture. Rarely did I encounter a vocabulary in any of these spheres that ruptured or challenged the material relations of racism or the stereotypes and prejudices that reinforced race and class divisions. It was only later, as I entered the sixties, that I discovered in the midst of the civil rights and antiwar movement languages of dissent and possibility that helped me to rethink my own memories of youth, racism, and class discrimination.

In many ways, this book is an attempt to engage in a form of memory-work—exploring how I was positioned and how I located myself within a range of discourses and institutional practice—in which it has become clear that racial and class differences fueled by bigotry, intolerance, and systemic inequality were the disruptive forces in my life. My own sense of what it meant to be a white male emerged performatively through my interactions with peers, the media, and the broader culture. The identifications I developed, the emotional investments I made, and the ideologies I used to negotiate my youth were the outcome of educational practices that appeared to either ignore or denigrate working-class people, women, and minority groups. Popular culture provided the medium through which we learned how to negotiate our everyday lives, especially when it brought together elements of resistance found in Hollywood youth films such as *Blackboard Jungle* (1955) or the rock n' roll music of Bill Haley and the Comets, Elvis Presley, and other artists. Moreover working-class street culture provided its own set of unique events and tensions in which our bodies, identities, and desires were both mobilized and constrained. We were the first generation of working-class kids for whom popular media such as television played a central role in legitimating not only our social roles but also the limited range of possibilities through which we could imagine something beyond the world in which we lived. The trauma I associated with negotiating between the solidarity I felt with Brother Hardy and my white working-class friends suggests that education works best when those experiences that shape and penetrate one's lived reality are jolted, unsettled, and made the object of critical analysis. In looking back on my experience of moving through the contested terrains of race, gender, and class, it is clear to me that power is never exerted only through economic control, but also through what might be called a form of cultural pedagogy. Racism and class hatred are a learned activity, and as a kid I found myself in a society that was all too ready to teach it.

PERFORMATIVE INTERPRETATIONS
AS PEDAGOGICAL PRACTICE

Looking back at my own journey through a culture steeped in racist and class divisions, I feel that I was very fortunate to have had the opportunities to challenge some of the dominant cultural practices shaping my life. While the racial boundaries among contemporary youth are more fluid, young people today inhabit a society that is largely indifferent to their needs and makes them scapegoats for many of the problems caused by deindustrialization, economic restructuring, and the collapse of the welfare state. Those youth who have come of age during the culture of Reaganism that began in the 1980s increasingly are used as either bait for conservative politics—blamed for crime, poverty, welfare, and every other conceivable social problem—or "defined [largely] in . . . relation to [the] processes and practices of commodification."[4] The attack on youth, coupled with an insurgent racism in America, has transformed the popular sphere—of representations, images, and practices through which youth are constructed and experience themselves—into a battleground. Targeted as trouble and troubling, dangerous and irresponsible, youth face a future devoid of adult support, maps of meaning, or the dream of a qualitatively better life for their own families.

At the core of this book is the issue of how youth and race are constructed within new realities that offer both a warning and a challenge to all those concerned about furthering political and economic democracy in the United States. But this is more than a matter of naming or bringing to public attention the conservative attack on youth and the insurgent racism that parades without apology across the American landscape. There is also the matter of what Jacques Derrida calls "performative interpretation." That is, "an interpretation that transforms the very thing it interprets."[5] As an educational practice, "performative interpretation" suggests that how we understand and come to know ourselves and others cannot be separated from how we are represented and imagine ourselves. How youth and race are imagined can best be understood through the ways in which pedagogy weaves its "performative interpretation" of youth within all those myriad educational sites and electronic technologies that are redefining and refiguring the relationship among knowledge, desire, and identity. Youth and racial identity are constituted within and across a plurality of partially disjunctive and overlapping communities. Such communities or public spheres offer creative critiques and possibilities even as they work to constrain and oppress youth and others through the logic of commodification, racism, and class discrimination. This suggests reclaiming the political as a performative intervention that links cultural texts to the institutional contexts in which they are read, critical analysis to the material grounding of power, and cultural production to the historical conditions that give meaning to the places we inhabit and the futures we desire.

Channel Surfing is an attempt to understand how constructions of youth and race function within and across the media as educational and political discourses. At stake here is more than simply providing a critical reading of different cultural texts. On the contrary, I am more concerned about how such texts contribute to our understanding of the educational and political role of cultural spheres that often are treated as if their only purpose is to entertain or promote the latest consumer hype. Central to this concern is how such spheres can be rearticulated as crucial educational sites actively shaping how youth are named and produced in this society. Youth in this instance becomes more than a generational marker; it also becomes an ethical referent reminding adults of their political, moral, and social responsibility as public citizens to address what it means to prepare future generations to confront the world we have created. The growing demonization of youth and the spreading racism in this country indicate how fragile democratic life can become when the most compassionate spheres of public life—public education, health care, social services—increasingly are attacked and abandoned. Part of the attempt to undermine those public spheres that provide a safety net for the poor, children, and others can be recognized in the ongoing efforts of the right to "reinstall a wholly privatized, intimate notion of citizenship."[6] In the new world order, citizenship has little to do with social responsibility and everything to do with creating consuming subjects. Such a constrained notion of citizenship finds a home in an equally narrow definition of education that abstracts equity from excellence and substitutes a hyperindividualism for a concerted respect for the collective good. While the immediate effects of this assault on public life bear down on those most powerless to fight, the greatest danger will be to democracy itself—and the consequences will affect everyone. Now is the time for progressives, educators, and community members to address these critical issues and to once again assert that education for critical citizenship is, in part, about assuming responsibility and bearing witness, combining intellectual rigor with social relevance, and sustaining those public spheres where democracy can flourish and sustain itself.

The first section of this book focuses on how youth are both scapegoated and commodified in the world of advertising and Hollywood films, with specific analyses of the recent controversial Calvin Klein Jeans advertising campaign and Larry Clark's film *Kids*. In Chapter 3, specifically, I examine how the rebellious culture of the sixties has been appropriated by conservatives to demonize young people and how its legacy might be useful in understanding the despair, exemplified by the death of Kurt Cobain (and more recently Tupac Amaru Shakur), that is developing among large segments of young people.

In the second section of the book, I examine the emergence of the new scholarship on whiteness and its implication for refashioning the meaning of racial identity in oppositional terms; I also look critically at the media hype over the rise of black public intellectuals in the United States and how this topic has been constructed within a largely white press. Next, I focus on the racially divided response to the outcome of the legal trial of O. J. Simpson. Finally, I examine the resurgence of race talk in the highly publicized book, *The Bell Curve,* and examine its reception and public success as symptomatic of the growing crisis of democracy and racial justice that plagues the United States.

The two sections of the book are connected by a consideration of how race and class are coded as powerful normative and political categories shaping contemporary youth. For example, as the discourse on youth shifts from an emphasis on social failings in the society to questions of individual character, social policy moves from the language of social investment—creating safety nets for children—to the language of containment and blame. Instead of talk about eradicating poverty, building decent schools, creating viable jobs, and establishing affordable housing for young people, conservative and liberal policymakers invoke the punitive-driven demand for building more prisons and sending the children of unwed teen mothers to the Victorian workhouse. Against the image of demoralized and dangerous working-class, urban youth, public officials invoke the mythic morality of the Cleaver Family and moral panics over living with cultural and racial differences. This book marks a tentative and partial attempt to bring critical attention to the class and racial divisions that bear down on young people and circulate through a politics of representation in the broader culture. Moreover, it offers an educational and political challenge for progressive cultural workers and others to rewrite the narrative in which race, youth, and class are currently being constructed in the United States. Such a challenge represents one small step in provoking, disrupting, and challenging those representations and institutional forms of power that are waging a sustained attack on all levels of public life. This is not merely a theoretical or textual problem, but one that invokes the need for social movements to seize the initiative in recovering the space of democracy as more than a formalistic ritual or an instrument of free market logic. The attempt to expand relations of democratic practice across economic, political, and cultural spheres is less an expression of utopian desire than an urgent challenge for all cultural workers to reclaim the promise of democracy for the lived majority of citizens, especially those who traditionally have been excluded and who stand on the frontier of a future that has yet to be envisioned in a language of critique, racial and social justice, and possibility.

SECTION I

FASHION, DEMONIZATION, AND YOUTH CULTURE

SOMETHING COMES BETWEEN KIDS AND THEIR CALVINS
YOUTHFUL BODIES AND COMMERCIALIZED PLEASURES

A merican youth face a world of increasing poverty and unemployment and diminished social opportunities. They have few opportunities to make their voices heard as they witness a growing culture of violence, with its assault on public life, deterioration of cities, and seeming indifference toward civil rights. At the same time, their collective image stands as a reminder of lapsed social responsibility, a disturbing sexual presence, and a symbol of powerlessness. As such, youth become an easy target for a public discourse in which the dual strategies of scapegoating and commodifying take on the proportions of a national policy and minor revolution in the media.

In the profit-driven world of advertising and fashion, the image and culture of youth are appropriated and exploited for the high pleasure quotient they evoke. The body in this fashionscape does not represent the privileged terrain of agency, but serves as a site of spectacle and objectification, where youthful allure and sexual titillation are marketed and consumed by teens and adults who want to indulge a stylized narcissism and coddle a self that is all surface. In this public sphere of simulated yearning and sexualized images, advertisers inventively present the fragmented bodies of youth as the site where pleasure, desire, and commodification intersect in a commercial display "that fetishizes and marginalizes the body as the locus of spectacle."[1]

A recent, highly publicized example of this is the controversial 1995 Calvin Klein Jeans advertising campaign. In these images, photographed by Steven Meisel, young models are presented in various stages of undress, poised to offer both sensual pleasure and the fantasy of sexual availability. In a departure from the signature black-and-white photography and self-conscious artistry of Calvin Klein's high-end product advertising, the young models are set against a backdrop of dated purple carpeting and wood-paneled walls, rife with connotations of a particular class and lifestyle. In these advertisements, coquettish girls flash their breasts and white panties, and lounging boys display black nail polish, tatoos, and bulging briefs.

The images of these kids resonate with a cultural perception of the sexuality of poor, white, urban youth. In the televised ads, a low, gravelly off-camera voice prods the kids with questions such as: "Do you like to take direction?" and "Ya think you can rip that shirt off ya? That's a nice body. You work out? Yeah, I can tell," evoking the dialogue of a low-budget porn flick. The ads present a romanticized vision of the dangerous and seedy world of desperate kids on the make; the youthful bodies portrayed suggest kids who are powerless and poor, perhaps forced to negotiate their sexuality as the only currency they have to exchange for profit or the promise of glamour. These images not only test the limits of using sexuality to sell jeans; their use legitimates a "hip" promiscuousness and invites the "most intrusive of gazes."[2] I would argue that this advertising campaign is symptomatic of a broader representational struggle being waged against youth, one that needs to be understood for both the political and pedagogical lessons it can provide for artists, educators, and other cultural workers.

Current representations of youth need to be addressed as part of a broader struggle over how "technologies of power produce and manage . . . the individual and social body through the inscription of sexuality" by means of the pedagogical machinery of advertising and consumer culture.[3] Within such pedagogical practices, the bodies of youth are no longer seen as the privileged site of moral and political agency. Scorned as a threat to the existing social order, working-class and inner-city black youth are pushed to the margins of political power within society. Increasingly denied opportunities for self-definition and political interaction, youth are located within a range of images that largely disavow their representational status as active citizens. The current assault on youth increasingly takes place through a media culture whose educational functions are often ignored. In this case, the Calvin Klein ad campaign represents a provocative example of cultural pedagogy that attempts to educate young people about what to think, believe, desire, and feel and how to behave. By questioning the educational practices at work in advertising and other cultural spheres, progressive cultural workers can begin to challenge the representational politics used to frame, commodify, and exploit the social formation of youth.

One wonders which social groups were considered the target market for this suite of Calvin Klein's ads. Is it working-class youth—youth who can barely afford Calvin Klein's merchandise—who are meant to find themselves in the images of the hustled? Or is it a more elite social group, who might view the working class as an exotic other, that is meant to be titillated by the fantasy of sexual slumming? The ads resonate with a broader conservative politics in which one-dimensional and ahistorical representations of youth erase the complexities and contradictions of place, style, language, and individual histories. Without these complexities, the social formations at work in the shaping and reshaping of societal subjectivities, desires, and needs magically disappear.

The controversial Calvin Klein advertising campaign was met with a swift and uniformly critical response. Angry critics—including parents, social-welfare groups, conservative politicians, and President Bill Clinton—called the images suggestive and exploitative and condemned Calvin Klein for using children as sexual commodities. Other critics likened the ads to child pornography. The public outcry eventually prompted the Justice Department to launch a Federal Bureau of Investigation inquiry to determine if the advertising campaign had violated any legal statute by using underage models. No evidence was found and the investigation eventually was dropped, but the massive public criticism forced Calvin Klein, Inc., to halt the advertising before its scheduled end.[4]

Many critics, artists, and activists have correctly pointed out that advertising images of seminude youth are not new, certainly not in Calvin Klein's campaigns—after all, jeans, perfume, and underwear commercials featuring Brooke Shields, Kate Moss, and Marky Mark have helped to situate the designer's "corporate image right on the razor edge between propriety and titillation."[5] Many of the same critics have argued that critical responses to the Calvin Klein ads are less about the rights of children than about the hypocrisy exhibited by right-wing conservatives who rally around the sanctity of family values when attempting to enact antipornography legislation (which would undermine First Amendment rights) but (with President Clinton's assent) pass federal legislation that adds over a million children to the poverty rolls, eliminates basic health care coverage for seven million young people, and disadvantages fourteen million additional children as a result of cuts in federally funded food and nutrition programs.[6]

"Family values" in this scenario becomes a metaphor for legitimating "the systematic denigration, stereotyping, and stigmatizing of millions of poor women and their children."[7] Similarly, antipornography legislation has been used by many conservatives to reinforce rigid gender roles and particular interpretations of sexuality, attack lesbian and gay civil rights, and eliminate progressive sex education programs in the public schools. From this view, the attack on Calvin Klein's ad campaign is seen as an opportunistic political strategy to undermine artistic freedom and promote political censorship.

Camille Paglia added another twist to the criticism surrounding the ads. Paglia took Calvin Klein to task for portraying the models as looking "caught and caged by manipulative, jaded adults" and for trivializing the "pedophiliac homoeroticism [that] suffuses the Western high art tradition." Paglia complained that "if Klein and Meisel want to borrow the iconography of pedophilia, they should have the courage to step forward to admit it."[8] Missing from this analysis, however, is any mention of power, ideology, human rights, or the historical legacy of child abuse in the interests of capital. Also absent is any challenge to representations of youth that reinforce a commodified and thus fragmented notion of the body or any exploration of the limitations that should be placed on fulfilling desire that is based on exploitation, degradation, and domination. On the contrary, Paglia narrowly defends an aesthetics that, posturing as a liberated politics, supports the homoerotics of pedophilia. But she has nothing to say about either the needs/rights of children or the glamorization in the mass media of a not-so-hip violence in which kids are sexually preyed upon by adults.

By focusing exclusively on representations of children as sexual objects, Paglia situates youth within a representational politics that links their bodies solely to the virtues of other people's pleasure and consumption. This is exactly what Calvin Klein does, but Paglia seems unaware of the convergence between her defense of aesthetic representations of pedophilia and Klein's cultural politics of depicting the body for voyeuristic consumption and financial profit. Similarly, if the overt commodification of young children can be dealt with so irresponsibly, it seems conceivable that fashion companies such as the Gap, Esprit, Levi Strauss, Benetton, and others who promote themselves as "socially responsible" have little to worry about in attracting public attention, especially from intellectuals like Paglia, over violating child-labor laws.[9] Kathie Lee Gifford's remorse over discovering that her Wal-Mart clothing line was being produced in sweatshops by overworked and underpaid kids testifies less to her sense of social responsibility than it does to the refusal of a public to acknowledge the other dirty little secret regarding how the fashion industry engages in child abuse.[10] The commodification of children in ads such as those produced by Calvin Klein makes it easier for the public and the fashion industry to believe that the commodification of child labor has little to do with morality because it is about aesthetics, art, and fashion.

Eluding such connections comes easily for industry apologists parading as cultural critics. For instance, among Calvin Klein's defenders, Dave Mulryan, a partner at Mulryan/Nash Advertising, likened the campaign to a moving target on which the blame for all of society's ills was being pinned. "People are concerned about teens having sex, but instead of focusing on the real problem, they're attacking the fictional portrayals in such movies as *Kids* and in advertising like Calvin Klein's."[11] Michael Musto, writing in *Artforum,* proudly proclaimed that the ads "were the most delicious media event of the year" and that "Bringing teenage sexuality to the front half of everyone's brains, they pushed buttons and made people livid, the way a great, nasty, confrontational ad campaign should. . . . I considered them a major breakthrough in advertising in front of which I sat in awe."[12] It seems that Musto defends the use of children's sexuality as a vehicle for commercialism through an appeal for the freedom of visual representations. Seemingly indifferent to the operations of power that hide behind advertising's use of images of children within a stylized aesthetics, Musto ignores how representations of sexuality work as part of a broader public discourse in which children's bodies are defined exclusively through "the commercial imperative of spectacle, commodification, and objectification."[13]

My concern with such representations of youth lies not in deciding whether they are "good" or "bad" but in analyzing them in relation to the pedagogical work they are doing. That is, what knowledge, values, and pleasures do such representations invite or exclude? What particular forms of identity, agency, and subjectivity are privileged, and how do they help to reinforce dominant reactions, messages, and meanings? What do they say about the representers, the context in which they are produced, and the meanings they circulate? What do such representations say about the relationship between children's bodies and the AIDS crisis, the use of drugs by young children, the disciplining of children's bodies by any number of authority figures, or the symbolic violence waged by Hollywood films that present, in graphic detail, the bodies of young, inner-city black youth steeped in violence and stylized gore? Situating Calvin Klein's ads in the broader assault being waged against subordinated youth makes it clear that kids are one of the most visible targets for neglect, exploitation, commodification, and abuse by adults. These ads do more than play on our fear about the loss of innocence; they provide images of teens that resonate with current right-wing attacks on youth, who become symbols of menace, aberrant promiscuity, and social degeneracy.

Calvin Klein publicly responded to criticisms of his jeans campaign by issuing an advertisement in the *New York Times* in which he argued apologetically that the ads were meant to convey a media generation of youth who are savvy and "have a real strength of character and . . . strongly defined lines of what they will and will not do—and have a great ability to know who they are and who they want to be."[14] One wonders: How are strength, character, and independence represented in pictures of Marky Mark clutching his crotch, or in images of bare-breasted young women exhibiting their underwear while posing suggestively?

In an interview in *New York* magazine, Klein compared himself to Larry Clark, the photographer and director of the feature film *Kids*.[15] Klein justified the ads on the grounds that he, like Clark, used unaffected kids to represent to an adult world something that was both real and frightening; that is, a youthful sexuality that lacked artifice. Klein appropriates the goals and rhetoric of realism as a pedagogical tool to inform society about the supposed desires of and possibilities available to young teens. But Klein's, and Clark's, claim to a lack of artifice rings false. This is a realism that is all surface, without context, voyeuristic. It peddles a hollow aesthetic defiance, refusing to address how kids might narrate themselves rather than yield to the power of adults such as Klein, who markets kids in the image and fantasies of adult drives and desires.

In the slick world of advertising, teenage bodies are sought after for the exchange value (or profit) generated through the marketing of adolescent sexuality, which offers a marginal exoticism and ample pleasures for the largely male consumer. Commodification reifies and fixates the complexity of youth along with the range of possible identities they might assume while simultaneously exploiting them as fodder for the logic of the market. This may not be pornography, but it has little to do with civic virtue or the responsible construction of youth identities within a broader project of substantive citizenship and civic responsibility.

When situated within the broader context of social and political life, Klein's transgressive images fail to challenge dominant, conservative codings of youth as sexually decadent, drug-crazed, pathological, and criminal. Representations of youth in Klein's ads are reduced to aesthetics, style, and promotion; such images lack the mediating mechanisms of historical reflection or critical analysis and fail to challenge conservative depictions of youth. In fact, Calvin Klein has more in common with Newt Gingrich and the family values crowd than he realizes. Moreover, both Klein and Gingrich privilege market values over human value. That is, both ideologies subordinate human needs to the laws of the free market, with its endless drive to accumulate profit, and ignore, if not undermine, the notion of social responsibility and the reinvigoration of democratic public life. Those artists, educators, and cultural workers who defend Klein in the name of artistic freedom run the risk of simply retreating, as Andrew Ross argues, into a "safe haven [that] is simply a quarantine zone, in which artists [and others] are not only immune from public accountability but are also excluded from public dialogue."[16]

This is not, however, meant to suggest support for the right wing's empty call for censorship. For many on the right, attempts to censor the media primarily serve as a way of keeping the progressive social agenda (institutional, material, and political) out of the discussion for social change. For progressives, discussing the limits of public representations, especially regarding children, would be a way of analyzing underlying economic, political, and social concerns while reinvigorating the possibility for public debate and political action.

However, there is a curious lack of such rigorous discussion—if not outright silence—from progressive and other radical cultural workers about the ways in which children and sex are portrayed in advertising and other forms of media culture in general. Often demeaning and sexually prurient in their portrayal of young teens, such stylish jeans ads are found not only in the fashionscape world of Calvin Klein, but also in the advertisements of Guess?, Gap, Buffalo, and Benetton; moreover, such representations also abound in Hollywood. Consider films ranging from *Lolita* in the 1960s to the more contemporary *Interview with the Vampire,* with its portrayal of a nine-year-old vampire girl who exhibits the sexuality of an adult, or *The Professional,* which casually narrates the sexually charged attraction between a cold-blooded hit man and the twelve-year-old Lolita-ish girl he befriends.

The primary issue is not whether such images of children might be labeled pornographic or invite questionable pleasures in their audiences. On the contrary, the more interesting issue, educationally and politically, is how such images in the media work to purge desire of its constitutive possibilities (desire as more than pathology and as an enabling force for love, solidarity, and community), portray the bodies of urban youth as dangerous, and celebrate an excessive hedonism that rejects personal and social responsibility. What is refused in such representations as the Calvin Klein ads is the ethical imperative for educators, artists, and other cultural workers to provide complex images, ideas, narratives, and sites of struggle where youth can invest in a sense of commitment and possibility.[17]

If media culture is to become a vibrant sphere that enables debate, dialogue, and critical education, parents, educators, and other concerned citizens need to reclaim a progressive cultural politics that refuses to cede the terrain of ethical and educational discourse to right-wing conservatives. More specifically, it is crucial for artists, educators, and others on the cultural left to see that popular representations of children are social discourses grounded in public struggles and often tied to corporate interests. A critically informed citizenry needs to raise questions regarding whose point of view is being legitimated by such representations, what pleasures/desires are being mobilized, and what the limits of such pleasures might be in terms of how they play out in public life. Within the visual and aural world of popular culture, cultural progressives must be willing to make judgments about how certain moral scripts are being narrated and used to push back the possibilities of democratic public life.

Educationally and politically, young people need to be given the opportunity to narrate themselves, to speak from the actual places where their experiences and daily lives are shaped and mediated, such as alternative music spheres, neighborhood subcultures, mass-mediated electronic cultures, underground magazines, and other sites. Educators and others need to recognize the importance of providing opportunities for kids to voice their concerns, but equally important is the need to provide the conditions—institutional, economic, spiritual, and cultural—that will allow them to reconceptualize themselves as citizens and develop a sense of what it means to fight for important social and political issues that affect their lives, bodies, and society. Writing in *Spin,* columnist Eurydice goes right to the heart of the matter in arguing:

> Millions more kids are abused by silence than by leering pedophiles, and kids who are kept ignorant are kept exploitable. Our society retards the emotional growth of kids so their physical and psychological maturities don't coincide. Instead of scrambling explicit programming on cable and the Net, blocking the distribution of condoms at school, and in every way making it difficult for kids to act responsibly, we should give them charge of their bodies. In the nationwide discussion about protecting kids from the sickos who prey on them, the kids are missing. And by refusing kids our trust, we encourage them to refuse us theirs.[18]

As artists and educators, we must develop educational practices in which discourses and representations of the adolescent body in its relationship to others are mediated by considerations of power, politics, and ethics. Popular culture increasingly teaches kids to gaze inwardly at the body as a fashionscape, a stylized athletic spectacle, or as a repository of desires that menace, disrupt, and undermine public life through acts of violence or predatory sexuality. Young people need to become critical agents able to recognize, appropriate, and transform how dominant power works on and through them. To achieve this, they need forms of educational practice steeped in respectful selfhood that do not collapse social into personal problems or systematic oppression into the language of victim-blaming. In short, they need a pedagogy that provides the basis for improvisation and responsible resistance.

But any educational discourse about youth must take as one of its central concerns the ways in which authority and power are wielded by adults. This is particularly true for those aspects of public space where teens and other youth learn how to define themselves outside of the traditional *spheres* of instruction such as the school and the home. Learning in the postmodern age is located elsewhere—in popular spheres, organized around rap music, daytime television, fanzines, Hollywood films, sprawling shopping malls, and computer hacker culture, that shape young people's identities through forms of knowledge and desire that are absent from what is taught in schools.[19] The literacies of the postmodern age are electronic, aural, and image-based; it is precisely within this diverse terrain of popular culture that educational practices must be established as part of a broader politics of public life—practices that will aggressively subject dominant power to criticism, analysis, and transformation as part of a broader reconstruction of democratic society.

Of course, popular culture is contradictory; it is also responsible for unleashing a torrent of youthful creativity in the arts, public access radio, dance, video, film, underground journals, and computer bulletin boards. Education and politics can combine in a fruitful way to seize upon this creativity not simply as a hip aesthetic, but as a creative source for recovering an ethical discourse in which cultural justice and rights can be seen as integral to expanding and democratizing popular forms and public spaces. In this instance, there is no politics without pedagogy, and no pedagogy without a politics of critique and possibility. Similarly, this is not to suggest that reading cultural texts such as Calvin Klein's advertising campaign has no value beyond recognizing how they reinforce right-wing attacks on subordinate teens in the broader culture.

Finally, media culture must be seen as a source of cultural pedagogy in the dual sense. Educators and other progressives must not only provide students with the knowledge and skills to read the media critically, they must also equip them with the skills to develop counter-media spheres in which students can produce their own radio and television programs, newspapers, magazines, films, and other forms of public art. Students need to learn all aspects of media production, including business management and the diverse technologies. The point, of course, is that artists, educators, and other cultural workers need to reinvent spaces for ethical, political, and pedagogical practices through which they can build alliances and produce social practices and policies that rewrite the importance of what it means to treat youth with dignity and respect. Unlike cultural workers such as Calvin Klein, who offer children the cheap satisfactions of stylized bodies and commodified pleasures (what Ernst Bloch once called the swindle of fulfillment), progressive educators and other cultural workers need to challenge such limited representations of youth through an "integrative critical language in which values, ethics, and social responsibility can be discussed in terms" of how youth are constructed within such images.[20] In addition, artists and other cultural workers need to create pedagogical practices that provide the conditions through which young people actually learn about and understand their personal stake in struggling for a future in which social justice and political integrity become the defining principles of their lives.

TWO

HOLLYWOOD AND THE DEMONIZATION OF YOUTH
BEATING UP ON KIDS

REPRESENTING YOUTH AS A PROBLEM

Representations of youth in popular culture have a long and complex history and habitually serve as signposts through which American society registers its own crisis of meaning, vision, and community. The presentation of youth as a complex, shifting, and contradictory category is rarely narrated in the dominant public sphere through the diverse voices of the young. Prohibited from speaking as moral and political agents, youth becomes an empty category inhabited by the desires, fantasies, and interests of the adult world. This is not to suggest that youth don't speak; they simply are restricted from speaking in those spheres where public conversation shapes social policy and refused the power to make knowledge consequential with respect to their own individual and collective needs.

When youth do speak—the current generation, in particular—their voices generally emerge on the margins of society, in underground magazines, alternative music spheres, computer-hacker clubs and other subcultural sites. The places youth inhabit, especially since the beginning of the 1980s, increasingly point to the dangerous erosion of civil society and the undermining of safety nets and nurturing systems that historically have provided some sustenance and hope for young people.[1] Quality public schools, youth clubs, religious institutions, public art programs, urban shelters, and drug-and crime-free urban neighborhoods seem to have receded and been replaced, in part, by public spaces largely marked by the absence of adult support. The basketball court, the shopping mall, the darkly lit street corner, the video arcade, the urban dance hall, the suburban home inhabited by latchkey children, the decaying housing projects, and the secondhand automobile have become the privileged sites for working-class youth. In alarming numbers, young people in the 1990s are being distanced from the values, language, and practices necessary to shape a democratic social order and those public terrains that traditionally have been used to promote and embody civic discourse and critical reflection.

Lauded as a symbol of hope for the future while scorned as a threat to the existing social order, youth have become objects of ambivalence caught between contradictory discourses and spaces of transition. While pushed to the margins of political power within society, youth nonetheless become a central focus of adult fascination, desire, and authority. Increasingly denied opportunities for self-definition and political interaction, youth are transfigured by discourses and practices that subordinate and contain the language of individual freedom, social power, and critical agency. Symbols of a declining democracy, youth are located within a range of signifiers that largely deny their status as active citizens. Associated with coming-of-age rebellion, youth become a metaphor for trivializing resistance. At the same time, youth attract serious attention as both a site of commodification and a profitable market. For many aging baby boomers, youth represent an invigorated referent for a midlife consciousness aggressively in search of acquiring a more "youthful" state of mind and lifestyle.[2]

At stake here is not merely how American culture is redefining the meaning of youth, but how it constructs children in relation to a future devoid of the moral and political obligations of citizenship, social responsibility, and democracy. Caught up in an age of increasing despair, youth no longer appear to inspire adults to reaffirm their commitment to a public discourse that envisions a future in which human suffering will diminish while the general welfare of society will increase. Constructed primarily within the language of the market and the increasingly conservative politics of media culture, contemporary youth appear unable to constitute themselves through a defining generational referent that gives them a sense of distinctiveness and vision, as did the generation of youth in the 1960s. The relations between youth and adults always have been marked by strained generational and ideological struggles, but the new economic and social conditions that youth face today, along with a callous indifference to their spiritual and material needs, suggest a qualitatively different attitude on the part of many adults toward American youth—one that indicates that the young have become our lowest national priority. Put bluntly, American society at present exudes both a deep-rooted hostility and chilling indifference toward youth, reinforcing the dismal conditions under which young people increasingly are living. Donna Gaines is insightful in her claim that the 1980s represented a decade in which "young people were devalued, dismissed and degraded at every turn," and that children and teenagers currently are losing ground in securing a decent present and future for themselves and others.

> In post-Vietnam America, young people have experienced an erosion in their cultural prestige, their impact as a social force

has diminished, they are losing ground in their rights and civil liberties. The nature of the nuclear family, the global economy and the world stage is in rapid transition. The American working class is disappearing as a social entity. There now exists a permanent subclass of American citizens we call "the homeless." Half the kids in America don't go to college, and the ones who do spend six years getting degrees, after which they cannot find jobs, or afford housing, health care or cars.[3]

For many young people, especially those who experience ruthless subordination and oppression, nihilism often translates into senseless violence, racism, homophobia, drug addiction, date rape, suicide pacts, escalating homicide rates, and a refusal to participate in building communities of hope and alliances with other oppressed groups. This is not meant to portray youth merely as reproducing a larger social pathology, but to make visible the political, economic, and cultural conditions that undermine democratic public life and take the young and the very old as its first victims.

Of course, conditions of oppression produce not only victims and ongoing forms of resistance, but also ethically frozen social systems that are indifferent to the forms of political courage and civic responsibility necessary to engage critically the most pressing problems of the times. The distinctive change of attitude toward working-class and black youth in America, while rooted in histories of racism and class struggle, can be seen, in part, by the dismal statistics concerning the quality of life of children in this country that reflect new economic and ideological realities. Statistics are often too abstract to capture the day-to-day suffering they attempt to register; nonetheless, they serve as reminders of what can only be judged as a national crisis regarding the deteriorating conditions in which many children currently find themselves.

> Nationwide, the number of children living in poverty in-
> creased by 2.2 million between 1979 and 1989. Child poverty
> among European-Americans increased from 11.8 percent to
> 14.8 percent, among Latinos from 28 percent to 32 percent,
> and among blacks from 41.2 percent to 43.7 percent. . . . The
> United States has one of the worst infant mortality rates among
> industrialized nations. Out of every thousand babies born in
> the U.S., 9.8 die in infancy—a rate worse than sixteen other
> nations. Black children die at almost twice the national aver-
> age—18.2 per thousand births.[4]

Not only are there fourteen million children living in poverty in the
United States, but also the United States ranks in the lower half of
Western industrialized countries in providing services for family
support. Moreover, the United States has experienced an alarming
growth in cases of child abuse. It is also a country where more
teenagers "die from suicide than from cancer, heart disease, H.I.V.
infection or AIDS, birth defects, pneumonia, influenza, stroke and
chronic lung disease combined."[5] Similarly, behind the meager distribution of resources allotted for children of the poor looms an
oppressive and exploitative structure of economic inequality in which
the top 1 percent of the population "holds 46.2 percent of all stocks
and 54.2 percent of all bonds."[6] In a recent study by the Organization
for Economic Cooperation and Development it was revealed that the
United States, out of the top seventeen wealthiest industrial countries,
has the biggest gap between the rich and poor.[7] It appears that for the
richest and most powerful groups in American society young people
represent one of their lowest priorities.

A striking example of such callous indifference can be seen in
the actions of the 1996 Republican Party congressional budget-
cutters who, as noted earlier, promoted legislation that adds 1.2

million children to the poverty rolls, eliminates basic health care coverage for 7 million young people, and disadvantages 14 million additional children as a result of cuts in federally funded food and nutrition programs.[8] Even more disturbing is the fact that the largest growing population of homeless in this country are children and the average age of such children is nine years old. For white working-class youth, prospects are also bleak; they can look forward to dead-end jobs, unemployment without the benefit of health care, or perhaps homelessness.

Black teenagers face an unemployment rate of 57 percent and unprecedented levels of poverty while impoverishment and hunger become the rule of the day.[9] But what sets black youth off from their white counterparts is that the preferred method of containing white teenagers is through constitutional controls exercised through schooling where working-class youth suffer the effects of school choice programs, tracking, and vocationalization. Further, black youth increasingly are subjected to the draconian strategies of "tagging," surveillance, or more overt harassment and imprisonment through the criminal justice system.[10] Recent statistics based on Justice Department figures reveal the full scope of this policy by indicating that one in three black men in their twenties are either imprisoned, on probation, or under the supervision of the criminal justice system on any given day in America.[11]

As the political tide has turned against support for the well-being and happiness of working-class white and black children, further weakening basic support for the very young in troubled families and social circumstances, a new form of representational politics has emerged in media culture fueled by degrading visual depictions of youth as criminal, sexually decadent, drug-crazed, and illiterate. In short, youth are viewed as a growing threat to the public order.

HOLLYWOOD YOUTH AND
THE POLITICS OF REPRESENTATION

Traditionally, for youth the body has been one of the principal terrains for multiple forms of resistance and a register of risk, pleasure, and sex. It has been through the body that youth displayed their own identities through oppositional subcultural styles, transgressive sexuality, and disruptive desires. The multiple representations and displays of the body in this context were generally central to developing a sense of agency, self-definition, and well-placed refusals.[12] The body as a potent marker of youthful resistance served to set youth off from the adult world and suggested that the body was outside of the reach of dominant forms of moral regulation and sexual containment. Many adults responded with trepidation to the youth resistance of the 1950s, to what was viewed as the mutually reinforcing phenomena of juvenile delinquency and rock and roll.[13] Hollywood and other conduits of media culture capitalized on such fears by conceiving of youth as both a social threat and a lucrative market. With the redefinition of teen culture as both separate and in opposition to adult society, youth became the embodiment of alienation, anger, and potential danger. Hollywood films provided a new youth market with romantic images of antiheroes such as James Dean and Marlon Brando to both identify with and emulate. Films such as *Rebel Without a Cause* (1955), *Blackboard Jungle* (1955), and *Rock Around the Clock* (1956) portrayed youth as icons of defiance and rock and roll as the subversive space where sexual desire was explored and its excesses were indulged. The social and political turmoil of the sixties was explored in films such as *Easy Rider* (1968), *Alice's Restaurant* (1968), *Zabriskie Point* (1968), and *The Strawberry Statement* (1970).

Following the sixties, Hollywood employed different representational strategies to portray middle- and working-class youth. Films such as *Mean Streets* (1972), *Taxi Driver* (1976), and *Saturday Night Fever* (1977) increasingly presented the city as a space of violence, pathology, and resistance inhabited largely by dangerous, white working-class youth facing dead-end futures. At the same time, as the exhaustion of the politics of the sixties had become manifest along with a growing conservative backlash, Hollywood resurrected white, suburban, middle-class youth in the nostalgic image of Andy Hardy and Frankie Avalon, but with a twist. In a historical rendering of youth in the 1950s, films such as *The Last Picture Show* (1971), *American Graffiti* (1973), and *Diner* (1982) combined white-bread angst with the comforts of the cool, ordered nostalgia of the decade. Hollywood's fascination with middle-class youth was predicated on a claim to public memory that bypassed the radical politics of the sixties by portraying youth within a historical and sociological context that erased moral and political considerations while reducing the realm of the social to utterly privatized and personal narratives. Films such as *Love Story* (1971) and *Summer of '42* (1971) produced an image of youth in which ethical perspectives and public politics became unimaginable.

At the same time, when youth engaged the political sphere, as in popular films such as *Woodstock* (1970), *Harold and Maude* (1971), and *Hair* (1979), considerations of power and domination were replaced by either a quirky cynicism or a fatuous rendering of youth resistance as "turned on and tuned out." Erased from such representations were those diverse institutional spaces through which youth of the 1960s had linked a politics of meaning to strategies of engagement. Young people in the latter films appear without a politics, living out their lives according to someone else's countercultural script. Youth films in this period are constructed in narrowly experiential terms that appear to "transcend different styles, classes, desires and activities."[14] Within this Hollywood scenario, public memory is constructed in the service of a "past [that] appears as both pervasive and apparently irrelevant."[15]

As the recession of the 1970s gave way to the conservatism that burst forth with the election of Ronald Reagan in the 1980s, films such as *Breaking Away* (1979), *Risky Business* (1983), *The Breakfast Club* (1985), and *Sixteen Candles* (1984) provided a sympathetic portrait of white working-class and middle-class youth as confused but innocent, doing their best to come of age in a dramatically changing world. This was a period that witnessed a wide variety of youth films, many of which focused on alienated and confused youth either on the rampage or plodding their way through the end of their adolescence. Some of these included *Over the Edge* (1979), *Quadrophenia* (1979), *Fame* (1980), *Fast Times at Ridgemont High* (1982), and *Flashdance* (1983). These films, as cultural critic Larry Grossberg points out, are less about delinquency than "about a certain kind of loneliness and uncertainty and the possibilities of identity and belonging."[16] But in the late 1980s, the image of youth became more apocalyptic as Hollywood increasingly began to move from associating youth with a kind of ennui and meaninglessness to connecting them with a world that is increasingly irrational and hopeless.

The anti-teen impulse that surfaced in Hollywood films in the 1980s and 1990s had begun to emerge in dramatic Hollywood style in slasher films such as *Halloween* (1978), *Friday the 13th* (1980), and *Nightmare on Elm Street* (1984). While a hateful misogyny swept through the horror genre films, a dismal depiction of working-class youth spread across the Hollywood screens in the late 1980s and seemed to forecast a new politics of representation through which dominant media culture would attempt to rewrite and represent the identities and social status of youth by persistently placing them in communities "whose older local support institutions had been all but demolished."[17]

If a crisis of representation regarding youth has emerged in the 1990s, it is rooted less in a transformation of representational ideologies than in a host of complex national and global forces changing the face of the contemporary urban landscape: a downward-spiraling economy, a resurgent racism, a diminishing allocation of funds for crucial public services, the creation of Tipper Gore's Parents' Music Resource Center, and the hostile public response from many white adults to rap and urban contemporary music as it entered the mainstream. These factors, among many others, appear to register a shift from media culture's simplistic but sometimes sympathetic portrayal of youth as a lens through which to analyze the social and political dynamics at work in the larger society to its current more racist and brutalizing view. Young people are no longer seen as a symptom of a wider social dilemma—they are the problem.

A representational politics began to emerge that strongly resonated with a growing neoconservative demonization of urban white and black youth in the commercially dominated sectors of media culture. In films such as *River's Edge* (1987), *My Own Private Idaho* (1991), and *Natural Born Killers* (1995), white youth are framed and presented through the degrading textural registers of pathological violence, a deadening moral vacuum, and a paralyzing indifference to the present and future. On the other hand, Hollywood blockbusters such as *Wayne's World* (1992), *Dazed and Confused* (1993), and *Dumb and Dumber* (1995) project onto post-Watergate youth a long legacy of anti-intellectualism that has been a defining principle of American culture. In this script, idiocy and hilarity become a sign of what's in as Jim Carrey portrays the teenager who eventually will grow out of a fascination with Beavis and Butthead and emulate the simple-headed but responsible Forrest Gump, who has become the conservatives'

1990s model of family values, motivation, and patriotism. Needless to say, simplistic Hollywood portrayals of working-class youth as either potential muggers or dead from the neck up legitimate real futures in prisons, mental hospitals, or local fast food outlets. As youth are conceived in images of demonization, sexual decadence, and criminality, the only public sites that appear available to them are unskilled work, highly policed public spaces, or the brute reality of incarceration.

Hollywood representations of black youth in the 1990s seem to be inspired largely by the dynamics of class hatred as well as the powerful resurgent racism in American society. Even in the films of black filmmakers, films such as *Boyz N the Hood* (1991), *Menace II Society* (1993), and *Clockers* (1995), black male youth are framed through narrow representations that fail to challenge and in effect reiterate the dominant neoconservative image of "blackness as menace and 'other.'"[18] Within these films, violence resonates with the popular perception that everyday black urban culture and the culture of criminality mutually define each other. If white working-class youth are seen as a problem to be contained, black youth are seen as a dangerous threat to be eliminated.

FASHIONING TEENAGE SEXUALITY

Media representations of white and black working-class youth in the 1990s differ from the portrayal of such youth historically in that the contemporary construction of youth appears to be limited to a politics of demonization through which sexuality is defined as either a commodity or as a problem. Within current representational politics, teenagers are largely defined in terms of their sexuality. What fuels their limited sense of agency and the brutality and violence it produces is an adolescent libido out of control.

Within the new representational politics of youth, the body increasingly is being commodified and disciplined through a reactionary, postmodern cultural politics. The struggle over the body and sexuality as a sign becomes as important as the more traditional practices of containing and disciplining the body as a threat to the social order. In part, the new crisis of representation erases the body of youth as a site of resistance, whether expressed through a transgressive sexuality, an appropriation of popular culture, or in the formation of underground cultural formations. The bodies of youth in the age of Newt Gingrich and the Christian Coalition signify one of the most unsettling threats to American society as an increasingly conservative agenda dominates the discourse about the rights of children and the nature of the social problems facing the United States. Surely there is more than irony at work in a conservative discourse that defines its notion of family values, in part, on an image of the completely pure and sexually innocent child (read white and middle-class) while it refuses to acknowledge the "immense sexualization of children within consumer capitalism."[19] The hypocrisy of such a discourse cannot be easily dismissed. As social critic Marilyn Ivy points out, "For to think about the child as a sexual object in capitalism is already to have violated the pristine space the child must occupy to guarantee the crumbling social order, with its insistence on the sanctity of the nuclear family and standardized gender relations."[20]

In what follows, I want to analyze the representations of teenage sexuality in the bleak depiction of urban youth in Larry Clark's film *Kids*. The representations of youth presented in this film need to be addressed as part of a broader public struggle over how "technologies of power produce and manage . . . the individual and social body through the inscription of sexuality" within the visual and pedagogical machinery of Hollywood culture.[21] The primary issue is not whether artists, educators, and the general public should be condemned for finding pleasure in representations of youth as depicted in films such as *Kids*. Finding pleasures in sexually charged images of children does not make people morally culpable. At the same time, the emergence of a representational politics in which youth are no longer seen as capable of critical thinking, agency, resistance, or productive desires raises important questions regarding the moral responsibility and limits of one's pleasures at a time when subordinate young people are under massive assault by conservatives. In doing so, I want to illuminate how Larry Clark's *Kids* functions educationally within a broader discourse about youth, focusing specifically on how its representations resonate with specific conservative attacks on related issues of sexuality, race, and gender. Central to this analysis is a critique of a transgressive art that serves to depict teenage sexuality as decadent and predatory.

Related to this criticism is the call to challenge the current fascination of many cultural workers with forms of aesthetic and textual criticism and the ways in which such criticism fails to discuss children's culture and bodies as part of a larger debate about power, ideology, and politics. Textual criticism that celebrates the formal aesthetic principles at work in "realistic representations" of teenage sexuality often provides justification for flaunting the commodification of young bodies. Moreover, portraying teenage sexuality as decadent and predatory is neither critically transgressive nor worthy of being labeled as progressively transformative. Artists, critics, and others who respond to these representations by retreating to an ideologically "neutral" defense of aesthetics and artistic freedom often reproduce the very problems such representations legitimate. That is, by failing to engage in a broader public dialogue about the messy political realities of exploitation and social injustice that result from current attacks on poor, urban, white and black youth, such critics often legitimate rather than challenge the current conservative agenda for dispensing with those youth they view as disposable, if not dangerous, to the imperatives of the free market and global economy.

I will conclude by offering some suggestions for a pedagogy that addresses popular culture and the representational politics of youth in a progressive way. The film *Harlem Diary* (1996) will serve as one example of a representational politics in which a politics and pedagogy of the popular make it possible to understand the ways in which working-class youth can attempt "to open social and cultural spaces in which to express themselves,"[22] as well as engage and transform the conditions of poverty and racism.

KIDS AND THE POLITICS OF DIMINISHED HOPES

> Seeing comes before words. The child looks and recognizes before it can speak. But there is also another sense in which seeing comes before words. It is seeing which establishes our place in the surrounding world; we explain that world within words, but words can never undo the fact that we are surrounded by it. The relation between what we see and what we know is never settled.[23]

One of the most controversial films to appear about teenage sexuality and youth in 1995 was *Kids*, a film directed by Larry Clark from a script written by nineteen-year-old Harmony Korine. Most of the characters in the documentary-like film are not actors and are skateboarding friends of Korine. The film opens with a closeup of a teenage boy and girl loudly kissing each other. This image is crucial both aesthetically and politically. Aesthetically, the camera focuses on open mouths and tongues working overtime, and a sucking noise highlights the exchange of saliva—the scene is raw, rubbing against the notion of teenage sex as "a scaled down version of adult couplings, glamorized and stylized."[24] And it seems to go on forever, positioning the audience as voyeurs watching sex explode among kids who look too young to be acting on their own passions. In voice-over, Telly (Leo Fitzpatrick), the fifteen-year-old known to his friends as the Virgin Surgeon, says "Virgins. I love 'em." After seducing a young blonde virgin in her bedroom, Telly bolts from the Manhattan brownstone and joins his friend, Casper (Justin Pierce), who has been waiting for him. Telly provides an account of his conquest in intimate detail, and so begins Clark's rendition of urban teenage youth in the 1990s.

After Telly's initial seduction, he and Casper head out to wander through the streets of Manhattan. Along the way, they knock off a 40-ounce bottle of beer, urinate in public, jump over subway turnstiles, and steal some fruit from a Korean grocer. They end up at a friend's apartment where they do drugs, talk sex, and watch skateboarding movies. The action becomes more violent as Telly and his friends end up at Washington Square Park where they smoke some more dope, insult two gays who walk by, and viciously beat with their skateboards a black youth with whom Casper has been arguing. After stealing some money from Telly's mother, the youths break into the local YMCA for a swim. The day's activities culminate in a night of excessive drinking and drugs at a party given by a kid whose parents are out of town. The party degenerates into a haze of narcotized and drunken bodies, hands plunged randomly into crotches. Telly scores his second virgin. In the meantime, Jennie (Chloe Sevigny) appears at the party looking for Telly to inform him that she has tested positive for the H.I.V. virus, but she is too drugged to prevent him from infecting another young girl. Too numb to do anything, she falls asleep on a couch. In a grotesque and perverse reversal of the fairy-tale plot, Clark's sleeping beauty, Jennie, is not awakened with a kiss and the promise of living happily ever after. Rather, she suffers the brutal humiliation of a rape by Casper and will awaken to the nightmare reality of her eventual death and potentially his as well. The scene ends with Casper looking directly into the camera and asking "Jesus Christ, what happened?"

Irresponsible sex changes to lethal violence as it becomes clear that Jennie contracted the H.I.V. virus from Telly, who now emerges as the infector, "the ultimate villain of American culture in the age of AIDS."[25] If Telly's story is one of sexual conquest, Jennie's is one of tragedy and powerlessness in the face of a ruthless urban youth culture that celebrates reckless sexuality and violence while it reduces young girls to one of two sexist stereotypes. They are sexual objects to be taken up and put down at will or they are sex-crazed and on the make. When the girls come together in the film, they sit around talking about oral sex, titillating the guys or each other, or get set up to be exploited, as in the case of Telly's last sexual conquest, Darcy, and to become another AIDS statistic.

As for the younger generation of preteens, their future is foreshadowed as the camera focuses on a quartet of dope-smoking eleven-year-old boys who watch the older kids drink and drug themselves into a stupor at the party. The future they will inherit holds no positive role models nor encouraging signs of hope.[26] For even younger girls, there is the ominous and disturbing message that they soon will become sexual trophies for the predatory males who stalk them in the dangerous space of the city. Film critic Michael Atkinson captures this sentiment in noting that the camera "lingers on a stepside moptop three-year-old girl as if to grimly intone, it's only a matter of time."[27] Clark's gaze, which captures the bodies of young girls as wholly gendered and sexualized, sustains "the representation of the female body as the primary site of sexuality and visual pleasure."[28] Passivity and helplessness become the privileged modes of behavior as the girls in the film follow the lead of the male characters, silently observe their expressions of brutality, and plead tearfully when they become the objects of such violence. Predatory sexuality permeates the ruthless world of misogynist teenage males who are filled with a sense of themselves and their desire to prey on young girls who wait passively to be pulled into a ritual of seduction and possible death.

DECONTEXTUALIZED YOUTH
AND THE SWINDLE OF AGENCY

Floating on the surface of a dead-end cynicism, Clark's film refuses to probe where identity resides for the urban youth he represents. The teenagers in *Kids* are portrayed as if they live in a historical, political, and cultural vacuum. Lacking any depth, memories, or histories, Clark's teenagers are drawn in personal and stylized terms. For example, he provides no larger context for understanding the cultural, social, and institutional forces working on the lives of these urban teenagers. In this severely decontextualized perspective, it is almost impossible to understand the absence of adults in the film, the at-risk sexuality, the rabid homophobia, or the random violence practiced by these teenagers. Representing teen life as if it existed outside the forces of history, politics, and the dominant culture too easily resonates with a dominant, conservative ideology that blames the "psychological instability" of the poor, especially black urban youth, for the social decay, poverty, and endless disruptions that influence their everyday lives. Not unlike the Calvin Klein Jeans advertising campaign, Clark's narrative about youth plays on dominant fears about the loss of moral authority while reinforcing images of demonization and sexual license through which adults can blame youth for existing social problems and be titillated at the same time.

Clark's realism is too easily used—under the pretext of historical and social consideration—to transform the jolting experiences of
the teenagers he represents into raw, celebratory, and stylized
evocations of shock and transgression. Failing to come to grips with
considerations of politics, power, and ideology, Clark avoids serious
questions regarding how the viewer can account for the simultaneous aggression and powerlessness portrayed by teenagers in *Kids*,
and he offers no resistance to the brutality and limited options that
define their lives. Lacking depth and detail, the teenagers who
inhabit Clark's film are one-dimensional to the point of caricature.
Film critic David Denby is right in insisting that Clark "turns the
youth of his subjects into aesthetic shock. His teens have arrived at
decadence without passing through maturity. They seem to have no
dimensions—intellectual, spiritual, even physical—apart from car-
nality. They're all tongues."[29] Clark's attempt to let the film speak for
itself results in a stylized aesthetic of violence that renders the reality
of violence voyeuristic, spectacular, and utterly personal rather than
social and political. *Kids* avoids a central educational lesson in
dealing with any segment of teenage culture: unsafe sexual practices, violence, and drug use are learned behaviors that "society
seems to be going all out to teach."[30] Similarly, Clark seems
unacquainted with the notion that any serious portrayal of teens in
this culture "that wishes to force a shift in ways of seeing, feeling and
perceiving begins by questioning established power."[31]

In the end, pathology and ignorance become the basis for
defining the identity and agency of urban youth in Clark's world of
casual violence, rampant nihilism, and incorrigible depravity. While
Clark has been quick to defend his film as a cautionary tale about safe
sex as well as an indictment of adults who either don't understand
teenagers or simply are not around to provide guidance for them, he
fails to understand—or at least represent—that it is precisely adult

society with its celebration of market values, market moralities, and
its attack on civil society that "undermines the nurturing system for
children."[32]

REALISM AND THE POLITICS OF TEENAGE SEXUALITY

Clark's framing of *Kids* in pseudodocumentary style—an aesthetic
rendition of representing the world directly as it is—serves to
legitimate his claim that *Kids* provides a full-blown, "no-holds-barred"
journey into the culture of contemporary urban youth. But the cinema
verité approach and loosely structured narrative cannot salvage
Clark's surface exploration of a typical twenty-four hours in the lives
of some drug- and sex-crazed, morally rudderless adolescents, regardless of the aura of "truth" that structures *Kids*. Clark's use of and appeal
to realism as a testimony to the film's authenticity obscures Clark's
own political and ethical responsibility in depicting a brutal and bitter
portrait of a specific group of young people.[33] The invocation of truth
that accompanies appeals to gritty realism serves to sanction the
severity of right-wing images of urban youth at work in broader
popular representations.

Clark's reliance on the verisimilitude of documentary-like-narra-
tive, playing on the audience's fears and anxieties, and his positing of
sexuality and hedonism as the driving forces of agency among urban
youth reveal the ideological conservatism that undergirds *Kids*. The
consequence of portraying youth through the "transparent" lens of
realism is a viewpoint marked by the absence of a reflective moral
perspective, a viewpoint that offers critics and viewers a dose of media
sensationalism and serves as an apology for a specific view of reality
by making it appear natural, matter-of-fact, and outside of human
control.[34] Teen sexuality in Clark's discourse becomes a metaphor for

insincerity, crudeness, violence, and death. Missing from this perspective is a political understanding of the relationship between violence and sexuality as a daily experience for those who inhabit the places that promote suffering and oppression. The dangers of such a position are exemplified in a review of *Kids* by Amy Taubin, the film critic writing for *Sight and Sound*.

Fascinated by Clark's use in *Kids* of light, shade, and color and the film's realistic portrayal of teenage sexuality, Taubin adds an ideological twist to Clark's chic aesthetic by suggesting that adolescent socialization is determined less by culture than by biology—that is, high-powered libidos out of control. For Taubin, it is precisely this high-intensity libidinal energy that gives Clark's representations of teenage youth "their feverish energy, their mad humor, their extravagantly blunt language . . . [making them] mean, sordid, hungry and radiant at the same time."[35] Taubin's fascination with the aesthetics of teen sexuality excludes ideological considerations even as they are invoked, betraying the conservative politics—or the perversion—underlying her analysis. This is particularly clear when she describes the horrible rape scene of Jennie at the end of the film. Taubin writes that "it seems to take forever, leaving one time to feel as helpless as the semi-conscious Jennie, and perhaps (if one is totally honest) slightly turned on."[36] Not unlike Clark, Taubin is fascinated with teenage sexuality even when it legitimizes voyeuristic titillation in the face of a ruthless and gruesome rape. What the perspectives of Clark and Taubin have in common is that they both view teenage sexuality as a negative force in teens' lives and also push the limits of an aestheticism that provides fodder for the celebration of stylized perversion and teen lust. What such thinking shares with current right-wing attempts to demonize youth is the assumption that young people are primarily identified with their bodies, especially their sexual drives. Stripped of any critical capacities, youth are defined primarily by a sexuality that is viewed as unmanageable and in need of control, surveillance, legal constraint, and other forms of disciplinary power. Similarly, this reductionist rendering of sexually active youth is a short step from stereotypical portrayals of black sexuality in which sexuality becomes a metaphor for disease, promiscuity, and social decadence.

RACE TALK AND CONTAMINATING YOUTH

There is another disturbing aspect of *Kids* that has received little attention in the popular press. Though Telly and Casper are white, they communicate in black street lingo and call each other "nigger." Their clothes, walk, and street style mimic the black cultural fashion of hip-hop. Though the black characters in *Kids* are not central to the film, they are either the recipients of violence or serve as a comic backdrop for sexual stereotyping. The role of blackness is not an incidental aspect of Clark's film because it resonates too strongly with the broader dominant view that black culture is responsible for the self-destructive journey that white youth are making through the urban land mines of drugs, sex, and violence. Film critic Marcus Reeves captures this sentiment explicitly.

> Taken alongside the right's urgent moves to demonize and eliminate African American cultural influences in America and abroad (especially hip-hop music, language, and fashion) Clark's unyielding and "verité" focus on the summer-day transgressions of two hip-hop dressing/street slang-wielding/40 ounce-drinking/blunt-smoking/pussy-conquering white teenage males . . . provides a focus on what's making white American youth so crazy: Dey hanging out and acting

like dem nasty, demoralizing niggas. That the race baiting is unintentional doesn't help.[37]

While Clark's alleged racism and demonization of youth may be unintentional, it participates in what Toni Morrison calls race talk: "The explicit insertion into everyday life of racial signs and symbols that have no meaning other than pressing African Americans to the lowest level of the racial hierarchy . . . the rhetorical [and representational] experience renders blacks as noncitizens, already discredited outlaws."[38] The pertinent question is not whether one can accurately declare Clark a racist, but whether the effects of his cinematic representations perpetuate racist discourse and practices in the wider society. Clearly his representations about working-class and black youth hint at an ideological irresponsibility rooted in an over-identification with the recklessness of the young.

Clark's own tortured childhood reveals in part his infatuation with teenage culture. Ignored by his father and forced to accompany and aid his mother who went door-to-door peddling baby photography, Clark started using his own camera to shoot his friends, many of whom were petty hoodlums, speed freaks, and thugs. Eventually Clark produced a number of books of photography, including *Tulsa* (1971), *Teenage Lust* (1983), *Larry Clark* (1992), and *The Perfect Childhood* (1993). The first two books secured Clark's image as a tough-guy photographer. Despite his notoriety, Clark drifted around in the seventies and eventually spent nineteen months in jail in Oklahoma on an assault and battery charge. After the jail stint, he headed for New York and became a professional photographer. By Clark's own account, he came into puberty too late and suffered a lousy adolescence for not measuring up to his peers. In part, this experience explains his obsession with adolescence and the horror, excitement, and intensity it reflects.[39] In a revealing comment to writer

Terrence Rafferty, he says "Since I became a photographer I always wanted to turn back the years. Always wished I had a camera when I was a boy. Fucking in the backseat. Gangbangs. . . . A little rape. In 1972 and 1973 the kid brothers in the neighborhood took me with them in their teen lust scene. It took me back."[40] Clark reveals more than nostalgia about adolescence in general; he uncritically romanticizes the very violence he portrays in *Kids*. Clark's film replicates the erotic compulsion of the middle-aged male voyeur whose infatuation with teen sex is more narcissistic than socially or politically revealing, more symptomatic than productively educational.

Where *Kids* fails in this sense, the popular British film *Trainspotting* (1996), directed by Danny Boyle, offers a more complex and politically nuanced portrayal of youth. *Trainspotting* chronicles the lives of six young people in an economically impoverished Scotland as they descend into the world of heroin, drugs, alcoholism, and despair. Favoring the surreal over social realism, Boyle tries to capture the exhilarating highs and the debilitating lows of heroin addiction. Kids lose themselves in ecstatic numbness and dissipate into Christ-like figures as the heroin pumps through their veins to the sound of Iggy Pop's "Lust for Life." Faithful to depicting the pleasures that draw young people to smack, the film begins early on with a junkie in the shooting gallery rhapsodizing about heroin: "Take the best orgasm you've ever had, multiply it by a thousand, and you're still nowhere near." Whereas *Kids* dwells on the surface of free-floating hormones, drug use, AIDS, and rage, *Trainspotting* depicts the horrors of addiction, withdrawal, and indiscriminate violence. In one scene, Renton (Ewan McGregor) plunges into a shit-filled toilet to retrieve the heroin-laced suppositories he has lost. Trying to kick his habit, Renton is haunted by distorted images of his life on the streets, violent friends, and the horrifying memory of a neglected baby who died in the shooting gallery he occupied with his heroin-addicted mates.

Trainspotting refuses the cheap voyeurism of Larry Clark's *Kids*. Instead, it explores with humor, surreal images, and unflinching sensitivity the complex dynamic of pleasure, pain, and unchecked narcissism that accompanies heroin use.

Crackling with dead-end grittiness, *Trainspotting* posits a similarity between drugs and the stifling repression of ruthless capitalism. Conventional tensions between critique and celebration are bypassed in this film, just as the politics of the film refuses a preachy moralism. *Trainspotting* never lets the audience forget that behind the drugs, pleasure, narcissism, and violence is a society that creates the economic, social, cultural, and historical conditions for youth who engage in such behavior. Bob Dole got it wrong when he claimed in his 1996 presidential campaign that *Trainspotting* celebrates heroin use. On the contrary, Boyle's film argues that heroin usage is not going to go away by telling young people to "just say no" as long as civic life is modeled on crass consumerism and young people live under impoverished economic and social conditions. With society dominated by a particularly harsh and hypocritical form of capitalist accumulation, drugs will retain their allure within a broader cycle of extremity and hopelessness.

RECOVERING ETHICAL DISCOURSE
FOR A PEDAGOGY OF REPRESENTATIONS

For too long, progressives have viewed the struggle over meaning as less significant than what is often referred to as the "real" world of politics, that is, the world of material suffering, hunger, poverty, and physical abuse. While such a distinction rightly suggests that representations of rape, for example, and its actual experience cannot be confused, it is imperative to understand how physical reality and discourse interact. Cultural critic John Fiske is insightful on this issue. He writes: "There is a physical reality outside of discourse, but discourse is the only means we have of gaining access to it."[41] At the same time, it is important to stress that I am not suggesting that questions of power be limited to the realm of discourse. But without discourse it becomes difficult both to make sense of reality and to engage its power-bearing functions. Furthermore, it is only through discourse that we are able to give meaning to reality, or as Fiske points out "what is accepted as reality in any social formation is the product of discourse."[42] The struggle over naming and constructing meaning is also about how we constitute moral arguments and judge whether institutions, social relations, and concrete human experiences open or close down the possibilities of democratic public life. In short, the politics of meaning cannot be separated from the politics of the "real" world. How we constitute ourselves as engaged citizens to deal with that world is a defining principle of cultural politics and critical agency. Struggles over popular culture, for instance, represent a different but no less important site of politics. For it is precisely on the terrain of culture that identities are produced, values learned, histories legitimated, and knowledge appropriated.

Culture is the medium through which children fashion their individual and collective identities and learn, in part, how to narrate themselves in relation to others. Culture is also the shifting ground where new and old literacies—ways of understanding the world—are produced and legitimated in the service of national identity, public life, and civic responsibility. As a site of learning and struggle, culture becomes the primary referent for understanding the multiple sites in which pedagogy works, power operates, and authority is secured or contested. More specifically, Hollywood films represent more then weak politics or innocent entertainment. In fact, they are powerful educational sites where children and adults are being offered specific lessons in how to view themselves, others, and the world they inhabit. In this sense, such films must be seen as a serious object of social analysis by anyone who takes education seriously. But recognizing that Hollywood films function as teaching machines demands more than including them in the school curricula; it also demands that educators and other cultural workers bring questions of justice and ethics to bear on the form and content of such films. This becomes particularly important when raising questions about the limits of such representations, particularly those that portray children in degrading terms, legitimate the culture of violence, and define agency and desire outside of the discourse of compassion and moral responsibility.

As the right wing wages war against sex education, condom distribution in schools, sex on the Internet, and video stores that carry pornographic films, there is a curious silence from progressive and other radical cultural workers about the ways in which children and sex are portrayed in films, advertising, and media culture in general. While it is important for progressives to continue to argue for freedom of expression in defending films or other cultural forms that they might find offensive, they also need to take up what it means to provide an ethical discourse from which to criticize those images, discourses, and representations that might be destructive to the psychological health of children or serve to undermine the normative foundations of a viable democracy. Appeals to the First Amendment, the right of artistic expression, and the dignity of consent are crucial elements in expanding cultural democracy, but they are insufficient for promoting an ethical discourse that would cultivate an ethics of concern, self-responsibility, and compassion. Progressives must demonstrate more commitment to exposing the ways that structures of oppression operate through the media and particularly through those public spheres that shape children's culture. Given the ubiquitous presence of the media in our society and the educational influence it has on children, it is crucial that those who control media culture in this society become accountable for the knowledge, values, and desires they produce. Cultural workers such as Larry Clark have a responsibility, both political and moral, to reflect upon the possible implications of their work. The obligation here is not legal, it is moral—to consider whether young people will benefit from images and representations of sexuality that legitimate a "callous culture of self-centered individuals for whom physical pleasure is all."[43] What is at stake are issues of both power and public responsibility: Who decides what messages and representations will emerge from media culture? If media culture is to be viewed as a site of political struggle, how might such a struggle be linked to broader attempts to improve the quality of democracy itself?

My reading of texts such as Larry Clark's film *Kids* does not mean that their only significance is their reinforcement of right-wing attacks on urban youth. They are also ripe with potential for exploring what Eve Sedgwick calls a "scornful, fearful, patheticizing reification of ignorance."[44] For Sedgwick, ignorance cannot be treated as passive or innocent and needs to be explored not merely as an absence but as a defining pedagogical "presence" that signals the exclusion from cultural texts of particular ideologies, histories, and social practices. Central to Sedgwick's notion of ignorance is the theoretical possibility for developing educational practices that critically address the relationship between knowing and ignorance, the relationship between power and knowledge as mediated by that which is not named, spoken, or represented. For example, can we offer informed alternatives to refusals to know while exploring the ways in which refusals reinforce the right wing's agenda—including their advocacy of censorship and fight against adult discussions of sexual desire and schools' distribution of condoms?

Finally, educators, artists, and other cultural workers must address the challenge of developing educational approaches that teach kids how to use media as a mode of self-expression and social activism. We need to find new ways to translate pedagogy into an activist strategy that will expand the opportunities for young people to acquire the knowledge and skills that will help them extend their participation into, and control over, those cultural, economic, and social spheres that shape daily life (mass media, schools, media, workplace, policy making institutions, the arts). Evidence of such work can be found in films such as Jonathan Stack's *Harlem Diary* (1996), which narrates the complexities, struggles, and hopes of nine black youth attempting to reclaim their lives within a destructive culture of violence and drugs. Stack is no romantic, but he lets the kids' voices capture the complexities of their lives and their courage and strength by giving them video cameras to provide representations of their own experiences. These narratives become the basis for the students to engage in dialogue with others and to debate the meaning of the ideologies that influence their daily lives and discuss the implication of such influences on their futures. This is a remarkable cultural document, full of complexities, tensions, and subtleties; moreover, it is acutely aware of its own politics and the dangers these kids face. At the same time, it refuses to romanticize resistance and the power of critical pedagogy, and Stack holds firm in the belief that progressive educational and political interventions might give rise to possibilities and real achievements for kids too often viewed as throwaways.

Stack's film moves beyond the simplistic call for positive images of black youth; instead, it captures the complexities of how such youth are produced within certain social, economic, and political circumstances while simultaneously working to transform such conditions. Stack's politics are clear and he refuses to hide behind the alleged "neutral" appeal to realism. This is a film with an up-front project that takes seriously the challenge of developing a language of critique and possibility, one that confronts both racist representations of youth and a representational politics in which youth are blamed for society's failures. *Harlem Diary* provides an example of a representational politics that shows how a politics of the popular can enable black youth "to open social and cultural spaces in which to express themselves"[45] and engage and transform the conditions through which they push against the constraints of poverty and racism.

Harlem Diary is much less interested in "realistically" portraying domination than in revealing its contradictions, cracks, and fissures and showing how within such spaces teenage youth fight domination and racism rather than simply yield to it. This is a film in which the pedagogical inserts itself into a representational politics, and in doing so expands and deepens the democratic possibilities for producing films that resist rather than reinforce the current racist and demonizing portrayals of subordinate youth.

THREE

BASHING THE SIXTIES
PUBLIC MEMORY AND
THE LOST HOPE OF YOUTH

> What of the millions of children who grow up in this rich
> society hungry, poor, undereducated, and surrounded by
> violence? What are their hopes and dreams? Can they
> afford to dream?
>
> —Ruth Sidel[1]

SCAPEGOATING YOUTH

Ruth Sidel's question as to whether children, especially those
who are poor and uneducated, can afford to dream appears
both provocative and problematic at the current historical conjuncture: provocative because it forces adults to take seriously as moral
agents a generation of young people who need to play a role in
shaping their own lives if they are to fulfill their obligations as active
and critical citizens; problematic because the more specific issue of
what conditions adults need to provide for children in order for them
to narrate and act upon their dreams of a better world seems far
removed from public consciousness. Hence, an interesting contradic-

tion emerges as adults appear to have given up on their responsibility to nurture, educate, and provide the spiritual, political, and economic conditions for kids to see themselves as citizens capable of living principled lives while expanding the general well-being of the larger society. Rather cynical representations abound in the media and other public spheres that pigeonhole young people as a generation mired in nihilism, sloth, and narcissism.

Public pronouncements that students have become profoundly cynical are less an accurate description of today's youth than a strategy for discounting explicitly political discussions that insist that "our battle is with a society that fails to do all it can for young people—then lays the blame on them."[2] Many of these critiques are being waged by young people fueled by a hopelessness and despair that has reached crisis proportions in light of the current collapse of the welfare state, the shrinking opportunities for decent work, shelter, social justice, and the ongoing "systematic denigration, stereotyping, and stigmatizing of millions of poor women and their children."[3]

The reckless stereotyping of young people as politically insensitive and morally irresponsible cannot be separated from conservative attacks on other groups who are equally powerless in this society. The dominant media and conservative pundits dismiss the generation of youth that has emerged in the 1980s and 1990s as "slackers": idle, self-absorbed, and indifferent to the value of paid work as an end in itself. Conservatives such as Allan Bloom, E. D. Hirsch, William Bennett, and others have repeatedly suggested that many of today's (white and middle-class) college youth are self-indulgent, ignorant, and lacking in fundamental cultural knowledge. Moreover, they rail against minority youth who allegedly have retreated into the discourse of separatism, the underground culture of crime, and violence as part of an unholy effort to undermine the basic values of Western civilization and the principles of corporate culture. The demonization of large segments of working-class white and black youth goes hand-in-hand with the increasing attacks on the entitlements and benefits that have provided a safety net for the poor, the aged, immigrants, and young children. Teenage pregnancy, welfare dependency, black poverty, crime, and drug and alcohol abuse are now traced either to genetic and cultural factors that imply racial inferiority, or to the liberal permissiveness of the sixties. The sixties have become more than a threat—they have become for many conservatives the all-encompassing factor in undermining America's domestic prosperity and international leadership in the world.

For many adults, the crisis of youth represents a moral failing on the part of kids rather than an ethical failure on the part of adults who are unwilling to provide the economic and social resources as well as the spiritual support necessary for young people to function effectively as critical citizens capable of self-determination, social responsibility, and individual compassion in the twenty-first century. Youth behavior rather than the social conditions that promote such behavior occupy center stage in the media and provide the text for politicians such as Bob Dole to condemn teenage drug use on the one hand, while slashing school programs and calling for the construction of more prisons and tougher sentences for teenage offenders on the other. Punishment-driven proposals ignore the underlying forces behind the violence, drugs, and rage that frustrated youth exhibit.[4] There is no imaginative leap or risk-taking on the part of right-wing ideologues and politicians to understand or recognize the human suffering experienced by large numbers of young people trapped in a desperate cycle of poverty, violence, and despair. Compassion in this instance has given way to a monumental indifference and disregard for human life. The message that youth receive in the nineties has been aptly described by cultural critic Donna Gaines:

Stuck without hope, dreaming of jobs that no longer exist, with the myths of better days further convincing them of their individual fate as "losers," kids today are earning almost one third less, in constant dollars, than comparable groups in 1973. For white kids, the drop in income is almost 25 percent; for black kids, it's 44 percent. The scars of race discrimination run deep, and minority youth feel hopeless because they get the message that this nation does not value its nonwhite citizens. White kids have scars too, but with no attending socioeconomic explanation, they personalize their plights. They are "losers" because they are shit as people. They are failures because they are worthless. Either way, it hurts.[5]

The attack on youth with respect to policy measures is summed up by conservative commentator James Q. Wilson. He writes that youth represent a menacing cloud beyond which lurks "30,000 more muggers, killers, and thieves than we have now," all of whom come from dysfunctional families, exhibit "wrong behavior," and come from "disorderly neighborhoods."[6]

A reminder of failed social responsibility, a disturbing sexual presence, and a symbol of powerlessness, youth have become an easy target for conservatives and liberals advocating a public discourse in which scapegoating and surveillance take on the proportions of a national policy and minor revolution in the media. Conservative tough-love policies and a siege-like mentality increasingly have resulted in legislation aimed at lowering the age at which children can be tried as adults in the criminal justice system (currently in Vermont and Wisconsin ten-year-olds can be tried as adults for murder.) Similarly, more and more states are passing laws that allow kids under the age of eighteen to receive the death penalty. Mike Males and Faye Docuyanan point out that "Juveniles convicted of drug offenses in adult court receive lengthy mandatory sentences . . . [and in] California, studies by the state corrections department show that youths serve sentences 60 percent longer than adults for the same crimes."[7] Emulating the discipline-and-punish policies of the criminal justice system, 3,000 public schools now utilize some form of electronic surveillance. But punishment and surveillance are not the only strategies that register society's scorn for the rights and welfare of children, especially working-class and black urban youth.

The highly publicized suicide of Kurt Cobain, a spate of deaths among musicians who have overdosed on heroin, and the downward slide of actor Robert Downey, Jr. into heroin addiction serve as disturbing indicators of how youth are faring in relation to economic downsizing and a political climate hostile to their needs. These incidents also support the federal government's recent claim that drug addiction among children twelve to seventeen years old rose 78 percent from 1992 to 1995, a statistic that made the "war on drugs" one of the central issues of candidate Bob Dole's 1996 failed presidential campaign. Until recently, drugs were seen as a black problem in spite of the fact that "nationally, more than seven times as many whites (24 million) use cocaine."[8] Unfortunately the racist stereotypes that feed popular assumptions about drug use mean that if you are using or selling drugs and are black or Latino, you will more than likely go to jail. But if you are white, you will be able to go into a drug treatment program. Hence, blacks and other people of color have been hauled off to prisons on drug-related charges in record numbers, and as Derrick Z. Jackson, an editorial writer for the *Boston Globe* has pointed out, "The so-called war on drugs is hugely responsible for the quadrupling of inmates in the last 20 years to 1.5 million in state and federal prisons. In the last two years alone, the number of prisoners in local jails has doubled from 223,500 to 490,000."[9] The answer to the drug crisis among black and Latino youth is increasing criminalization and longer prison terms. Now that there is a new drug crisis represented by a growing number of white kids hooked on heroin, there are increased calls for twelve-step programs, educational reform efforts, and other preventive measures to keep kids off drugs.

While the drug issue is symptomatic of the double standard applied to black and white youth, it further testifies to the moral panic that has been growing in this country along with hostile and punishing attitudes that suggest adult society is no longer willing either to invest in its children or to provide the social services and safety nets for those who are at risk as a result of poverty, physical and sexual abuse, exploitation, and perpetual unemployment. Bob Dole and others believe that juvenile crime, rising homicide rates, and teenage pregnancies are produced by a lapse of character, the growing popularity of rap music, and the influence of media violence—circumstances that for Bob Dole resulted from the moral degeneracy of the sixties. Factored out of this language is a concern with the rising rate of poverty among children, an increasingly dysfunctional educational system for those who are poor, the lack of employment opportunities for youth, lack of health coverage for the young, and a welfare system that is largely designed to scapegoat single, teenage mothers and their children by mandating work when there is none, and when work is provided offering no financial support for child care.[10]

Examples of scapegoating youth, as opposed to corporate greed or repressive social policies, have become so commonplace in the media that they suggest the emergence of a new literary trope. For example, the liberal magazine, *George,* in its June/July 1996 issue, ran a series of stories under the headline "Why Kids are Ruining America." Spearheading the assault, novelist Bret Easton Ellis argues that the budget crisis, collapsing middle class, and rising crime do not represent the biggest threat to America. On the contrary, he claims, "Kids are ruining all of our lives." Of course, kids are not entirely to blame; Ellis also impugns the sixties as an era that ushered in the decline of family values and the rising divorce rate. Smugly invoking his own elite experience of youth as a model of nostalgic yearning, Ellis's resentment of working-class, urban youth is utterly unrestrained; he argues that government-sponsored legislation and controls should decide what's best for this generation of kids. Issues regarding freedom, autonomy, responsibility, and active citizenship become irrelevant in his discourse. Ellis's co-contributors reinforce his stereotypes with stories about why kids kill, blow money, control the entertainment industry, and are in need of more laws and regulations. Echoing the ideological sentiments of the Bob Dole/Ralph Reed crowd, the contributors of *George* are indifferent to the social, political, and economic realities that most poor and black kids have to face in an age marked by downsizing and deindustrialization, the dismantling of public services, and a rabid commitment by Washington policymakers to continue to shift income and wealth from the poor and the middle classes to the rich and privileged classes.[11] Rather than attempt to expose and break the cycle of poverty, despair, and hopelessness that many young people face in America, Ellis and his co-contributors shamelessly mobilize adult fears and hysteria by constructing youth as an invading army of killers and drug fiends against which society is going to have to defend itself. Unfortunately, magazines such as *George* are not alone in bashing youth. *Education Week* claims on the front page of its June 5, 1996 issue that "Teen Culture is Impeding School Reform." Inadequate resources, segregated schools, overcrowded classrooms, outdated curricula, and a crumbling infrastructure disappear in this account as the complex causes of school failure are reduced to the psychological profiles of disgruntled youth.

Similarly, Hollywood's view of youth is exemplified in films such as *Dumb and Dumber* (1994), *Clerks* (1994), *Clueless* (1995) *Bio-Dome* (1995), and *Kids* (1996). In these films and in the spate of cloned films that followed their release, kids are portrayed either as vulgar, disengaged pleasure-seekers or as over-the-edge violent sociopaths. Television sitcoms such as *Friends* portray young people as shallow, unmotivated, navel-gazing slackers intent on making do without the slightest interest in a larger social and political world. While many of the characters frequently experience unemployment, low-wage jobs, and high credit debts, such experiences become at best fodder for comic relief and at worst completely nullified by their sporting hundred-dollar haircuts, expensive makeup, and slick Greenwich Village–like apartments. These white middle-class youth are defined largely through their role as conspicuous consumers, their political indifference, and their intense lack of motivation to engage a world beyond their own self-indulgent interests. On the other hand, represented through a celluloid haze of drugs, crime, and sex, black youth are viewed as menacing and dangerous. In the popular press, representations of youth take on a decidedly racial register as they move between celebrations of the cynicism and rage of white singers such as Alanis Morrisette and Michael Stipe (of REM), on the one hand, and condemnations of the violent-laden lyrics and exploits of black rappers such as Snoop Doggy Dog and the recently deceased Tupac Shakur.

Caught between representations that view them as either slackers, consumers, criminals, or sellouts, youth increasingly are defined through the lens of commodification, scorn, or criminality. The only groups that appear attentive to youth are market researchers. One such company, Sputnik, sends "youthful spies" to seventeen cities to find out what youth wear, like, buy, and desire. Identifying five youth subcultures, it offers its "research" findings to clients such as Reebok,

Levi Strauss, and Pepsi-Cola. Whether seen as a market for commodities or commodified as in the recent Calvin Klein underwear ads, kids are stripped of their specificity, agency, and histories. And yet, the popular press rarely questions how children are exploited by a market that grinds up youth as fodder in order to expand the profit margin of the large corporations. This may constitute the real violence being waged against kids in the dominant media, but it is a violence that is rarely acknowledged.[12] In this scenario, young people are important as consumers rather than as critical, social subjects.

BASHING THE SIXTIES

The current assault on kids through media and the courts, policy initiatives, and legislation often is legitimated by pointing to the sixties as an era that ushered in a moral plague, the effects of which are largely responsible for many of the social problems currently facing youth and others in American society. In effect, the legacy of the sixties has become an excuse for putting a low priority on those members of society who lack resources to defend themselves, while scapegoating poor white kids and large segments of black youth. Civic life along with its most important public spheres and social infrastructures wanes as politicians, corporations, dominant media conglomerates, and conservative ideologues refuse to deal with the real problems threatening American democracy while simultaneously blaming youth for living out the legacy of what has become a mythical rendering of the sixties. As the national government dismantles services that traditionally have constituted a safety net for the poor, children, and the aged, the state becomes hollow as its most compassionate functions are eliminated.[13] With the ascendancy of the "hollow state" and changing economic and political conditions, kids have become the enemy of those in power and the state apparatuses that address their problems are increasingly reduced to the police, criminal justice system, armed forces, and other agencies of military surveillance and control.

The loss of compassion and hope among large segments of adult society has not been lost on the kids themselves. Angst, despair, and disillusionment have become a popular marker for large segments of an entire generation of young people. While the cynicism and despair are perhaps overplayed in the popular press, there is a disturbing quality to the message coming from major segments of youth. Rock and roll legend Patti Smith captures this concern in her comment "When I saw River Phoenix and Kurt Cobain die, I worried for young people, how they would take it. Each generation suffers different pain; the thing young people seem to suffer now is a lack of comprehension at how beautiful life is. I've experienced a lot of personal sorrow, but I still feel constant amazement at how beautiful life is."[14]

Patti Smith's suggestion that such despair among youth is generational offers a sharp contrast to views, however inflated, of her own generation of sixties youth, who experienced the possibilities of the future on a more radically political and hopeful register. In part, the sixties was a time when agency, optimism, and political action appeared to move a diverse population of youth. I am referring, of course, to the widespread political and moral urgency that guided many young people to take up the legacy of civil rights, to renew a sense of struggle against patriarchy, oppressive poverty, and a brutal war in Vietnam and to condemn the ravages of economic inequality on democracy. The challenges these student movements posed to the political leadership of the time, to the moral conscience of the country, and to the ethical limits of a rapacious, consumer society became a significant force for shaping and expanding the precepts and practices of American democracy. But I am also struck by how significant this legacy of struggle has been in efforts to reshape public memory and prevailing political opinion in the 1990s, particularly as it has become a negative referent used by many conservatives to forge a new political language about youth, education, and democracy that appears to be the antithesis of the values and hopes expressed by many young people in the 1960s.

What social and political conservatives would like to forget is that the sixties activists represented what author James Carroll calls a "social weather shift that swept the [country] and . . . belonged to the sons and daughters of the middle class. It belonged to the students. They were the ones who intuitively embraced the cultural change, but then they were blamed for it."[15] Carroll captures the sense of hope and belief in social justice and collective action that inspired so many young people to challenge the transformation of the university into a "knowledge factory," the immorality of America's presence in Vietnam, and the ravages of racism and sexism at home. Central to the student protest movement of the period were the burning issues of democracy, civil rights, and related concerns about what purpose the university and other public spheres should fulfill as agencies for learning and social change. Linking the struggles of the southern Civil Rights movement with the Free Speech movement—a movement that emerged out of student protests against the House Un-American Activities Committee with its red-baiting of critical intellectuals both in and outside of the university—students rapidly extended their concerns for social justice to a critique of the corporate university and the emptiness of consumer society. Seizing upon the work of theorists such as Paul Goodman, C. Wright Mills, Thorstein Veblen, and Herbert Marcuse, student protesters argued against the legitimating function of the state and university as an adjunct to the needs of corporate culture and the military-industrial complex. Appealing to the language of participatory democracy and equality, student protesters attempted simultaneously to reimagine civil society and, most important, the university as a critical public resource for civic responsibility and to define themselves as a force for informed citizenship rather than as simply consumers of knowledge.

Currently, however, the sixties have fallen on hard times. The optimism that motivated a generation of students and adults in the sixties appears to have been replaced in the nineties, as Patti Smith suggests, by a widespread sense of nihilism, fragmentation, and alienation among large segments of the American public. What is so paradoxical about this age of diminishing hopes is that many people, especially cultural conservatives and the religious right, claim that the highly charged and culturally resonant sixties are *responsible* for undermining Western values, for the erosion of the traditional work ethic, and for the loss of U.S. prominence in the competitive global market. Missing from this discourse is the role the government has played in the last thirty years in providing corporate welfare, shifting the tax burden to the middle and working classes, aiding the migration of manufacturing overseas, supporting corporate deregulation, and, if recent reports are to be believed, smuggling cocaine into largely black neighborhoods in the United States in order to raise money for Nicaraguan contras in the early 1980s.[16]

Bashing the sixties has become a full-time sport not only in the dominant media but also on the national political scene. Neoconservatives such as Rush Limbaugh, Newt Gingrich, and Pat Buchanan suggest that the legacy of the sixties is responsible for most of the disruptions that plague contemporary social, economic, and political life. In fact, Newt Gingrich argues in his best-selling book, *To Renew America,* that it is because of the 1960s that Americans have lost faith "in the core values, traditions, and institutions of our civiliza- tion."[17] Gingrich claims that prior to the sixties, America was held together by a common-sense consensus of what it meant to be an American, and that the norms and conventions that informed such an understanding could be found in an unquestioned set of ideas transmitted to schoolchildren and adults in daily rituals, from "the Pledge of Allegiance, the opening prayer, 'The Star-Spangled Banner,' [the observance of] historic holidays (the study of the Pilgrims at Thanksgiving, Washington and Lincoln on their birthdays) to stories in the schoolbooks."[18] According to Gingrich, the breakdown of this consensus has resulted in a crisis in education and public life over "whether there is anything in the American past worth transmitting."[19] Gingrich doesn't critically analyze the issues and values raised, challenged, and affirmed during the sixties as much as he uses that historical period as a referent for making a claim on public memory to support a particularly conservative rendering of the present. Gingrich "runs" through the sixties like the makers of *Forrest Gump,* who shaped the historical period as if their script had been funded by the Conservative Olin Foundation.

For many conservatives, America can best be understood by returning to the 1950s when national identity was best exemplified in the middle-class, "family" values of the Ward and June Cleaver family. It hardly matters to ideologues such as Newt Gingrich, William Bennett, Lynne V. Cheney, and Dinesh D'Souza that such a past amounts to nothing more than sentimental fiction. But this golden-age fable of life before the rise of student protest does more than misrepresent the cultural and political legacy of the sixties; it also suggests a process of organized forgetting that constructs comfortable myths about the past as an antidote to a historical period that is deemed both dangerous and un-American. Organized forgetting functions to rewrite the past through a process of omission and mythification. History becomes in this instance a vehicle to represent the nation not in terms of a democratic community, but in terms of a mythical view of family, best personified in the image of Father-Knows-Best-Leave-It-to-Beaver America. But as Ruth Sidel points out, what conservatives leave unsaid in their politics of nostalgia is that the fifties were:

> a time in which 25 percent of the population was officially poor, a time when 60 percent of Americans over the age of sixty-five had incomes below $1,000, a time when the poverty rate of two-parent black families was 50 percent. . . . It was also a time when millions of women lost the jobs they held during the war and were forced to retreat to domestic roles in relatively isolated suburban tracts. It was a time when tranquilizers were developed; by 1959, consumption, mostly by women, had reached 1.15 million pounds. It was a time when teen birth rates soared.[20]

Contradictions aside, for many conservative ideologues, the sixties represent an era of antisocial behavior that can only be offset by returning to the values of Victorian England, embodied in the United States in the decade of the fifties. As conservatives claim that the sixties were a period of pathological rebellion and social anarchy, the politics of nostalgia they so fervently embrace becomes a convenient mask through which to construct a picture of white youth in the nineties as either depoliticized "slackers" as in the widely popular film *Slackers,* or as sex- and drug-crazed teens as in the film *Kids.* On the other side of the racial divide, the political legacy of civil rights and social justice for those most in need, especially the children of the poor, is undermined through the scapegoating of single, black teenage mothers who are portrayed as part of a culture of illegitimacy. At the same time, young black males are increasingly defined through a menacing culture of social decay and criminality. A casualty of right-wing rhetoric, the meaning of the sixties is frozen in a claim to public memory that rewrites the present through a reading of the past that turns history into caricature while suggesting that dissent and critical agency are unpatriotic. At the same time, America is being reinvented as a Disney theme park at the end of history—without class divisions, poverty, homophobia, anti-Semitism, genocide of Native Americans, unjust wars, or widespread alienation.

Many of the critiques made by young people in the sixties seem just as relevant today as they were twenty-five years ago, especially in light of the sustained assault on the democratic foundations of political, social, and cultural life that have emerged since the Reagan revolution began in the 1980s. As a claim on public memory, the legacy of sixties activists in many ways represents a valuable reminder of the important role that youth can play in keeping the spirit of social criticism alive. But sixties activism also posed a threat to those who believed in business and politics as usual. And it is precisely because of such a threat that the sixties have become a source of heated political debate and criticism within the last decade. Not only has sixties-bashing become respectable in the last fifteen years, but also it has become a central motif for portraying youth as both anguished and troubling, irresponsible and dangerous. Seen less as a period that generated greater expression of democratic values than as one that promoted "excessive forms of mindless militancy, drugged Euphoria, or narcissistic self-indulgence,"[21] the sixties are now blamed for many of our current social and cultural ills, including the drug crisis and the decline of standards in higher education. Scapegoating the sixties, of course, does more than divert attention away from the real economic and social forces undermining democracy in this country; it also provides, in part, a rationale to wage a concerted assault on young people who are seen as either lazy, nihilistic, or indifferent.

I want to argue that the legacy of sixties activism provides a lesson for engaging in a dialogue with the past rather than viewing it in either reductionistic or absolute terms. Remembering in this instance renders memory as an act of interpretation, one that necessitates an ability to decipher, exercise critical judgment, and intervene in the construction of the present. Remembering as a critical act does not conceive of knowledge as an inheritance and history, as something that "cannot be taught, but only imparted."[22] On the contrary, historical inquiry as an act of remembering recognizes the partiality of traditions in order to enter into critical dialogue with them, amplifying the multiple perspectives that make social memory the site of contestation, struggle, and critical engagement.

Because the sixties were a "noisy time" in history, many conservatives argue that the debates and conflicts they generated represent a threat to moral decency as well as national law and order. A very different reading might view such turbulence as an expression of democratic public culture, one that gave full range to multiple voices, vociferous speech, and critical inquiry. It seems to me that the student protests of the sixties, though in a sometimes ambiguous, confusing, and contradictory way, captured something crucial to what democracy is about. By linking a language of critique with a personal desire for self-fulfillment and social justice, many young people in the sixties reclaimed a space for defining themselves as moral agents capable of shaping history while keeping alive a renewed faith in the spirit of equity and collective action. For all of its flaws—a rampant sexism, an uncritical acceptance of the political wisdom of those individuals and groups deemed to be oppressed, and an overly romanticized view of Third World revolutions (i.e., Cuba)—the legacy of sixties activism continues to stand out as an attempt on the part of a large number of young people to raise critical questions about ethics, freedom, the substance of representative government, and the relevance of the university for deepening and expanding the possibilities for substantive democracy. Moreover, as Nicholas Bromell points out, "the political and social movements of the '60s were a revolt against . . . cynicism. Their 'failure' is not so much a testament to their inadequacy as an indication of the power with which the social and political elites of the 1980s and '90s have distorted and controlled the public record of the '60s."[23]

This is not meant to suggest that we should either romanticize the sixties or ignore the complexity and contradictory forces at work in that highly charged and spirited decade. What seems more crucial to recognize is that the legacy of sixties activism is about more than fashion, nostalgia, or the demonization of young people who challenged some of the basic precepts of the dominant culture.[24] This legacy is also integral to a debate about how memory-work and education enable rather than stifle forms of ethical agency, critical analysis, and social responsibility. In spite of the debilitating images of youth rampant in the media or the all-too-real despair felt by many youth, there are many young people who are carrying on the political legacy of the sixties in terms that reaffirm "youth" within the discourse of critique and possibility rather than the narrow and often politically charged discourse of "crisis." In what follows, I want to explore briefly the political registers and issues some youth are engaging and conclude with a commentary on the importance of the legacy of the sixties for improving the quality of the lives of children in this country.

PEDAGOGICAL LESSONS AND POLITICAL HOPES

The spirit of hope and commitment to public life that marked the decade of the sixties is far from dead in the 1990s. While it is true that young people in the 1980s did not engage in broad-based social movements comparable to the antiwar crusade of the sixties, student protests did emerge around issues such as the environment, homelessness, racial and sexual politics, rising tuition rates, poverty, and illiteracy. Focusing their concerns on a range of issues crucial to questions of public and university life, students in many cases reacted against the widespread sentiment that they constitute a generation that is apathetic and greedy. In fact, such commentary seems to be either blind or unwilling to acknowledge that student protests in the mid-eighties played a crucial role in getting many American universities to either fully or partially divest their financial investments in South Africa. In addition, students actively protested the Gulf War and demonstrated against CIA recruitment efforts at schools such as Brown University, Rutgers, Princeton, Columbia, and others.[25] Moreover, many students were actively involved in local projects organized around establishing shelters for battered women and fighting anti-gay and -lesbian ordinances, as well as protesting the rising incidents of racist behavior on college campuses. While the political involvement of students in the eighties and nineties is more modest than the dramatic social movements and generational sweep of the 1960s, students have been much more active than popular mythologies suggest.

There is also an emerging culture of opposition among many students in the nineties within popular terrains made possible by the new electronic technologies. In addition to making a space for themselves in the spheres of music, cable TV, and the Internet, young people increasingly are producing their own magazines and newspapers as an intervention into public life. For example, independent newspapers such as *Vox,* created by teenagers in Atlanta, provide a launching pad for energetic writers, especially young people of color, to tell their own stories and combine political commentary with personal narrative. At least twenty youth-produced newspapers exist nationwide with an "estimated cumulative circulation of more than 1.5 million readers."[26] If the political activism of progressive youth suggests a new form of cultural politics, it also is being reasserted through traditional forms of protest on many of the nation's campuses, which now appear under siege as a result of the financial defunding and increasing vocationalization of higher education.

In many ways the "crisis" of American higher education resonates with criticisms lodged by young people against the university in the sixties and appears to apply just as forcefully today. Facing draconian cuts in student aid, increasing work loads for faculty, and the reorientation of the curriculum toward corporate. interests, many students, especially at public universities such as the City University of New York (CUNY), are once again raising questions about what the university should be and what kind of society young people are being prepared for in such institutions. Nor is the problem confined to the United States. In France, students and workers recently protested a similar attack on the universities by launching a three-and-a-half-week strike that brought the country to a standstill and forced the government to back off on planned cuts in financial aid and social benefits.[27] The dominant media in the United States generally disregarded this massive show of strength by French students.

In the United States, the dominant media culture has relied largely upon three strategies in addressing student activism. One strategy operates through the process of simple exclusion. That is, the media gives no serious coverage of the growing social concerns and emerging activism among young people on American campuses and in other public spheres. A second strategy mines the history of student activism in order to commodify it. For instance, marketing the sixties has not been lost on the likes of Frey Boots, Nike, and other companies who turn the political slogans of a time of social upheaval into ads for boots, shoes, and fragrances. But the most aggressive attempt to undermine student activism is expressed through demonizing and scapegoating. When the media does address campus activism or social protest movements, it generally dismisses such protests on the grounds that they are simply an expression of what conservatives label as multiculturalism or "political correctness" (a euphemism for disparaging anyone who takes a critical stand on a social issue).[28]

Revising the legacy of the sixties, a period in history which conservatives find both dangerous and indispensable, seems more urgent than ever if educators and others are to create alternative understandings of that period in order to reassess critically how we might once again regain a legitimate belief in the possibility of a vital and substantive democracy and the role that young people might play in shaping it. This should not suggest that we romanticize the sixties or treat the decade as a seamless whole. Nor should we overlook the economic, social, and cultural differences that distinguish sixties youth from their counterparts in the nineties. Kurt Cobain's suicide is an important, though extreme, reminder of the "no way in and no way out" attitude that characterizes a large segment of youth in this country. Confronting a future far more precarious than that a genera-tion of young people faced in the sixties, many youths feel powerless to change the world they have inherited. Author Paul Rogat Loeb captures the malaise in the voices of many of the college students he interviewed between 1987 and 1993. He writes:

> Most concluded that the world was inherently unfair, and that
> they had little possibility of changing it. Buried by outside jobs
> and by massive debt loads, threatened by a dubious economic
> future, these students feared they were on their own in terms
> of personal survival. They suspected they'd have to "work
> twice as hard" to match their parents' standard of living.
> Commitments of conscience "would only get in the way."
> Many also feared that if they failed in their struggle toward the
> top they'd end up unemployed and expendable, scraping to

get by. They needed to focus, they said, on learning to adapt
to whatever circumstances they'd encounter. They could not
afford to address the history that had shaped their lives.[29]

Such pessimism speaks less to the failure of a generation of young
people than to the unwillingness of adult society to address the
rampant poverty, racism, sexism, and lack of job opportunities facing
the current generation of youth. Hope in the sixties was rooted in both
a rejection of middle-class values and the recognition that material
affluence was available to large segments of youth. Rejecting the
middle-class lifestyle of baby boomers and the material affluence that
opened up various avenues of social and economic mobility is no
longer an option for many youth in the nineties. Too many youths,
especially blacks and the urban poor, occupy an uneasy interstice
between the adult world and the future, a world marked by conve-
nience stores, fast food chains, and desolate housing projects.

But in spite of such social and economic differences between
generations, there is much to be learned from the sixties in
addressing the "crisis" of youth as it unfolds in the streets, neighborhoods, schools, media, and state apparatuses. The legacy of sixties
activism provides a resource for understanding how the language of
critique and possibility opened up a new sense of agency for young
people to enter into a dialogue with power, history, and knowledge.
Contradictory and multiple in both how they took hold of their
sense of purpose and meaning, sixties activists suggested a notion of
youth linked not merely to an unbridled narcissism, but to a
redefinition of democracy as a vibrant dialogue in which young
people provided a prophetic vision and played a vital role in ending
both segregation and a morally dubious war and in promoting
democratic social change. In the current climate, childhood and
youth are no longer treasured for their role in providing a prophetic

vision, a multinarrated dream in which hope becomes the basis for critical agency and civic courage.

But history is open, and those adults who felt so comfortable in the fifties also were unaware of the coming storm of the sixties. Youth are symbolically central to the reproduction of society.[30] But even where youth in the past were seen as both troubled and troubling, adults used the "crisis" of youth to order, regulate, and appeal to future generations to take up the demands and relations of power of the existing social order. Seen as the "other," adults expressed concern and alarm in their attempt to assimilate youth to existing relations of power and dominant values. In this scenario, youth were in transit between being outside and coming inside. Something has changed in the last decade. Many youth not only are situated beyond the margins of acceptable society, but also are seen as irrelevant to the way in which society unfolds. The "crisis" of youth is really about the crisis of adult society and democracy in general. Fortunately, there is always an indeterminacy in youth, a vibrancy that seems to exceed the limits adults place on them; this is what makes youth appear dangerous and at the same time provides the ground for prophetic action. Maybe new storm clouds are forming so that the twenty-first century will awaken to a new generation of kids willing to put a stop to the suffering and oppression that has become so endemic to American society, willing to challenge a society that seems spiritually and ethically frozen with regard to its responsibilities to the present and its vision of the future.

SECTION II

RACE, MEDIA, AND WHITENESS

FOUR

WHITE NOISE
RACIAL POLITICS
AND THE PEDAGOGY OF WHITENESS

INTRODUCTION

The crisis of leadership in the white community is
remarkable—and terrifying—because there is, in fact, no
white community.

—James Baldwin[1]

"Whiteness" is no longer invisible. As a symbol of
cultural identity and an object of critical scholar-
ship, it has become both a symbol of resurgent racism and the subject
of a rising academic specialization. For conservative ideologues,
"whiteness" has been appropriated as a badge of self-identity and
fashioned as a rallying point for disaffected whites who claim they are
the victims of reverse racism in a country that is becoming increasingly racially diverse and hybridized. Under "attack" by multi-
culturalists, radicals, feminists, gays, lesbians, and other subordinate
groups, such whites feel besieged and persecuted.

At the same time, "whiteness" has become the object of critical analysis in a number of academic fields, including literary studies, anthropology, labor history, and feminist studies. This new scholarship, named by some as "whiteness studies," has attracted a great deal of media attention, and is best known for revealing how over time "whiteness" in its various ideological and institutional forms has worked to perpetuate relations of domination and oppression against nonwhites while simultaneously securing whites with a disproportionate amount of power and privilege.[2]

While the "old" view of "whiteness" as a signifier of privilege and power is enjoying a resurgence in the United States, it appears mainly as a rear-guard attempt to ward off those forces chipping away at the remaining, though far from weak, vestiges of racism that structure all aspects of public life. The new scholarship on "whiteness" provides an enormous theoretical and political service in revealing and deconstructing how the ideology of "whiteness" has worked historically in America and how it currently operates politically in the service of racism. And yet, the new scholarship is troubling in its inability to capture the complexity that marks "whiteness" as a form of identity and cultural practice. The distinction between "whiteness" as a dominating ideology and white people who are positioned across multiple locations of privilege and subordination is often sacrificed in this work to the assumption that "whiteness" is simply "the terrifying attempt to build an identity based on what one isn't and on whom one can hold back."[3] Being white in this context appears by default to make one a racist.

Defining "whiteness" largely as a form of domination, such scholarship, while rightly unmasking "whiteness" as a mark of ideology and racial privilege, fails to provide a nuanced, dialectical, and layered account of "whiteness" that would allow white youth and others to appropriate selective elements of white identity and culture as oppositional. This theoretical lacuna suggests that workers, educators, and students face the task of rethinking the subversive possibility of "whiteness." Such a pedagogical and political challenge means, in part, reimagining "whiteness" beyond both identity politics' fixed boundaries, defined primarily through a discourse of separatism and white supremacy, and the acts of bad faith—whites exhibiting what historian Eric Lott calls "blackface's unconscious return."[4]

While it is imperative that a critical analysis of "whiteness" address its historical legacy and existing complicity with racist exclusion and oppression, it is equally crucial that such work distinguish between "whiteness" as a racial identity that is nonracist or antiracist and those aspects of "whiteness" that are racist.[5] Where "whiteness" has been dealt with in educational terms the emphasis is almost exclusively on revealing "whiteness" as an ideology of privilege mediated largely through the dynamics of racism.[6] While such interventions are crucial in developing an antiracist pedagogy, they do not go far enough. I am concerned about what it means educationally for those of us who engage in an antiracist pedagogy and politics to suggest to students that "whiteness" can only be understood in terms of the common experience of white domination and racism. What subjectivities or points of identification become available to white students who can only imagine white experience as monolithic, self-contained, and deeply racist? What are the educational and political stakes in rearticulating "whiteness" in anti-essentialist terms so that white youth can understand and struggle against the long legacy of white racism while using the particularities of "their own culture as a resource for resistance, reflection, and empowerment?"[7]

At the same time, there are too few attempts to develop a pedagogy of "whiteness" that enables white students to move beyond positions of guilt or resentment. There is a curious absence in the work on "whiteness" regarding how students might examine critically the construction of their own identities in order to rethink "whiteness" as a discourse of both critique and possibility.[8] Cultural critics need to connect "whiteness" with a language of possibility that provides a space for white students to imagine how "whiteness" as an ideology and social location can be progressively appropriated as part of a broader politics of social reform. "Whiteness" needs to be theorized carefully in terms of its potential to provide students with a racial identity that can play a crucial role in refashioning an antiracist politics that informs a broader, radical, democratic project. In what follows, I want to delineate in more detail the dialectic of "whiteness" as it has been embraced both by conservative whites and in the new scholarship.

THE CONSERVATIVE POLITICS OF WHITENESS

In the early 1990s the debate over race took a provocative turn as "whiteness" became increasingly visible as a symbol of racial identity. Displaced from its widely understood status as an unnamed, universal moral referent, "whiteness" as a category of racial identity was appropriated by diverse conservative and right-wing groups, as well as critical scholars, as part of a broader articulation of race and difference, though in different ways and for radically opposed purposes. For a disparate group of whites, mobilized, in part, by the moral panic generated by right-wing attacks on immigration, race-preferential policies, and the welfare state, "whiteness" became a signifier for middle-class resistance to "taxation, to the expansion of state-furnished rights of all sorts, and to integration."[9] Threatened by the call for minority rights, the rewriting of American history from the bottom up, and the shifting racial demographics of the nations' cities, other whites felt increasingly angry and resentful over what was viewed as an attack on their sense of individual and collective consciousness.[10]

As "whiteness" came under scrutiny by various social groups as an oppressive, invisible center against which all else is measured, many whites began to identify with the "new racism" epitomized by right-wing conservatives such as talk show host Rush Limbaugh.[11] Winning over vast audiences with the roar of the "angry white male" bitter over imagined racial injuries committed against whites, Limbaugh's popularity affirmed that race had become the most significant social force of the 1980s and 1990s. In an era of unprecedented unemployment, poverty, and diminishing opportunities for most black Americans, right-wing whites had convinced themselves of their own loss of privilege. Thus, the discourse of race became a vehicle for appeasing white anxiety and undermining the forceful legacy of racial and "social justice." The progressive legacy of identity politics as "a crucial movement to expand citizenship to people of color and other subordinated groups" was either trivialized or dismissed as conservatives appropriated the politics of identity as a defining principle of "whiteness."[12] Cultural critic John Brenkman highlights this appropriation by claiming that "the constituency whose beliefs and fears have been most significantly molded to their racial identity in the 1980s are white."[13]

A siege mentality has arisen for policing cultural boundaries and reasserting national identity. The discourse of "whiteness" as an ambivalent signifier of resentment and confusion gives expression to a mass of whites who feel victimized and bitter while it masks deep inequalities and exclusionary practices within the current social order. Shifting the politics of race from the discourse of white supremacy, the historical legacy of slavery, and segregation as well as the ongoing burden of racial injustice endured by African Americans and other minorities in the United States, politicians such as Pat Buchanan,

David Duke, Jesse Helms, and Pat Robertson have mobilized a new populist discourse about family, nation, traditional values, and individualism as part of a broader resistance to multicultural democracy and diverse racial culture.

In the rapidly expanding medium of talk radio, conservatives bash blacks for many of the social and economic problems facing the country.[14] Conservative columnist Mickey Kaus exemplified this sensibility when he said that he wants "to live in a society where there is no alienated race and no racism, where I need not feel uncomfortable walking down the street because I'm white."[15] As race became paramount in shaping American politics and everyday life from the 1980s on, racial prejudice in its overt forms was considered a taboo. While the old racism maintained some cachet among the more vulgar right-wing conservatives (i.e., New York City's radio talk show host Bob Grant), a new racist discourse emerged in the United States. The new racism was coded in the language of "welfare reform, neighborhood schools, toughness on crime and 'illegitimate' births." Cleverly manipulated to mobilize white fears while relieving whites of any semblance of social responsibility and commitment, the new racism served to rewrite the politics of "whiteness" as a "besieged" racial identity. As the racial backlash intensified in the broader culture, "whiteness" assumed a new form of political agency visible in the rise of right-wing militia groups, white skinheads, and the anti-PC crusades of indignant white students and conservative academic organizations such as the National Association of Scholars and the Southern League.[16]

Rather than being invisible, as left-wing critics such as Richard Dyer and bell hooks have claimed, "whiteness" was aggressively embraced in popular culture in order to rearticulate a sense of individual and collective identity for "besieged" whites.[17] Celebrated in the mass media in the 1990s, the new cartography of race has emerged as the result of an attempt to rewrite the racial legacy of the past while recovering a mythic vision of "whiteness" associated with purity and innocence. Immensely popular films such as *Forrest Gump* (1994) attempted to rewrite public memory by cleansing the American past of racial tensions and endorsing "a preferred understanding of racial relations that work on the behalf of the public mourning of the 'victimized white male.'"[18] Widely discussed books such as *The Bell Curve* by Richard Herrnstein and Charles Murray and *The End of Racism* by Dinesh D'Souza revised and reaffirmed the basic principles of the eugenics debate of the 1920s and 1930s and provided a defense of racial hierarchies.[19]

In the popular press, the discourse of racial discrimination and social inequality gave way to lurid stories about black crime, illegal aliens taking jobs, the threat to the deficit posed by government welfare payments to single, teen mothers, and the assertion that black "gangsta" rap artists such as Snoop Doggy Dogg and Ice Cube corrupt the moral values of white suburban youth.[20] While liberal academic journals such as *The New Republic* and *The Atlantic Monthly* shunned the extremist discourses of David Duke, Ralph Reed, and Jerry Falwell, they produced editorials and stories legitimating the popular perception that black culture is a culture of crime, pathology, and moral degeneracy. *The New Republic* devoted an entire issue to an analysis of *The Bell Curve,* justifying its decision in a shameful editorial statement that declared, "The notion that there might be resilient ethnic differences in intelligence is not, we believe, an inherently racist belief."[21] Of course, the refusal to acknowledge that such a position grew historically from a eugenics movement that legitimated diverse racial hatreds as well as some of the most barbarous and atrocious massacres of the twentieth century appeared irrelevant next to the editorial's self-congratulatory assertion of intellectual flexibility. *The Atlantic Monthly* echoed similar racial fears in a barrage of sensationalist cover stories and articles about how crime, disease, gangsta rap, unwed (black) mothers, and the breakdown of public order were about to wreak havoc on "everyone—even white people in Back Bay."[22]

The tawdry representations of black experience that these magazines produced gained increasing currency in the dominant media. Racial coding parading as commonsense populism associated blacks with a series of negative equivalencies that denied racial injustice while affirming the repressed, unspeakable, racist unconscious of dominant white culture. Images of menacing black youth, welfare mothers, and convicts, framed by the evocative rhetoric of fearmongering journalists, helped to bolster the image of a besieged white middle-class suburban family threatened by "an alien culture and peoples who are less civilized than the native ones . . . a people who stand lower in the order of culture because they are somehow lower in the order of nature, defined by race, by color, and sometimes by genetic inheritance."[23]

While the popular press was signaling the emergence of a politics of identity in which white men defined themselves as the victims of "reverse" racial prejudice, academics were digging in and producing a substantial amount of scholarship exploring what it might mean to analyze "whiteness" as a social, cultural, and historical construction. Such work was characterized by diverse attempts to locate "whiteness" as a racial category and to analyze it as a site of privilege, power, and ideology, but also to examine critically how "whiteness" as a racial identity is experienced, reproduced, and addressed by those diverse white men and women who identify with its commonsense assumptions and values.

In some quarters, the call to study "whiteness" provoked scorn and indignation. For instance, *Time* magazine held up to ridicule a professor who named a standard American literature survey course she taught "White Male Writers."[24] *Newsweek* took a more mainstream position, constructing an image of white men in the United States as undergoing an identity crisis over their changing public image. According to the editors of *Newsweek,* white males were no longer secure in an identity that had been ravaged by "feminists, multi-culturalists, P.C. policepersons, affirmative-action employers, rap artists, Native Americans, Japanese tycoons, Islamic fundamentalists and Third World dictators."[25] *Newsweek* further lamented the clobbering that white men were taking in the media, buttressing its argument with comments from a "rancorous" female employee as well as a prominent psychiatrist who assured readers that "For white men in their 30s and 40s, this is not a joke at all. Their whole future is at stake, in their minds. They're scared."[26] While the demise of the power of white men seemed a bit exaggerated to the editors of *Newsweek,* they also made it quite clear that the current white panic was not entirely unfounded since in the next century whites may find themselves living in a society consisting largely of "diverse racial and ethnic minorities."[27]

THE RISE OF WHITENESS STUDIES

Building upon the work of W. E. B. DuBois, Ralph Ellison, and James Baldwin, scholars from a wide range of disciplines, including history, cultural studies, literary studies, sociology, and speech communication, have put the "construction of 'whiteness' on the table to be investigated, analyzed, punctured, and probed."[28] Rejecting the assumption that an analysis of race means focusing primarily on people of color, scholars Ruth Frankenberg, bell hooks, Toni Morrison, Howard Winant, Alexander Saxton, Fred Pfeil, and others address the historical and social construction of "whiteness" across a wide spectrum of spheres, identities, and institutions and redefine the necessity to make "whiteness" central to the broader arena of racial politics.[29] While it is impossible to analyze this large body of work in any great detail, I want to comment briefly on some of the theoretical directions it has taken and assess the implications of such work for those of us concerned with issues of representation, racial politics, and pedagogy.

Historians such as David Roediger, Noel Ignatiev, and Theodore Allen, among others, have built upon the work of previous historians of race by focusing less on the African-American roots of mainstream white culture than on the issue of how white identities were constructed, appropriated, and shaped historically. Challenging both what it means to be white and the experience of "whiteness" as an often unstable, shifting process of inclusion and exclusion, these historians have rearticulated and broadened the concept of racial identity while simultaneously challenging "whiteness" as a site of racial, economic, and political privilege. More specifically, such work brings a revisionist history to the highly charged debates about racial and national identity central to contemporary American politics. By focusing on how "whiteness" as the dominant racial identity shaped at different intervals the history of American labor and configured historical and political relations among ethnic groups (such as the Irish), Roediger and others have thrown into sharp relief "the impact that the dominant racial identity in the United States has had not only on the treatment of racial 'others' but also on the ways that whites think of themselves, of power, of pleasure, and of gender."[30]

Central to theoretical work on "whiteness" is the attempt to confront "the issue of white racial identity [and to raise] the questions of when, why and with what results so-called 'white people' have come to identify themselves as white."[31] No longer the stable, self-evident, or pure essence central to modernity's self-definition, "whiteness" in the work of such historians as David Roediger and Noel Ignatiev is unmasked as an attempt to arbitrarily categorize, position, and contain the "other" within racially ordered hierarchies. Dislodged from a self-legitimating discourse grounded in a set of fixed transcendental racial categories, "whiteness" is analyzed as a lived but rarely recognized component of white racial identity and domination.

These scholars have done more than add a historical component to the discourse about "whiteness"; they have expanded and deepened the relevance of politicizing the debates about the interrelationship between "whiteness" and race. Roediger, for example, provides three reasons for urging cultural critics who are involved in the social construction of race to focus their political energies on "exposing, demystifying and demeaning the particular ideology of 'whiteness'":

> The first is that, while neither whiteness nor Blackness is a scientific (or natural) racial category, the former is infinitely more false, and precisely because of that falsity, more dangerous, than the latter. The second is that in attacking the notion that whiteness and Blackness are "the same," we specifically undermine what has become, via the notion of "reverse racism," a major prop underpinning the popular refusal among whites to face both racism and themselves. The last is that whiteness is now a particularly brittle and fragile form of social identity and it can be fought.[32]

The notion that "whiteness" can be demystified and reformulated is a theoretical motif that links historical analyses of the construction of "whiteness" to the work of prominent theorists in a variety of other fields. For instance, Toni Morrison in her landmark book *Playing in the Dark* challenges critics to examine how "whiteness" as a literary category functions in the shaping and legitimating of a monolithic

"American identity." Morrison frames her interrogation of the imaginative construction of "whiteness" in the following way:

> the readers of virtually all of American fiction have been
> positioned as white. I am interested to know what that assumption has meant to the literary imagination. When does
> racial "unconsciousness" or awareness of race enrich interpretive language, and when does it impoverish it? . . . What parts
> do the invention and development of whiteness play in the
> construction of what is loosely described as "American"?[33]

In the field of cultural studies, Ruth Frankenberg, Richard Dyer, and bell hooks further probe the role of "whiteness" as a site of privilege and exclusion, recognizing that "whiteness" is produced differently within a variety of public spaces as well as across the diverse categories of class, gender, sexuality, and ethnicity. Frankenberg, for example, has explored how "whiteness" as a site of racial privilege works to shape the lives and identities of a diverse group of white women.[34] Dyer, on the other hand, challenges the representational power of "whiteness" "to be everything and nothing as the source of its representational power" through an analysis of the racial pedagogies at work in popular culture. He provides a theoretical service by analyzing "whiteness" as a guarantor of beauty and truth within the representational politics of three Hollywood films.[35]

One of the most trenchant criticisms of "whiteness" comes from bell hooks, who argues that too many white scholars focus on certifiable "others" in their analysis of race, but are doing very little "to investigate and justify all aspects of white culture from a standpoint of 'difference.'"[36] According to hooks, "It would be just so interesting for all those white folks who are giving blacks their take on blackness to let them know what's going on with whiteness."[37] Hooks further extends her critique by arguing that while whites are willing to analyze how blacks are perceived by whites, rarely are white critics attentive to how blacks view whites. For hooks, whites refuse to see blacks as political agents. Nor do whites, caught up in their own racial fantasies of murder and rape, recognize that in the black imagination "whiteness" is often associated with terror. But for hooks more is at stake than getting whites to recognize that representations of "whiteness" as pure, good, benevolent, and innocent are challenged by black imaginations' representations of "whiteness" as capricious, cruel, and unchecked. Hooks also calls into question "whiteness" as an ideology by exposing its privileged readings of history, art, and broader institutional power and its politically myopic forms of cultural criticism. Hooks builds upon this criticism by calling for whites to become self-critical about how "whiteness" terrorizes, to "shift locations [in order] to see the world differently."[38]

In a decisive theoretical and somewhat paradoxical twist, hooks urges whites not to go too far in focusing on "whiteness," particularly if it serves to downplay the effects of racism on blacks. First, she argues that attempts to see racism as victimizing to whites "in the hopes that this will act as an intervention is a misguided strategy."[39] Second, disavowing the discourse of white victimization as one that fails to distinguish between racial prejudice, as it is experienced by blacks and whites alike, and institutional racism, which victimizes people of color, primarily blacks, hooks agrees with the black theologian James Cone, who argues that the only way in which whites can become antiracist is "to destroy themselves and be born again as beautiful black persons."[40]

Hooks's criticism is echoed in the field of speech communication by Thomas Nakayama and Robert Krizek, who also argue that the primary task of whites is to demystify and unveil "whiteness" as a form of domination. In this case, Nakayama and Krizek go to great lengths to "deterritorialize the territory of 'white,' to expose, examine, and disrupt . . . so that like other positions it may be placed under critical analysis. . . . We seek an understanding of the ways that this rhetorical construction makes itself visible and invisible, eluding analysis yet exerting influence over everyday life."[41]

Heavily indebted to the assumption that "whiteness" is synonymous with domination, oppression, and privilege, the critical project that largely informs the new scholarship on "whiteness" rests on a singular assumption. Its primary aim is to unveil the rhetorical, political, cultural, and social mechanisms through which "whiteness" is both invented and used to mask its power and privilege. The political thrust of such work seeks to abolish "whiteness" as a racial category and marker of identity. Roediger echoes this sentiment in his comment that "It is not merely that 'whiteness' is oppressive and false; it is that 'whiteness' is *nothing but* oppressive and false."[42] This position is echoed by Noel Ignatiev, who provocatively writes in *Race Traitor* that "the key to solving the social problems of our age is to abolish the white race. . . . So long as the white race exists, all movements against racism are doomed to fail [and] treason to 'whiteness' is loyalty to humanity."[43] Similar arguments conflating "whiteness" with white racism can be found in the work of Derrick Bell and Andrew Hacker.[44] In what follows, I want to analyze some of the political and educational problems based on the assumption that "whiteness" is synonymous with domination and the only alternative that progressive white kids have to constructing a racial identity is to, in fact, renounce their own "whiteness." I develop this critique by examining three considerations. First, I focus on some of the issues at stake in understanding the racial backlash that is taking place among many white students in the United States. Second, I address how representations of "whiteness" in two films exemplify the limits and possibilities of analyzing the social construction of "whiteness." Third, I explore how these films might be used pedagogically to rearticulate a notion of "whiteness" that builds upon, but also moves beyond, the view of "whiteness" as simply a fixed position of domination. In doing so, I attempt to address the possibility of fashioning a tentative and strategic educational approach to "whiteness" that offers students the possibility for rearticulating "whiteness" rather than either simply accepting its dominant normative assumptions or rejecting it as a racist form of identity. While white students may well feel traumatized in putting their racial identities on trial, trauma in this case can become a useful pedagogical tool in helping them locate themselves within and against the discourse and practice of racism. White youth need a more critical and productive way of construing a sense of identity, agency, and race across a wide range of contexts and public spheres. However, linking "whiteness" to the project of radical democratic change should not be a rationale for evading racial injustice and the deep inequalities between blacks and whites.

YOUTH AND THE REARTICULATION OF WHITENESS

Race increasingly matters as a defining principle of identity and culture as much for white students in the 1990s as it did for youth of color in the 1970s and 1980s. As a marker of difference, race significantly frames how white youth experience themselves and their relationships to a variety of public spaces marked by the presence of people of color. In contrast to the position popular among white educators who claim that "We [whites] do not experience ourselves as defined by our skin color,"[45] white youth have become increasingly aware of themselves as white. Two major forces affecting the racial divide have served to make "whiteness" more visible and fragile as a site of privilege and power, while at the same time limiting opportunities for youth to be both white and oppositional.[46] The first is the emergence of identity politics in the United States from the 1960s to the present. While contradictory and diverse in its manifestations, identity politics has largely resulted in the formation, consolidation, and visibility of new group racial identities. But such identities have emerged within a highly charged public debate on race, gender, and sexual orientation and have made it more difficult for white youth to either ignore "whiteness" as a racial category or to "safely imagine that they are invisible to black people."[47] White students may see themselves as nonracist, but they no longer view themselves as colorless. As Charles Gallagher points out, "whiteness" has become "a salient category of self-definition emerging in response to the political and cultural challenges of other racialized groups."[48]

Contrary to its advocates' claims, identity politics has not promoted the transformation of society in general, but a politics of difference that asserts itself through the separate and often essentialized banners of race, gender, sexuality, ethnicity, and nationality. Within this recoding of the politics of recognition and difference, the experiences, rights, and histories of subordinate groups have been affirmed. However, these groups have been simply unable to articulate a new social vision rooted in the principles of equality and solidarity that would organize progressive "interactions between white and black people in addressing such a politics."[49]

Unfortunately, for many white youth whose imaginations have been left fallow, unfed by a larger society's vision or quest for social justice, identity politics has engendered a defensive posture. White students have assumed that the only role they can play in the struggle against racism is either to renounce their "whiteness" and become black or suffer the charge that any claim to white identity is tantamount to racism. Within this paradigm, racism has been configured through a politics of representation that has analyzed how whites have constructed, stereotyped, and delegitimated racial others, but it has had practically nothing to say about how racial politics might address the construction of "whiteness" as an oppositional racial category. Moreover, while the debate within identity politics has made important theoretical gains in rewriting what it means to be black, it has not questioned the complexity of "whiteness" with the same dialectical attentiveness. Although "whiteness" has become an object of critical scrutiny, it appears to have no connotation except to "signify the center which pushes out, excludes, appropriates and distorts the margins."[50] Similarly, liberal ideology has provided only a one-item agenda for how blacks and whites might work together in the struggle for social and racial justice. It replaces the recognition of the importance of racial identities with calls for tolerance and appeals to a color-blind society.

Identity politics, in part, has served to undermine the possibilities for white youth to engage critically the liberal appeal to a color-blind society; it has also had the unintended consequence of reinforcing the divide between blacks and whites. Furthermore, the absence of an oppositional space between separatism and a power-evasive liberalism has provided an opportunity for conservatives and right-wing activists to step into the fray and appropriate "whiteness" as part of a broader backlash against blacks and people of color. In this case, conservatives and the far right have actively engaged in the process of recovering "whiteness" and redefining themselves as the victims of racial antagonism while simultaneously waging a brutal and racially coded attack against urban youth, immigrants, and the poor. Seemingly unresponsive to the needs of white youth, the white working class, and the white underclass, the discourse of "whiteness" has been easily appropriated as part of a broader reactionary cultural politics that in its most extreme manifestations has fueled the rise of white militia groups, the growing skinhead movement among white youth, and a growing anti–political correctness movement in both higher education and the mass media.[51]

The second force at work in reconstructing "whiteness" as a racial category among youth is the profound changes that have taken place regarding the visibility of blacks in the media. While it would be foolish to equate the increased visibility of blacks in the media with an increase in power, especially around issues of ownership, diverse representations of black culture throughout the media have made issues of white identity inextricably more fragile and fluid. This is evident in the ways in which popular culture increasingly is being reconfigured through the music, dance, and language of hip-hop. Similarly, the emergence of Black Entertainment Television (BET), MTV, and cable television testifies to the ubiquitous presence of people of color in television dramas, sports, and music while the popular press touts the emergence of the "new" black public intellectuals in academia. All of these changes in the media signal that whites can no longer claim the privilege of not "seeing" blacks and other people of color; white youth now have to confront cultural difference as a force that affects every aspect of their lives. Coupled with the rise of an incendiary racial politics, the racialization of the media culture, and growing economic fears about their future, a significant number of white American youth increasingly are experiencing a crisis of self-esteem. Similar to cultural critic Diana Jester's comment about British youth, white American youth "do not feel that they have an 'ethnicity,' or if they do, that it's not one they feel too good about."[52]

Jester has further suggested that white youth have few resources for questioning and rearticulating "whiteness" as an identity that productively narrates their everyday experiences. This seems to be borne out in the ways in which many white college students have reacted to the racial politics of the last decade. One indication of the way in which "whiteness" is being negotiated among students is evident in the rising racist assaults on students of color on campuses across the United States in the last few years. As a resurgent racism becomes more respectable in the broader culture, racist acts and assaults once again have become a staple of college life. At the same time, large numbers of white students appear to support the ongoing assaults on affirmative-action programs that have been waged by the courts and state legislatures. Moreover, white students increasingly express a general sense of angst over racial politics and an emphatic indifference to politics in general.

Gallagher's ethnographic study of white college students suggests that many of them view the emergence of multiculturalists, feminists, and other progressive groups as an attack on "whiteness" and as a form of reverse discrimination. For example, Gallagher writes, "It is commonly assumed among many white students that any class that addresses issues of race or racism must necessarily be antiwhite. More specifically, students believe that the instructors of these classes will hold individual white students accountable for slavery, lynching, discrimination, and other heinous acts."[53] Many of the white students that Gallagher interviewed did not see themselves as privileged by virtue of skin color; some went so far as to claim that given the rise of racial preferences, whites no longer had a fair chance when competing with minorities in the labor market. Gallagher asserts that white students are resentful over being blamed for racism and that "ignoring the ways in which whites 'get raced' has the making of something politically dangerous . . . [and that] [w]hiteness must be addressed because the politics of race, from campus clubs to issues of crime to representation in the statehouse, permeate almost every social exchange."[54] Unfortunately, Gallagher offers little in the way of suggesting how "whiteness" might be rearticulated in oppositional terms. In fact, he concludes by suggesting that as "whiteness" becomes more visible it will be further appropriated and mediated through a racist ideology, and that any notion of white solidarity will result in a reactionary politics. Hence, "whiteness" as a marker of identity is confined within a notion of domination and racism that leaves white youth no critical lens or vocabulary through which they can see themselves as actors in creating an oppositional space to fight for equality and social justice.

Central to any pedagogical approach to race and the politics of "whiteness" is the recognition that race as a set of attitudes, values, lived experiences, and affective identifications has become a defining feature of American life. However arbitrary and mythic, dangerous and variable, the fact is that racial categories exist and shape the lives of people differently within existing inequalities of power and wealth.[55] As a central form of difference, race will neither disappear, be wished out of existence, nor become somehow irrelevant in the United States and the larger global context. Howard Winant insightfully argues:

> Race is a condition of individual and collective identity, a permanent, though tremendously flexible, element of social structure. Race is a means of knowing and organizing the social world; it is subject to continual contestation and reinterpretation, but it is no more likely to disappear than any other forms of human inequality and difference. . . . To rethink race is not only to recognize its permanence, but also to understand the essential test that it poses for any diverse society seeking to achieve a modicum of freedom.[56]

Educationally this implies providing the conditions for students to address not only how their "whiteness" functions in society as a marker of privilege and power, but also how it can be used as a condition for expanding the ideological and material realities of democratic public life. Moreover, it is imperative that all students understand how race functions systemically as it shapes various forms of representations, social relations, and institutional structures. Rather than proposing the eradication of the concept of race itself, educators and other cultural workers need to fashion pedagogical practices that take a detour through race in order to address how "whiteness" might be renegotiated as a productive force within a politics of difference linked to a radical democratic project.

Analyzing "whiteness" as a central element of racial politics becomes useful in exploring how "whiteness" as a cultural practice promotes race-based hierarchies, how white racial identity structures the struggle over cultural and political resources, and how rights and responsibilities are defined, confirmed, or contested across diverse racial claims.[57] "Whiteness" in this context becomes less a matter of creating a new form of identity politics than an attempt to rearticulate "whiteness" as part of a broader project of cultural, social, and political citizenship.

I want to begin to take up this pedagogical challenge by building upon James Snead's pertinent observation that the emergence of mass visual productions in the United States requires new ways of seeing and making visible the racial structuring of white experience.[58] The electronic media—television, movies, music, and news—have become powerful pedagogical forces, veritable teaching machines in shaping the social imagination of students in terms of how they view themselves, others, and the larger society. Central to the formative influence of the media is a representational politics of race in which the portrayal of black people removes them from their real histories while reinforcing all too familiar stereotypes ranging from lazy and shiftless to menacing and dangerous.

Recent films from a variety of genres, such as *Pulp Fiction* (1995), *Just Cause* (1995), and *Ace Ventura: When Nature Calls*

(1996) offer no apologies for employing racist language, depicting black men as rapists, or portraying blacks as savage or subhuman. Antiracist readings of these films often prompt white students to view racism as the product of dominant racist stereotypes or individual prejudices that unfairly depict black identities, experiences, histories, and social relations. As important as these critiques are in any antiracist discourse, they are severely limited theoretically because they do not address how "whiteness" as a racial identity and social construction is taught, learned, experienced, and identified within certain forms of knowledge, values, and privileges. Nor do such critiques analyze racism as a systemic and institutional issue. Hollywood films rarely position audiences to question the pleasures, identifications, desires, and fears they experience as whites viewing dominant representational politics of race. More specifically, such films rarely reveal either the structuring principles that mobilize particular pleasures in audiences or how pleasure as a response to certain representations functions as part of a broader public discourse. At worst, such films position whites as racial tourists, distant observers to the racist images and narratives that fill Hollywood screens. At best, such films reinforce the liberal assumption that racism is something that gives rise to black oppression but has little or nothing to do with promoting power, racial privilege, and a sense of moral agency in the lives of whites.[59]

In what follows, I want to explore the educational implications for examining representations of "whiteness" in two seemingly disparate films, *Dangerous Minds* (1995) and *Suture* (1993). Though I will focus primarily on *Dangerous Minds* (1995), it is through a juxtaposition and intertextual reading of these films that I hope to provide some pedagogical insights for examining how "whiteness" as a cultural practice is learned through the representation of racialized identities;

how it opens up the possibility of intellectual self-reflection; and how students might mediate critically the complex relations between "whiteness" and racism not by repudiating their "whiteness," but by grappling with its racist legacy and its potential to be rearticulated in oppositional and transformative terms. I also want to stress that I am not suggesting that *Dangerous Minds* is a bad film and *Suture* is a good film given their different approaches to "whiteness." Both have weaknesses that are notable. What I am suggesting is that these films are exemplary as dominant readings of "whiteness" and as cultural texts that can be used educationally to address the shortcomings of the recent scholarship on "whiteness," in particular the jaundiced view of "whiteness" as simply a trope of domination.

At first glance, these films appear to have nothing in common in terms of audience, genre, intention, or politics. *Dangerous Minds,* a Hollywood blockbuster starring Michelle Pfeiffer, was produced for a general audience and grossed millions for its producers within its first week. The film's popularity, in part, can be measured by the appearance of a pilot television series called *Dangerous Minds* that premiered in the fall of 1996. In contrast, *Suture* was an independent film that played primarily to highbrow audiences with a penchant for avantgarde cinema. While some may argue that *Dangerous Minds* was too popular and too unoriginal to be taken seriously as a cultural text, it is precisely because of its popularity and widespread appeal that it warrants an extended analysis. Like many Hollywood films, *Dangerous Minds* is offensive not only in terms of its racial politics but also in its fundamentally debased depiction of teaching and education. The 1995 summer hit is also symptomatic of how seemingly "innocent" entertainment gains its popularity by taking part in a larger public discourse on race and "whiteness" largely informed by a right-wing and conservative notion of politics, theory, and pedagogy.

DANGEROUS MINDS AND
THE PRODUCTION OF WHITENESS

Dangerous Minds resembles a long tradition of Hollywood movies recounting the sorry state of education for dispossessed kids who bear the brunt of poverty, crime, violence, and despair in the inner cities of the United States. Unlike earlier films such as *Blackboard Jungle* (1955), *To Sir With Love* (1967), and *Stand and Deliver* (1988), which also dealt with the interface of schooling and the harsh realities of inner-city life, *Dangerous Minds* does more than simply narrate the story of an idealistic teacher who struggles to connect with her rowdy and disinterested students. *Dangerous Minds* functions as a dual chronicle. In the first instance, the film attempts to represent "whiteness" as the archetype of rationality, "tough" authority, and cultural standards in the midst of the changing racial demographics of urban space and the emergence of a resurgent racism in the highly charged politics of the 1990s. In the second instance, the film offers viewers a mix of compassion and consumerism as a solution to motivating teenagers who have long since given up on schooling as meaningful to their lives. In both instances, "whiteness" becomes a referent not only for rearticulating racially coded notions of teaching and learning, but also for redefining how citizenship can be constructed for students of color as a function of choice linked exclusively to the marketplace.

Providing an allegory for representing both the purpose of schooling and the politics of racial difference as they intersect within the contested space of urban public schools, *Dangerous Minds* skillfully mobilizes race as an organizing principle to promote its narrative structure and ideological message. Black and Hispanic teenagers provide the major fault line for developing pedagogical classroom relations through which "whiteness," located in the authority of the teacher, privileges itself against the racially coded images of disorder, chaos, and fear. The opposition between teacher and student, white and nonwhite, is clearly established in the first few scenes of the film. The opening sequence, shot in grainy monochrome, depicts a run-down urban housing project teeming with poverty, drug dealing, and imminent danger. Against this backdrop, disaffected black and Hispanic children board a school bus that will take them to Parkmont High School and out of their crime- and drug-infested neighborhood. This is one of the few shots in the film that provides a context for the children's lives, and the message is clear: the inner city has become a site of pathology, moral decay, and delinquency synonymous with the culture of working-class black life. The soundtrack, featuring hip-hop music by artists such as Coolio, Sista, and Aaron Hall, is present only as a backdrop to the film. While the driving beat of hip-hop reinforces the gritty urban realism that provides a tidy summation of these kids' everyday lives, it is completely ignored as a cultural or pedagogical resource for learning about their histories, experiences, or the economic, social, and political limits they face daily. Rather, LouAnne's teaching focuses on the (white) subaltern icon of her generation, Bob Dylan. The musical score's marginality to the plot of *Dangerous Minds* notwithstanding, the popularity of gangsta rap has served to reinforce the right-wing assumption that equates black culture with crime and violence.

Since the beginning of the movie is framed by racial iconography and a musical score that construct minority students as both the objects of fear and subjects in need of discipline and control, the audience is prepared for someone to take charge. Enter LouAnne Johnson, a good-hearted ingenue thrust into the classroom of "at-risk" kids like a lamb led to the slaughter.

A divorced ex-marine, LouAnne Johnson turns up at Parkmont High in order to student-teach and finish her degree. She is immediately hired as an English teacher in the "Academy School," a euphemism for the warehouse for students who are considered unteachable. Dressed in frowzy tweeds and white lace, LouAnne enters her class triumphant and full of high hopes, only to meet a room filled with Hispanic and black kids who have brought the "worst" aspects of their culture into the classroom. Music blares amidst the clatter of students shouting, rapping, and dancing, presenting LouAnne with a classroom in an inner-city school that appears to be out of control. Leaving the safety of her white, middle-class culture in order to teach in a place teeming with potential danger, LouAnne Johnson is presented to the audience as an innocent border-crosser. This image of innocence and goodwill is used to provide white America with the comforting belief that disorder, ignorance, and chaos are always somewhere else—in that strangely homogenized racial space known as the urban ghetto.[60] The students respond to LouAnne's attempt to greet them with the taunting epithet "white bread." Confused and unable to gain control of the class, LouAnne is accosted by a male student who makes a mockery of her authority by insulting her with a sexual innuendo. Frustrated, she leaves the class and tells Hal, a friend who teaches next door, that she has just met the "rejects from hell." He assures her that she can reach these students if she figures out how to get their attention.

These opening scenes work powerfully to link black and Hispanic kids with the culture of criminality and danger. They also make clear that "whiteness" as a racial identity, embodied in LouAnne Johnson, is both vulnerable and under siege, as well as the only hope these kids have for moving beyond the context and character of their racial identities. In other words, these scenes construct "whiteness" as a racial identity through the stereotypical portrayal of black and

Hispanic kids as intellectually inferior, hostile, and childish while coding "whiteness" as a norm for authority, orderliness, rationality, and control.

The structuring principles at work in *Dangerous Minds* perform a distinct ideological function in their attempt to cater to white consumers of popular culture. Pedagogy performs a double operation as it is used in this film. As part of the overt project, the film focuses on teaching in an inner-city school and constructs a dominant view of racial others as embodied in the lives of urban black and Hispanic children. On the other hand, the hidden project of the film works to recover and mark the ideological, cultural, and dominant values that construct "whiteness" as a dominant form of racial identity. Hollywood has been producing films about teaching for over forty years, but rarely do such films use the theme of teaching in order to legitimate a conservative view of "whiteness" as a besieged social formation and subordinate racial identities as a threat to public order. *Dangerous Minds* stands as an exception to the rule. The conservative and ideological implications of how "whiteness" is constructed in this film can be seen through a series of representations.

Dangerous Minds tells us nothing about the lives of the students themselves. The audience is given no sense of their histories or experiences outside of the school. Decontextualized and dehistoricized, the cultural identities of these students appear marginal to the construction of race as an organizing principle of the film. Racial differences in this film are situated within the spatial metaphor of center and margins, with the children of color clearly occupying the margins. At the center of the film is the embellished "true story" of LouAnne Johnson, who not only overcomes her initial failure to motivate these students but also serves as a beacon of light by convincing them that who they are and what they know needs to be ditched if they are to become more civilized and cultured (and more white). Racial conflict in this context is resolved through a colonial model in which white paternalism and missionary zeal provide the inspiration for kids from deprived backgrounds to improve their character and sense of responsibility by reading poetry. The kids in this movie simply appear as a backdrop for expanding LouAnne's own self-consciousness and self-education; the film shows no interest in their development and ignores the opportunities for understanding their coming of age and examining how racism works in the schools and larger society. Whenever these kids do face a crisis—an unwanted pregnancy, the threat of violence, or dropping out of school—LouAnne invades their homes and private lives, using the opportunity to win the kids' allegiance or draw attention to her own divorce, physical abuse, or sense of despair. If any notion of identity occupies center stage, it is not that of the kids but that of a white woman trying to figure out how to live in a public space inhabited by racialized others.

The notion of authority and agency in *Dangerous Minds* is framed within a notion of "tough love" that serves to mask how racial hierarchies and structured inequality operate within the schools to connect them to the larger society. Authority in *Dangerous Minds* is asserted initially when LouAnne Johnson shows up on the second day of class wearing a leather jacket and jeans. Reinventing herself as a military officer on leave, she further qualifies her new "tough," no-nonsense look by informing her students she is an ex-marine who knows karate. Suggesting that fear and danger are the only emotions her students recognize as important, LouAnne crosses a racial divide by rooting her sense of authority in a traditionally racist notion of discipline and control. Once she gets the group's attention, she moves onto more lofty ground and begins the arduous task of trying to develop a pedagogy that is both morally uplifting and educationally relevant. Choice becomes for LouAnne the theoretical axis that organizes her classroom approach. First, on the side of moral uplift (complete with a conservative nineties whitewashing of history), she tells her students that there are no victims in her class. Presumably, this is meant as a plea to rouse their sense of agency and responsibility, but it rings entirely hollow since LouAnne has no understanding of the social and historical limits that shape their sense of agency on a daily basis. Of course, some students immediately recognize the bad faith implicit in her sermonizing call and urge her to test it with a dose of reality by living in their neighborhood for a week.

Moreover, LouAnne appears to confuse her own range of choices—predicated, in part, on her class and racial privileges—with those of her students, even though they lack the power and resources to negotiate their lives politically, geographically, or economically with the same ease or options. She has no sense that choice springs from power and that those who have limited power have fewer choices. The subtext here reinforces the currently popular right-wing assumption that character, merit, and self-help are the basis on which people take their place in society. Of course, within a hierarchical and social structure organized by race, as well as economic power, gender, and other key determinants, "whiteness" emerges as the normative basis for success, responsibility, and legitimate authority. By suggesting that white educators can ignore how larger social considerations impact on racial groups, white privilege, experience, and culture is relieved of complicity with, if not responsibility for, racist ideology and structural inequalities.

Choice is not only trivialized in LouAnne's classroom, it provides the basis for a pedagogy that is as indifferent to the lives of poor inner-city kids as it is demeaning. Relying on the logic of the market to motivate her kids, LouAnne rewards classroom cooperation with candy bars, a trip to an amusement park, and dinner at a fancy restaurant. Baiting students with gimmicks and bribes does more than cast a moral shadow on the educational value of such an approach or the teacher as a kind of ethical exemplar; it also makes clear how little LouAnne knows about the realities of her students' lives. Indifferent to the skills they need to survive, LouAnne is unconcerned about their experiences, interests, or cultural resources. This becomes clear in three pivotal instances in the movie.

In the first instance, LouAnne attempts to motivate the students by giving them the lyrics to Bob Dylan's "Mr. Tambourine Man." Indifferent to the force of hip-hop culture (though, in designing the soundtrack, marketing executives appeared to know the draw and impact of hip-hop on the film's audience), her attempt to use popular culture appears as nothing less than an act of cultural ignorance and bad pedagogy. But more revealing is her attempt to relate Dylan's lyrics to the most clichéd aspects of the students' culture—namely violence and drugs. Not only does she ignore her students' own cultural resources and interests, but she also frames her notion of popular culture in a text from the 1960s—almost twenty years before these kids were born. Rather than excavating the traditions, themes, and experiences that make up her students' lives in order to construct her curriculum, she simply avoids their voices altogether in shaping the content of what she teaches. Beneath this form of symbolic violence there is also the presupposition that whites can come into such schools and teach without theory, ignore the histories and narratives that students bring to schools, and perform miracles in children's lives by mere acts of kindness.

In LouAnne's romantic version of schooling and teaching, there is no sense of what it means to give urban youth survival skills. The teacher's ignorance is reflected in another scene in which she visits the grandmother of two black students who have been missing from school for several days. The boys' grandmother has pulled them out of school and LouAnne decides to reason with her in order to get the students back into her class. The grandmother meets her in the yard and refers to her as a "white-bread bitch." The grandmother is indignant over what the boys have brought home for homework and tells LouAnne that "her boys have got bills to pay and that she should find some other poor boys to save." Regardless of the fact that Bob Dylan's lyrics are irrelevant to the kids' lives, the black grandmother is represented as an obstructionist. Yet, she is actually closer to the truth in suggesting that what LouAnne has passed off as useful knowledge will not help the boys survive life in the ghetto, nor will it change the conditions that give rise to urban squalor.

LouAnne's teaching is in actuality a pedagogy of diversion—one that refuses to provide students with skills that will help them address the urgent and disturbing questions of a society and a culture that in many ways ignores their humanity and well-being. These students are not taught to question the intellectual and cultural resources they need to address the profoundly inhuman conditions they have to negotiate every day. How to survive in a society, let alone remake it, is an important pedagogical question that cannot be separated from the larger issue of what it means to live in a country that is increasingly hostile to the existence of poor white and black kids in the inner cities. But LouAnne ignores these issues and offers her students material incentives to learn, and in doing so she constructs them as consuming subjects rather than social subjects eager and able to think critically in order to negotiate and transform the world in which they live. In one pivotal exchange, students ask LouAnne what reward they are going to get for reading a poem. She surprises her students and the wider audience by insisting that learning is its own best reward. In doing so she switches her teaching strategy, completely unaware of the consequences or limitations of the marketplace approach she has employed most of the semester.

LouAnne's sense of privilege also becomes evident in the boundless confidence she exhibits in her authority and moral superiority. She believes that somehow her students are answerable to her both in terms of their classroom performance and in terms of their personal lives; her role is to affirm or gently "correct" how they narrate their beliefs, experiences, and values. LouAnne takes for granted that she has an unquestioned right to "save" them or run their lives without entering into a dialogue in which her own authority and purity of intentions are called into question. Authority here functions as a way of making invisible LouAnne's own privileges as a white woman, while simultaneously allowing her to indulge in a type of moralizing commensurate with her colonizing role as a white teacher who extracts from her students love and loyalty in exchange for teaching them to be part of a system that oppresses them.

The inability of LouAnne to enter into a dialogue with her students is apparent in two important interchanges with them. In one scene, LouAnne breaks up a fight between Emilio and some other students, then demands from Emilio a full explanation:

> LouAnne: Was it worth it? You like to hit people? Why? You feel angry?
>
> Emilio: You're trying to figure me out. You going to try to psychologize me. I'll help you. I come from a broken home, and we're poor, okay. I see the same fucking movies you do.
>
> LouAnne: I'd like to help you, Emilio.
>
> Emilio: Thank you very much. And how you going to do that? You going to give me some good advice—just say no—you going to get me off the streets? Well forget it. How the fuck are you going to save me from my life?

Emilio is trying to educate her, but LouAnne is not listening carefully. She assumes a moralizing posture that is totally indifferent to understanding the complex forces shaping Emilio's life. Nor can this great white hope consider the idea that her students' histories and world views might be incorporated usefully into her pedagogy in order to teach kids like Emilio the survival skills and knowledge they need to cope with the conditions and contexts of their surroundings. In another exchange, LouAnne takes Raul, a promising student, to a fancy restaurant because his group won a poetry contest. LouAnne mistakenly presupposes that it will be as easy for Raul to cross class borders as it is for her. But Raul is uncomfortable in such a context; he tells LouAnne that, in order to dress properly and avoid humiliating himself and her, he has bought his expensive leather jacket from a fence. In this scene is the underlying suggestion that, to succeed in life, working-class kids such as Raul need the cultural capital of white upper-middle-class people like LouAnne.

Dangerous Minds mythically rewrites the decline of public schooling and the attack on poor, black, and Hispanic students within a broader project that rearticulates "whiteness" as a model of authority, rationality, and civilized behavior. The politics of representation at work in this film reproduces a dominant view of identity and difference that has a long legacy in Hollywood films, specifically Westerns and African adventure movies. As historian Robin Kelley points out, the popularity of many Hollywood films, especially those of these two genres, is as much about constructing "whiteness" as it is about demonizing the alleged racialized Other. He notes that within this racialized Hollywood legacy, "American Indians, Africans, and Asians represent a pre-civilized or anti-civilized existence, a threat to the hegemony of Western culture and proof that 'whites' are superior, more noble, more intelligent."[61]

Dangerous Minds is an updated defense of white identity and racial hierarchies. The colonizing thrust of this narrative is highlighted through the image of Michelle Pfeiffer as a visiting white beauty queen whose success is, in part, rendered possible by market incentives and missionary talents.

Against LouAnne Johnson's benevolence and insight is juxtaposed the personality and pedagogy of Mr. Grandy, the black principal of Parkmont High. Grandy is portrayed as an uptight, bloodless bureaucrat, a professional wannabe whose only interest appears to be in enforcing school rules (Hollywood's favorite stereotype for black principals). Grandy rigidly oversees school policy and is constantly berating Johnson for bypassing the standard curriculum, generating nontraditional forms of teaching, and taking the students on unauthorized trips. As a black man in a position of leadership, he is depicted as an obstacle to the success of his charges and as ruthlessly insensitive to their needs. When Emilio visits Grandy's office to report another student who is trying to kill him, Grandy orders him out because he failed to knock on the office door. After leaving the building, Emilio is shot and killed a few blocks from the school.

Racial politics in this film are such that black professionals come off as the real threat to learning and civilized behavior, and whites, of course, are simply there to lend support. In contrast to Grandy, Johnson's "whiteness" provides the racialized referent for leadership, risk-taking, and compassion. This is borne out at the end of the film when the students tell her that they want her to remain their teacher because she represents their "light." In this context, *Dangerous Minds* reinforces the highly racialized, mainstream assumption that chaos reigns in inner-city public schools and that white teachers alone are capable of bringing order, decency, and hope to those on the margins of society.

SUTURING WHITENESS

Directed by David Siegel and Scott McGehee, *Suture* (1993) explores the location of identity within a dominant racial politics. Central to the politics of the film is the way in which it organizes the unfolding of its plot around two narratives. On the one hand, the directors use the discursive narrative, which develops through character dialogue and adopts the conventional form of the crime thriller. On the other hand, they construct a visual narrative that introduces racial identity as a defining principle of the movie by casting one of the two central characters (two brothers) as black and the other as white. Set within a plot about murder and framed identity, *Suture* presents the story of these two brothers, Vincent Towers and Clay Arlington. Under police investigation for killing his father, the rich and ruthless Vincent sets up a scheme in which he first plants his driver's license and credit cards in his working-class half-brother's billfold. He then convinces Clay to drive his Rolls-Royce to the airport. Clay does not realize that Vincent has placed a bomb in the car that can be triggered by remote control through the car phone. Vincent waits until Clay leaves for the airport and then calls him, setting off the bomb. After the explosion, Vincent leaves town, assuming that the police will mistake Clay for himself. Unfortunately for Vincent, Clay survives the explosion, though he has to undergo massive reconstructive surgery on his face. In fact, the damage to Clay is so extreme that the police and doctors who attend to Clay believe he is Vincent.

Clay survives the ordeal but is amnesiac and believes that he is Vincent. In fact, everyone who comes in contact with Clay believes he is Vincent. As he undergoes psychoanalysis and repeated bouts of surgery, he falls in love with Renée Descartes, a beautiful and renowned plastic surgeon. In the meantime, the real Vincent breaks into his old house to kill him, but Clay shoots him first and disposes of his body. By the time he kills Vincent, Clay has regained his memory but refuses to slip back into his old identity and give up the identity and life he has assumed.

What is so remarkable about *Suture* is that it is mediated by a visual narrative that is completely at odds with the discursive narrative and unsettles the audience's role as "passive" spectators. Clay does not look anything like Vincent. In fact, Clay is black, but is treated throughout the film as if he is white. In a scene fraught with irony and tension, Renée Descartes takes off Clay's bandages and tells him that he has a Greco-Roman nose, which allegedly proves that he "isn't inclined to deviant behavior, like killing people."

Memory and identity in this film are fluid and hybridized rather than fixed and sutured. Black identity is presented as a social construction that cannot be framed in essentialist terms. Clay assumes all the markings of white experience and culture, and it is only the audience that is able to mediate his newly assumed cultural capital by virtue of his blackness. But there is more at work in this film than a critique of black essentialism; there is also the ironic representation of "whiteness": it is invisible to itself and at the same time presents the norm by which everything else is measured. That is, "whiteness" in *Suture* becomes the racial marker of identity, power, and privilege. Playing the visual narrative against the discursive narrative, *Suture* evokes a peculiar form of racial witnessing in which it exposes "whiteness" as an ideology, set of experiences, and location of privilege. But it does so not by trading in binaristic oppositions in which bad whites oppress good blacks, but by calling into question the racial tension between what is seen and what is heard by the audience. The discursive narrative in the film privileges language while denying the defining principle of race, but the visual narrative forces the audience to recognize the phenomenological rather than political implications of race, identity, and difference. As film critic Roy Grundmann notes, "We initially want to jump out of our seats to scream at the characters who (mis?)take Clay for Vincent, especially upon such comparative 'evidence' as videos, photos, and a police lineup with a witness who knew Vincent."[62] Racial difference, in this case, is defined entirely through a representational politics of visual imagery that assails both the liberal appeal to color-blindness and a power-evading aesthetic of difference that reduces racial identities to lifestyles, marketing niches, or consumer products.

Rupturing the Hollywood cinematic tradition of presenting "whiteness" as an "invisible" though determining discourse, *Suture* forces the audience to recognize "whiteness" as a racial signifier, an "index of social standing or rank."[63] But in the end, *Suture* provides no means for framing "whiteness" outside of the discursive and visual politics of domination. The film's attempt to develop a representational politics certainly forces the viewer to demystify and debunk "whiteness" as invisible, outside of the modalities of power and identity, but it does nothing to develop a power-strategic politics that refuses to accept "whiteness" as a racial category that only has one purpose, which is closely tied to if not defined by shifting narratives of domination and oppression. This might explain why *Suture* eventually engages in a reductionistic moralizing by suggesting that Clay should be condemned for wanting to be white, without really engaging "whiteness" in a more dialectical or critical fashion.

TOWARD A PEDAGOGY OF WHITENESS

Dangerous Minds and *Suture* offer contrasting narratives of race that can be used educationally to critically deconstruct both racial othering and "whiteness" as part of a broader discourse on racial justice. The incongruous juxtaposition of these two films opens up a space for reading representations of "whiteness" as an ideology and site of power and privilege. Similarly, rupturing singular definitions of "whiteness" provides educators with the opportunity to construct more complex models for theorizing "whiteness" through a multiplicity of social relations, theoretical positions, and affective identifications.

Rather than being dismissed simply as a racist text by critical educators, *Dangerous Minds* should be read symptomatically for the ways in which it articulates and reproduces "whiteness" as a dominant racial identity within the public space of the inner-city classroom. Offering an unapologetic reading of "whiteness" as a trope of order, rationality, insight, and beauty, *Dangerous Minds* is an important educational text for students to use in addressing how "whiteness" and difference are portrayed in the film and how race consciously or unconsciously shapes their everyday experiences, attitudes, and world views. I am not suggesting that educators force students to view *Dangerous Minds* as either a good or bad film, but that they should encourage students to engage the broader social conditions through which the popularity of the film has to be understood. One pedagogical task is to get students to think about how *Dangerous Minds* bears witness to the ethical and racial dilemmas that animate the larger racial and social landscape, and how it reworks or affirms their own intellectual and affective investments as organized through dominant racial ideologies and meanings at work in this highly racialized text.

Students may offer a number of responses to a film such as *Dangerous Minds*. But given the popularity of the film and the large number of favorable reviews it received in newspapers across the country, it is reasonable to assume that the range of readings available to white students will fall within a mix of dominant and conservative interpretations.[64] Rather than stressing that students are diverse readers of culture, it is important to recognize that the ownership and control of the apparatuses of cultural production and distribution limits the readings made widely available to students and shapes the popular context from which dominant notions of racism are understood. When racist difference does enter into classroom discussion, it more than likely will focus on the disruptive behavior that black and Hispanic students exhibit in schools—behavior that often will be seen as characteristic of an entire social group, a form of cultural pathology that suggests minorities are largely to blame for the educational problems they experience. Similarly, when "whiteness" is destabilized or critically addressed by students, it more than likely will be taken up within a power-evasive discourse in which white racism often is reduced to an act of individual prejudice cleanly removed from the messy contexts of history, politics, and systemic oppression.[65] This suggests it is unlikely that white students will recognize LouAnne's teaching approach and insistence on the value of middle-class cultural capital as a racist attempt to teach black and Hispanic students that their own narratives, histories, and experiences are uncivilized and crude. And yet, however popular such dominant readings might be, they offer educators a prime educational opportunity to interrogate and rupture their codes and ideologies. For instance, the ideological link between the privileging of white cultural capital and the ongoing degrading representation of the Other in Hollywood films about Africa, in television sitcoms, or more recently in violent black youth films may not be evident to students on a first reading of the film, but certainly can become an object of analysis as various students in the class are provided with alternative readings.

At best, *Dangerous Minds* offers white students an opportunity to engage with a popular text that embodies much of what they generally learn or (mis)learn about race without initially putting their own racial identities on trial. A viewing and analysis of *Suture* reveals a different set of claims about "whiteness" that raises alternative possibilities for interrogating the relationship between "whiteness," race, and racism. *Suture* presents a critical reading of "whiteness" as a dominant social and cultural construction and attempts through an unsettling visual narrative to reveal how "whiteness" wages symbolic violence through its refusal to name its defining mechanisms of power and privilege. In doing so, *Suture* would force students, especially white students, to consider problematizing the assumption that issues regarding race and racial politics are largely about blacks as a social group. The dominant defense of "whiteness" as a universal norm is visibly thrown off balance in this film and makes "whiteness" a racial category open to critique. In rupturing "whiteness" as a racially and politically neutral code, *Suture* provides an educational opportunity for educators to talk about how white people are raced and how white experience is constructed differently within a variety of public spaces and mediated through the diverse but related lenses of class, gender, and sexual orientation.

Played off against each other, the two films engage in a representational politics that illuminates "whiteness" as a shifting, political category whose meaning can be addressed within rather than outside the interrelationships of class, race, ethnicity, and gender. In other words, the structuring principles that inform these films as they work intertextually provide a theoretical basis for challenging "whiteness" as an ideological and historical construction; it is precisely the tension generated between these films that invites entrance into a pedagogy that commences with what post-colonial critic Gayatri Spivak refers to as "moments of bafflement."[66] While such pedagogical tensions do not guarantee the possibility of decentering "whiteness" in order to render "visible the historical and institutional structures from within which [white teachers and students] speak,"[67] they do provide the educational conditions for students and teachers alike to question and unlearn those aspects of "whiteness" that position them within the privileged space and relations of racism.

While it is impossible to predict how students actually will react to a pedagogy of bafflement that takes "whiteness" and race as an object of serious debate and analysis, it is important to recognize that white students generally will offer enormous resistance to analyzing critically the "normative-residual space [of] white cultural practice."[68] Resistance in this case should be examined for the knowledge it yields and the possibilities for interrogating its silences and refusals. Educationally this suggests allowing students to air their positions on "whiteness" and race regardless of how messy or politically incorrect such positions might be. But there is more at stake here than providing a space for students to narrate themselves, to speak without fear within the contexts of their own specific histories and experiences. Rather than arguing that students simply be allowed to voice their racial politics, I am suggesting that they be offered a space marked by dialogue and critique in which such positions can be engaged, challenged, and rearticulated through an ongoing analysis of the material realities and social relations of racism.

Needless to say, the issue of making white students responsive to the politics of racial privilege is fraught with the fear and anger that accompany having to rethink one's identity. Engaging in forms of teaching that prompt white students to examine their social practices and belief systems in racial terms may work to reinforce the safe assumption that race is a stable category, a biological given, rather than a historical and cultural construction. For instance, AnnLouise Keating points out that when she teaches her students to interrogate "whiteness" critically, many of them come away believing that all whites are colonialists, in spite of her attempts to distinguish between "whiteness" as the dominant racial and political ideology and the diverse, contingent racial positions white people take up.[69]

In spite of the tensions and contradictions that any pedagogy of "whiteness" might face, it is imperative that teachers address the histories that have shaped the normative space, practices, and diverse relationships that white students have inherited through a legacy of racial privilege. Analyzing the historical legacy of "whiteness" as an oppressive racial force necessitates that students engage in a critical form of memory-work while fostering less a sullen silence or paralyzing guilt and more a sense of outrage at historical oppression and a desire for racial justice in the present. Keating illuminates the problems she faced when attempting to get students to think critically about racism and its systemic nature and to interrogate or reverse their taken-for-granted assumptions about "whiteness" and racial privilege. She writes:

> These reversals trigger a variety of unwelcome reactions in self-identified "white" students, reactions ranging from guilt to anger to withdrawal and despair. Instructors must be prepared to deal with these responses. The point is not to encourage feelings of personal responsibility for the slavery, decimation of indigenous peoples, land theft, and so on that occurred in the past. It is, rather, to enable students of all colors more fully to comprehend how these oppressive systems that began in the historical past continue misshaping contemporary conditions. Guilt-tripping plays no role in this process.[70]

However, Keating is not entirely clear on how educators can avoid guilt-tripping students or to what degree they are not to be held responsible for their present attitudes within this type of pedagogy.

Making "whiteness" rather than white racism the focus of study is an important educational strategy. Analyzing "whiteness" opens up a theoretical space for teachers and students to articulate how their own racial identities have been shaped within a broader racist culture and what responsibilities they might assume for living in a present in which whites are accorded privileges and opportunities (though in complex and different ways) largely at the expense of other racial groups. Yet, as insightful as this strategy may prove to be, more theoretical work needs to be done to enable students to critically engage and appropriate the tools necessary for them to politicize "whiteness" as a racial category without closing down their own sense of identity and political agency.

While both *Dangerous Minds* and *Suture* provide educational opportunities for students to see how dominant assumptions about "whiteness" can be framed and challenged, neither film addresses what it means to rearticulate "whiteness" in oppositional terms. Neither the portrayal of "whiteness" as a form of racial privilege nor its portrayal as a practice of domination necessarily establishes the basis for white students to rearticulate their own "whiteness" in ways that go beyond their overidentification with or desire to be "black" at the expense of their own racial identities.

Every student needs to feel that they have a personal stake in their racial identity (however fluid, multiple, and unstable), an identity that will allow them to assert a view of political agency in which they can join with diverse groups around a notion of democratic public life that will affirm racial differences through a "rearticulation of cultural, social, and political citizenship."[71] Linking identity, race, and difference to a broader vision of radical democracy suggests a number of important pedagogical considerations. First, students need to investigate the historical relationship between race and ethnicity. Historian David Roediger is right in warning against the conflation of race and ethnicity by critical theorists, especially in light of a history of ethnicity in which white immigrants saw themselves as white and ethnic. According to Roediger, the claim to ethnicity among white immigrants, especially those from Europe, did not prevent them from defining their racial identities through the discourse of white separatism and supremacy.[72] In this case, white ethnicity was not ignored by such immigrants; it was affirmed and linked in some cases to the dominant relations of racism.

The issue of racial identity can be linked to what cultural studies critic Stuart Hall has called the "new ethnicity."[73] For Hall, racial identities can be understood through the notion of ethnicity, but not the old notion of ethnicity, that depends in part on the suppression of cultural difference and a separatist notion of white identity. Hall's attempt to rewrite ethnicity as a progressive and critical concept does not fall into the theoretical trap described by Roediger. By removing ethnicity from the traditional moorings of nationalism, racism, colonialism, and the state, Hall posits the new ethnicity as a referent for acknowledging "the place of history, language, and culture in the construction of subjectivity and identity, as well as the fact that all discourse is placed, positioned, situated, and all knowledge is contextual."[74]

Extending Hall's insights about ethnicity, I want to argue that the diverse subject positions, social experiences, and cultural identities that inform "whiteness" as a political and social construct can be rearticulated in order for students to recognize that "we all speak from a particular place, out of a particular history, out of particular experience, a particular culture without being constrained by [such] positions. . . . We are all, in that sense, ethnically located and our ethnic identities are crucial to our subjective sense of who we are."[75] In Hall's terms, "whiteness" can be addressed not as a form of identity fashioned through a claim to purity or some universal essence, but as one that "lives with and through, not despite difference."[76]

Hall provides a theoretical language for racializing "whiteness" without essentializing it; he also argues, correctly, that ethnicity must be defined and defended through a set of ethical and political referents that connect diverse democratic struggles while expanding the range and possibilities of democratic relations and practices. Redefined within the theoretical parameters of a new ethnicity, "whiteness" can be read as a complex marker of identity defined through a politics of difference that is subject to the shifting currents of history, power, and culture. That is, "whiteness" no longer can be taken up as fixed, naturally grounded in a tradition or ancestry, but—as Ien Ang claims in another context—must be understood as a form of postmodern ethnicity, "experienced as a provisional and partial site of identity which must be constantly (re)invented and (re)negotiated."[77] The notion of "whiteness" as being transitory and hybrid, but at the same time grounded in particular histories and practices extends the political potential of Hall's new ethnicity thesis by providing a theoretical space for engaging racial identity as a fundamental principle of citizenship and radical democracy, the aim of which is the "expansion of egalitarian social relations, and practices."[78]

The new ethnicity defines racial identities as multiple, porous, complex, and shifting and in doing so provides a theoretical opening for educators and students to move beyond framing "whiteness" as either good or bad, racially innocent or intractably racist. "Whiteness" in this context can be addressed through its complex relationship with other determining factors that usurp any claim to racial purity or singularity. At the same time, "whiteness" must be addressed within power relations that exploit its subversive potential while not erasing the historical and political role it plays in shaping other racialized identities and social differences. Unlike the old ethnicity, which posits difference in essentialist or separatist terms, Hall's notion of the new ethnicity defines identity as an ongoing act of cultural recovery, acknowledging that any particular claim to racial identity offers no guarantees regarding political outcomes. But at the same time, the new ethnicity provides a theoretical service by allowing white students to go beyond the paralysis inspired by guilt or the racism fueled by the anxiety and fear of difference. In this context, "whiteness" gains its meaning only in conjunction with other identities such as those informed by class, gender, age, nationality, and citizenship. For progressive whites, "crossing over does not mean crossing out."[79] Whites have to learn to live with their "whiteness" by rearticulating it in terms that allow them to formulate what it means to develop viable political coalitions and social movements. Whites have to learn and unlearn, engage in a critical pedagogy of self-formation that allows them to cross racial lines not in order to become black but to begin to forge multiracial coalitions based on an engagement rather than a denial of "whiteness."

By positioning "whiteness" within a notion of cultural citizenship that affirms difference politically, culturally, and socially, students can take notice of how their "whiteness" functions as a racial identity while still being critical of forms of "whiteness" structured in dominance and aligned with exploitative interests and oppressive social relations. By rearticulating "whiteness" as more than a form of domination, white students can construct narratives of "whiteness" that both challenge and, hopefully, provide a basis for transforming the dominant relationship between racial identity and citizenship, a relationship informed by an oppositional politics. Such a political practice suggests new subject positions, alliances, commitments, and forms of solidarity between white students and others engaged in the struggle to expand the possibilities of democratic life, especially the affirmation of difference and the redistribution of power and material resources. George Yudice argues that as part of a broader project for articulating "whiteness" in oppositional terms, white youth must feel that they have a stake in racial politics that connects them to the struggles being waged by other groups. At the center of such struggles is both the battle over citizenship redefined through the discourse of rights and the problem of resource distribution. He writes:

> This is where identity politics segues into other issues, such as tax deficits, budget cuts, lack of educational opportunities, lack of jobs, immigration policies, international trade agreements, environmental blight, lack of health care insurance, and so on. These are the areas in which middle- and working-class whites historically have had an advantage over people of color. However, today that advantage has eroded in certain respects.[80]

As part of a wider attempt to engage these issues, Yudice suggests that white youth can form alliances with other social and racial groups who recognize the need for solidarity in addressing issues of public life that undermine the quality of democracy for all groups. As white youth struggle to find a cultural and political space from which to speak and act as transformative citizens, it is imperative that educators address what it means pedagogically and politically to help students rearticulate "whiteness" as part of a democratic cultural politics. Central to such a task is the need to challenge the conventional left-wing analysis of "whiteness" as a space between guilt and denial, a space that offers limited forms of resistance and engagement. In order for teachers, students, and others to come to terms with "whiteness" existentially and intellectually, we need to confront racism in all its complexity and ideological and material formations. But most importantly, "whiteness" must provide a diverse but critical space from which to wage a wider struggle against the myriad forces that undermine what it means to live in a society founded on the principles of freedom, racial justice, and economic equality. Rewriting "whiteness" within a discourse of resistance and possibility represents more than a challenge to dominant and progressive notions of racial politics; it provides an important challenge for educating cultural workers, teachers, and students how to live with and through difference as a defining principle of a radical democracy.

Howard Winant is right in simultaneously suggesting that racialized subjectivities are not going to disappear and that racial differences do not have to be equated with racism per se. On the contrary, the democratization of racial identity is central to the development of radical democracy itself. Winant's insight, which is crucial to Hall's call for redefining ethnicity as part of a broader attempt to liberate racial identities, is worth quoting at length:

> The liberation of racial identity is as much a part of the struggle against racism as the elimination of racial discrimination and inequality. That liberation will involve a revisioning of racial politics and a transformation of racial difference. It will render democracy itself much more radically pluralistic, and will make identity much more a matter of choice than of ascription. As the struggles to achieve these objectives unfold, we shall gradually recognize that the racialization of democracy is as important as the democratization of race.[81]

FIVE

IN LIVING COLOR
BLACK, BRUISED, AND READ ALL OVER

And where do intellectuals stand in relation to politics? . . .
[T]hose who are mindful of the ties that link everything in
this world together, who approach the world with humility,
but also with an increased sense of responsibility, who wage
a struggle for every good thing—such intellectuals should
be listened to with the greatest attention, regardless of
whether they work as independent critics, holding up a
much-needed mirror to politics and power, or are directly
involved in politics. . . . It does not follow that we should
bar such intellectuals from the realm of politics on the
pretext that their only place is in universities or the media.
On the contrary: I am deeply convinced that the more such
people engage directly in practical politics, the better our
world will be.

—Vaclav Havel[1]

In the last decade a multitude of books and articles have
lamented the demise of public intellectuals in the United
States. While the history of this discourse is too extensive to repeat, I
plan to highlight two theoretical interventions into the debate over the

current status of public intellectuals that raise important issues about their role and responsibility in American society on the one hand and, in light of the controversy surrounding academics as intellectuals, the relevance of defining higher education as an essential democratic public sphere on the other.

Russell Jacoby's widely read book *The Last Intellectuals* argued that the conditions that produced an older generation of public intellectuals in the post–World War II era had been undermined and displaced in the 1980s.[2] The unaffiliated intellectual functioning as a social critic writing accessible prose for such journals as *The Partisan Review* offers for Jacoby both an ideal of what it means to mobilize a popular audience and a model for the role of a public intellectual. Such intellectuals (and those from the public spheres that support them) have become an endangered species. In Jacoby's narrative of decline, such public intellectuals as Jane Jacobs, Edmund Wilson, Dwight Macdonald, Philip Rahv, C. Wright Mills, and Irving Howe have been replaced by 1960s radicals who have forsaken the role of the independent intellectual for the safe and specialized confines of the university.

But the university, according to Jacoby, neither represents a viable public sphere nor provides the conditions for intellectuals to speak to a broader public audience. More specifically, by sanctioning the privileges of professionalism, promoting overly technical jargon, and cultivating new forms of specialization, academics have been reduced to sterile technocrats, unable, if not unwilling, to address the responsibilities of public service.[3] If we believe Jacoby, the public intellectual has been replaced by the so-called radical academic interested more in career advancement and the cushy rewards of tenure than in acting as a proponent of social change.[4]

In a now famous essay in the journal *Cultural Critique* in 1985, Cornel West focused less on the demise of the public intellectual than on the emergence of a hostile climate for black intellectuals.[5] For West, society's recent political and social shift to the right, the widening gap between the black middle class and an ever-growing underclass, and universities' increasingly managerial logic, which is often intolerant of critical (especially black) scholars, all have hindered the development and support of black intellectuals in this country.

It is clear in retrospect that Jacoby and West correctly anticipated a significant set of issues that emerged late in the last decade as part of a larger debate over the role of intellectuals in the struggle for social change. Jacoby's argument that the university cannot nourish public · discourse resonates strongly with the current right-wing charge that the university is too political—the unhappy result of an influx of "tenured radicals."[6] For different reasons, both sets of critics posit the university as a depoliticized site and limit pedagogy to the arid imperatives of discipline-bound professionalization and specialization.

On the other hand, Jacoby sees the university, because of its complicity with dominant ideologies and practices, as a conservative sphere that buys off even its most critical intellectuals.[7] Conservatives like Roger Kimball, Charles Sykes, Lynne V. Cheney, and William Bennett translate a contempt for critical thinking and social criticism into appropriate educational behavior and see the ideal university as an apolitical public sphere inhabited largely by a disinterested faculty engaged in an ahistorical conversation among great minds and pedagogically bound to hand down the ideas and values of the classics to a new generation of would-be thinkers.[8] The university of this latter scenario becomes in instrumental terms largely a mechanism for social and cultural reproduction and a repository for transmitting both the timeless knowledge and skills of the culture of business and the high cultural values and ideals of the dominant society.[9]

In contrast, Cornel West's essay provides a theoretical service by injecting race into the debate over the meaning and role of public intellectuals in the United States. Expanding upon John Dewey's claim that "To form itself, the public must break existing public forms,"[10] West highlights the ways in which racism operates as a structuring principle of dominant public spheres and as a defining force in shaping the discourse on public intellectuals. West's argument provides a theoretical referent for challenging the context and content of much of the liberal discourse that has emerged around the well-publicized "discovery" of a group of black intellectuals almost a decade after West's piece first appeared.

In what follows, I want to address Jacoby's critique of public intellectuals and further analyze how his argument is being reinvented and aligned with broader conservative discourses that function largely to challenge and contain the notion of the academy as a viable democratic public sphere.[11] In opposition to these positions, I want to offer an argument for the university as a contested public sphere and for the importance of linking intellectual work to the moral horizon of public responsibility and progressive social change. I want to further extend West's argument by addressing how the recent media hype about black intellectuals blends celebrity discourse with a brand of white liberalism that displaces rather than engages the importance of making race a central component of the debate over the university as a public sphere. Finally, I want to address the necessity of linking the university as a public sphere and the vocation of intellectuals, on the one hand, with social issues and pedagogical practices that extend the needs of democratic life on the other.

MAPPING THE TERRAIN

The meaning and function of intellectuals in American society has been the source of controversy for much of the twentieth century.

Questions concerning the meaning, role, and responsibilities of such intellectuals are part of an often contentious tradition in scholarly work that on occasion spills over into the popular press. The literature is rich with theoretical work on the role of the intellectual and offers an ocean of insights from the early seminal work of Emile Durkheim, Thorstein Veblen, Upton Sinclair, and Antonio Gramsci to the later work of Jean-Paul Sartre, C. Wright Mills, Michel Foucault, Alvin Gouldner, H. Stuart Hughes, Noam Chomsky, Howard Zinn, and Edward Said. For many of these theorists, debates regarding the role of the intellectual often have functioned as part of a wider discourse about recovering the space of the political and deepening the possibilities for creating multiple democratic public spheres. In part, the concept of the critically engaged intellectual has served as a moral referent for gauging the limits and possibilities of cultural politics within dominant social and economic formations. Unfortunately, while the concept of the engaged public intellectual has occupied a respectable but problematic place in progressive ideological debates, cultural workers who assume the role of critical public intellectuals have not fared so well in the popular media and everyday life. Derided and praised, ignored and challenged, intellectuals have occupied that space in between politics and culture, having to contend with its ever-changing demands and expectations for committed social engagement and its simultaneous attempts to appropriate or silence the most progressive among them. More often than not artists, journalists, academics, and others who have been innovative and daring in their attempts to challenge the conventions of the dominant social and political order have fallen prey to ideological censorship among other political tyrannies, frequently garnering more scorn than respect.

Lampooned in their position as social critics of American society, intellectuals have been persecuted by the government, marginalized from apparatuses of power that shape public policy, and more recently denounced as subversives or as un-American.[12] Stereotyped as "eggheads" or dismissed as simply irrelevant to American life, intellectuals historically have been grist for the mill of popular media. Shaped by Cold War anticommunism, a long legacy of rampant anti-intellectualism,[13] and public antagonism toward criticism of that great monolith "the American way of life," public intellectuals rarely have been legitimated in the collective consciousness. Those who were given public acknowledgment have been stripped of their function as social critics and reduced to the status of technical workers,[14] such as stockbrokers, teachers, researchers, businesspeople, physicians, and other "professional" intellectuals who function as purveyors of culture in the limited technical sense of producing a specialized service within a narrow body of knowledge and who, as a group, are unlikely to rock the boat.

THE RETURN OF THE PUBLIC INTELLECTUAL

By the middle of the 1990s, the New York Times announced that the public intellectual had been reborn.[15] Claiming that a number of young liberal academics were aroused to battle because of the conservative assault on trends in education and public life, the Times praised University of Illinois academic Michael Berube for giving up the stodgy writing of the academy for the sound-byte prose of the op-ed pages. A similar story appeared in the Chronicle of Higher Education and touted Berube, Micaela Di Leonardo, Mark Edmunson, and others in the academy who were producing articles and books for broader public consumption. It seems both odd and gratifying that within the last few years academics, talk show hosts, the popular media, the national press, and a host of scholarly journals have heaped lavish attention on the meaning and relevance of an emerging group of public intellectuals in the United States. Such grand attention seems especially unusual given the assault that has been waged on all aspects of public life since the emergence of the political culture of Reaganism in the 1980s. The casualties are widespread and include public school systems, public transportation, public services, the public health system, and a vast array of social services designed to protect the poor, immigrants, elderly, and young children.[16] Given the ongoing attack on public life that has now become the hallmark of the conservative revolution of the 1990s, the attention given by the popular press to the rise of public intellectuals appears puzzling if not paradoxical. But on further analysis, it is clear that a number of conservative ideological principles have been at work in framing the rediscovery of the public intellectual.

For instance, as the rebirth of the public intellectual became a cause célèbre, the focus on character gained ascendance over any sustained analysis of the importance of the public spaces and the organization of audiences that provide the conditions for debate, dialogue, and social action. Focusing largely on personalities rather than on the conditions for the production and circulation of knowledge and values that allowed such intellectuals to intervene in diverse popular spheres, the press virtually ignored those structural and economic forces at work in the university that resulted in downsizing and massive layoffs of junior faculty as a considerable number of tenure-track jobs were replaced with short time contracts and adjunct professorships.[17] In light of the increasing influence of right-wing political culture in the 1990s, the discourse on the public intellectual as celebrity seems perfectly timed as a public-relations gimmick to obfuscate the pruning of the full-time university workforce.[18]

In addition, many conservative critics, already convinced the university is not the place for critical political analyses and practice, have seized upon the popular media's conflation of public intellectuals with media stardom to further fuel their aggressive opposition to academic work considered either at odds with a market-driven culture or perceived as a threat to the "high-minded, transcendent" values of Western culture. In this case, the very notion of public intellectual as social critic provides a venue for legitimating public intolerance and for extending the conservative assault on those academics who attempt to engage in critical and creative expression within higher education. The political nature of such an assault on academic freedom is captured in a speech that John Silber, president of Boston University, delivered to his board of trustees in 1993. He claims without apology:

> We have resisted relativism as an official intellectual dogma, believing that there is such a thing as truth, and if you can't achieve it, at least you can approach it. We have resisted the fad toward critical legal studies. . . . In the English Department and the departments of literature, we have not allowed the structuralists or the deconstructionists to take over. We have refused to take on dance therapy. . . . We have resisted revisionist history. . . . In the Philosophy Department we have resisted the Frankfurt School of Critical Theory. . . . We have resisted the fad of Afrocentrism. We have not fallen into the clutches of the multiculturalists. We recognize that Western culture, so called, is a fact of universal culture.[19]

This is more than ideological rigidity. It is symptomatic of how easily academic freedom can be dispensed with when politics is removed from considerations of how power and authority work in higher education and other institutional sites. In this instance, politics becomes the silent partner to forms of intellectual tyranny.

Of course, the news is not all bad. After a decade of relentless attacks by neoconservatives on multiculturalism, gender studies, political correctness, public schools, and funding for the arts and public radio, the attention that has emerged surrounding public intellectuals might appear as both a welcome relief and an opportunity to begin a national debate about what it means "to take one's life as a public person quite seriously."[20] Such a debate theoretically, at least, contains the promise of producing a vitalized language about public life and intellectual leadership. More specifically, public debate offers the potential for raising to a national level serious questions regarding the relevance of the university as a critical public sphere, the significance of cultural work taking hold across a variety of public spheres and pedagogical sites, and the necessity of vitalizing the language of the public as part of a broader discourse about democracy and social justice.

One extraordinary feature of the debate regarding the relationship between the intellectual and the academy is the degree to which progressives have been put on the defensive by the right. While the term "culture wars" often has been used to name the conflict, it more accurately refers to a conservative blitzkrieg, with the right wing dominating most of the channels of public access in shaping the debate. But as the right-wing offensive abates (or simply gets old), questions about the role of public intellectuals have been taken up by liberals such as Anthony Lewis, Lewis Menard, and Paul Berman who offer a discourse of rhetorical modesty in cautioning progressive academics not to take the issue of political struggle and academic reform too seriously. For example, Lewis Menard asserts that "talking about reforming the modern university is like talking about reforming a skyscraper. There's not much point in tinkering: you can knock the whole thing down, or you can go live somewhere else."[21] The most incisive example of this position can be found in the recent work of Stanley Fish and is worth examining at some length since it encapsulates similar arguments made by other critics.

TROPES OF DISPLACEMENT
AND THE POLITICS OF PROFESSIONAL CAUTION

For many liberal critics such as Stanley Fish, intellectuals who attempt to bridge the divide between academic and public life through a critical cultural politics primarily serve to undermine the enclave of professionalism while simultaneously indulging in a lame excuse for politicizing classroom practice.[22] Fish argues that literary studies should be defined primarily within the discourse of specialization and professionalism and that its practitioners have no business engaging in partisan politics. Fish doesn't deny the relationship between knowledge and power; he simply rejects the notion that literary studies has any consequential effects in the larger society—and in doing so relegates political practice in the university to the dustbin of irrelevance. More specifically, he argues that what academics say and do rarely leads to legislative and administrative changes in society. Hence, it is futile to establish politics as a fundamental dimension of any discipline other than politics or, by default, as a defining principle of teaching. The boundaries of the political in this case are reduced to the narrow sphere of administrative and legislative changes. Given this restrictive litmus test for legitimating the political as an essential academic and pedagogical category, the idea of the intellectual as adversary of the dominant culture becomes rather absurd. This, in turn, reinforces the assumption that the relationship among higher education, ideology, and power is relatively unproblematic.

Fish's call for professionalism may seem reasonable to some, but its effacement of the political in university life gains credibility only by ignoring the conflicts and struggles that historically have marked the university as a contentious political sphere in its own right. For example, Fish's account fails to acknowledge struggles over affirmative action and divestment, protests against U.S. intervention in Central America, struggles over gay and lesbian rights, and attempts by blacks, women, and other minorities to gain access and representation within the university curriculum. Fish's attack on politically engaged intellectuals conveniently excludes the degree to which the existing arrangements of social and economic power have contributed to the shaping of academic life. In short, his analysis dissolves the history of social and political struggles in the academy. This occurs as he ignores questions such as: What are the consequences of removing political considerations from the dynamics of canon formation, refusing to acknowledge the conditions through which institutions are invested with power, and ignoring the practices through which ideologies and values circulate in classroom relations? How does one analyze in any meaningful way the relationship of academics to public spheres outside of the university? What civic responsibilities do academics have in fostering pluralism and democratic relations, legitimating particular identities, and presupposing in their narratives of teaching particular visions of the future? What practices and ideologies are excluded in the classroom by removing politics from a broader understanding of how the university as a public sphere is defined in its own right by "specific relations of representation and reception, and as part of a larger social horizon . . . [of] overlapping local, national, and global, face-to-face and deterritorialized structures of public life?"[23] Needless to say, there are many other questions that can be raised given Fish's political myopia.[24]

It is crucial for public intellectuals to confront the questions Fish ignores. Without doing so, it is impossible to see how politics can work in the classroom to enable or foreclose young people's capacities to expand their sense of civic responsibility and critical agency. At stake here is a notion of political education that takes seriously the challenge of working within higher education to create interdisciplinary programs—whether grounded in ethnic, women's, black, or cultural studies—that enable students to understand critically the general dilemmas and concerns of the public cultures they share to rethink their role as active citizens whose responsibility it is to address and transform, when necessary, the dynamics of power, interests, and politics.

Jettisoning political and ethical considerations in favor of professionalism does little to encourage teachers and students to be attentive to how meaning, agency, and value shape classroom teaching, knowledge, and theoretical training. Erasing the political from the pedagogical, I believe, largely closes down the opportunities for teachers and students alike to engage and challenge the prevailing notions of authority and power that influence the selection of specific forms of classroom knowledge, legitimate particular pedagogical practices, and rationalize the exclusions of specific histories, experiences, and ideologies.

In Fish's narrow and overly pragmatic terms, the recovery of the political in higher education becomes almost futile. Of course, for neoconservative theorists such as Allan Bloom, William Bennett, Lynne Cheney, and others, Fish's commitment to professionalism resonates quite well with their ideological agenda to depoliticize the university in order to subordinate political and pedagogical considerations to a search for universal truth and transcendent beauty. But Fish's call for professionalism does more than reinforce an impoverished understanding of public politics' role in academic life; it also obscures the differences between academics who address their responsibility to public life and those who become identified as public celebrities.

INTELLECTUAL VOCATIONS AND PUBLIC CELEBRITIES

Focusing on what it means for academics to have a critical relationship to the public provides a heuristic tool for analyzing how academics connect their professional and pedagogical concerns to the broader considerations of public life. Central to such a relationship is what Stuart Hall calls the vocation of the intellectual life. At stake here is not the issue of upward mobility but how one's location in the academy is defined, in part, by insisting "on the necessity to address the central, urgent and disturbing questions of a society and a culture in the most rigorous intellectual way we have available."[25] By inserting the category of the political back into the vocation of intellectual life, Hall rightly insists that one of the fundamental tasks of academics is to weaken the boundaries between the disciplines and between the university and society. But linking the political and the public in our teaching and scholarly work will suggest more than raising new questions and models of study; it also implies "testing the fine lines between intellectual rigor and social relevance" in order to help our students understand and challenge "what keeps making the lives we live, and the societies we live in, profoundly and deeply antihumane."[26] Of course, recovering the space of the political and public in academic life does not deny the relevance of professionalism, nor does it suggest that the only knowledge worth teaching is tied directly to a narrow notion of social relevance.

Highlighting the public responsiveness of intellectuals suggests interrogating how knowledge is produced, circulated, and applied in order to secure particular forms of authority and expand or shut down a range of critical capacities integral to human agency. Such inquiry will facilitate students' ability to link what they learn to the demands of civic debate and public policy analysis.

The test of social relevance does more than gauge how knowledge should be judged useful as it impacts upon a broader society; it is also crucial for understanding how the university is itself constituted as a public sphere actively engaged in the production of knowledge, identities, values, and social relations. The university is a knowledge industry serving millions of young people and as such represents a locus of power that must be engaged, questioned, and, when necessary, challenged. Central to any viable notion of the academy as a public sphere is the recognition that educators play a crucial role in shaping the identities, values, and beliefs of students who impact directly upon society. This is especially true for those students who work in fields such as health care, public education, and the social services. Failing to recognize the important role the university plays as a public sphere, progressives underestimate the reasons and force of the current attack on higher education. They also run the risk of leaving unexamined how the university is being transformed and realigned with other commercial and market sectors of public life.

In step with declining revenues and the logic of downsizing, the university increasingly is being modeled by the culture of business. Within the last decade, the intellectual mission of the university has reinvented itself, becoming a kind of cheering squad for the culture and interests of the corporate sector.[27] While the corporate principles defining higher education always have been fundamental to its definition, the university's current vocationalization threatens to displace all other ethical and political considerations regarding its role in society. The progressive critique of the university as a workplace designed to educate and train students through the production and transmission of new knowledge-based products compatible with new global divisions of labor made possible by the new high-tech, information-based systems has taken on a new urgency in the 1990s. The political interests that underlie the production of university-based knowledge are not merely about equipping students with new literacy skills; they are also about training students to run the commanding apparatuses of the World Bank, the International Monetary Fund, insurance companies, independent think tanks, and other political institutions. How academics locate themselves vis-à-vis universities defined by corporate policies, instrumental pedagogies, and downsizing rationalities suggests that issues of politics, power, and ideology cannot be so easily displaced to spheres or audiences outside of the university.

Of course, one response to the claim that academics take seriously their responsibility to the imperatives of public life might follow Stanley Fish's claim that there really is no larger public that will listen to the specialized discourse of academics. For Fish, a public intellectual is not merely someone who "takes as his or her subject matters of public concern" but also someone who "has the public's attention . . . [and] academics, by definition, are not candidates for the role of public intellectual."[28] Fish does not fall into the trap of dismissing academics who gain media attention as posturing celebrities—he simply believes they have no significant effect upon public life. For him a public intellectual is "someone to whom the public regularly looks for illumination on any number of (indeed all) issues."[29] Academics are largely disqualified as public intellectuals because they do not have a "stage or pulpit from which their pronouncements, should they be inclined to make them, could be broadcast."[30] Even when academics such as Catherine Stimpson make an appearance on television programs such as the widely popular *Nightline* and engage a broader public, they are dismissed by Fish as "intellectuals for a day."

According to Fish, the measure of the public intellectual has less to do with what they actually believe, how they perform in the face of everyday injustices, or the issues they engage than it does with attracting consistently high Nielsen ratings.[31] This may be simply an expression of excessive irony, or a more serious attempt to professionalize scientific discourse in order to save the humanities from their increasing vocationalization, but Fish adds a cynical gloss to the public intellectual vs. celebrity intellectual debate by implying that public intellectuals can only function by becoming celebrities. Unfortunately, he is not kidding when he claims that "If 'public intellectual' is anything, it is a job description, and . . . it is not a job for which academics, as academics, are particularly justified."[32] If academics have a role to play as public intellectuals crossing the divide between the university and public life, there is little to be found in the work of liberals such as Fish to indicate how this role might be played out. Moreover, such work simply provides fodder for more extreme views, such as those of Leon Wieseltier, who argues in a recent issue of the *New Republic* that "Scholasticism is a noble calling, but it leaves the world as it found it. There is not a drug dealer in America who will give himself up to Deleuze and Guattari."[33]

Defining public intellectuals by their ability to mobilize national audiences, Fish effectively depoliticizes the work done by public intellectuals who move within much smaller public spheres engaging significant but smaller constituencies. A more expansive *and* political conception of the public intellectual focuses on the practices of educators and other cultural workers who construct, present, and engage various forms of images, texts, talk, and actions within and outside of the university.[34] Such practices point more specifically to creating educational conditions in which individuals might learn not only how to express themselves critically but also how to alter the structure of participation and horizon of debate within diverse public cultures. Clearly one important role of the public intellectual in higher education is to refuse dogmatism and cynical relativism while taking up the ethical and political responsibility of provoking students and diverse publics by giving them the opportunity to think critically about what it means to have a sense of vision and commitment and a passion for social justice.[35]

Public intellectuals often work within and across specific public spheres and address multiple audiences (of vastly different sizes). Such work can occur in grass-roots organizing, as in the work of

Robert Moses, who creates educational programs for black youth in inner city Boston, or at the level of policy initiatives, as in the work of Marcus Raskin at the Institute for Policy Studies. Or it can occur through the work of artists such as Bill Jones, Suzanne Lacy, Karen Finley, Barbara Kruger, and Guillermo Gomez-Pena whose work provokes an aggressive engagement with the status quo and functions pedagogically to organize counter-public spheres where serious debate can occur and provide the conditions for audiences to examine their roles "as socially concerned citizens of the world."[36] At a time when the university is under heavy attack by conservatives as a public forum for debate and critical analysis, the pivotal point on which academics might respond may have less to do with whether they can command a national audience than with organizing individually and collectively *in an effort to mobilize students, faculty, and others* to fight against the vocationalization of the university while linking such a struggle to broader assaults on other important sectors of the public sphere. Being a public intellectual in this case might begin by taking the notion of leadership, criticism, struggle, and solidarity as a starting point, a politics in transit fueled not by the promise of celebrity but by the possibility of revitalizing lost visions of social justice and future hopes of substantive democratic change.

MAKING THE PUBLIC POLITICAL

Acknowledging the public nature of our work as intellectuals means, in part, analyzing how power works within the university to give legitimacy to dominant ideologies while silencing or circumscribing other points of view. It also means making such power the object of social analysis as part of a language of critique and possibility. In part, this suggests that academics must expose the inconsistencies, omissions, and lies that a society conveniently excludes from public memory. This does not suggest a notion of the political in which intellectuals primarily represent or speak for others, nor does it suggest forms of pedagogical violence in which various audiences are silenced through the dogmatic assertion of alleged critical truths. What the political does invoke pedagogically is the need for public intellectuals to "name, reveal, and undermine the anonymous and obscure (although immediately present) operations of power as they negate . . . democratic possibilities."[37] But as Howard Zinn has noted so eloquently, academics need to do more than provide tools for those who may be willing to struggle against power as a constitutive element of subjugation; they also must hold up to students and others those "forgotten visions, lost utopias, unfulfilled dreams—badly needed in this age of cynicism."[38]

As modest as these political and pedagogical considerations may be, they suggest a form of political work in the academy that should be enabling, self-critical, and undogmatic. Central to this work is a critical attentiveness to forms of appropriation that incorporate intellectuals within dominant structures of the media and university so as to render them ineffective. The role of the public intellectual, as opposed to the public celebrity, demands a vigilant self-scrutiny that resists the seduction of star status—a status that works to enlarge public appeal while shrinking one's discursive repertoire to sound bites and curtailing collective struggle as well as one's own research with nonstop promotional tours. Not all public intellectuals in the academy become celebrities, nor does the conferring of celebrity status necessarily condemn one to selling out. The category of public intellectual as celebrity has little to do with the actual political and pedagogical work that many progressive educators perform on a daily basis. What it does often signal are forms of media hype that reduce serious social issues to discussions about personalities while serving up the category of public intellectual as a trope of displacement in which fashion becomes a substitute for analyzing the role that the university might play as an engaged public sphere. While the issue of whether academics command national attention as public intellectuals is not unimportant, the most important considerations should focus on changing the representation of public intellectuals. As Edward Said points out, intellectuals should not be viewed as experts but as social theorists raising critical questions, confronting orthodoxy, and engaging in public discourse.[39] But the struggle to change the existing representation of intellectuals must be grounded in more than a reworking of the discursive terms used to characterize public intellectuals; such a struggle also must engage in a practical politics of opposition to strengthen and revive those crucial public spheres "that help determine the forms and meanings of publicness in American society."[40]

By linking intellectual work to the struggle to sustain multiple public spheres that provide an "opening in which information, opinion, and criticism can thrive,"[41] it becomes possible to define such work as part of a broader public discourse about the importance of civic debate and the overturning of oppressive social structures rather than in terms of the intellectual's success in capturing the attention of a massive public audience. While such sentiments run the risk of sounding utopian or "politically correct" in the current age of political cynicism, the call for engaged political work in the university offers a counterweight to the conception of the professional as an expert or technician. Moreover, such a call serves as a reminder of the need for academics to "insist upon the broader moral horizon of professional responsibility."[42] In opposition to Stanley Fish, Cornel West views the vocation of the intellectual as both public and political, a practice born in the space between the university and public life, where claims on knowledge are indispensable for the demands of critical citizenship and social responsibility. According to West:

> The fundamental role of the public intellectual—distinct from, yet building on, the indispensable work of academics, experts, analysts, and pundits—is to create and sustain high-quality public discourse addressing urgent public problems which enlightens and energizes fellow citizens, prompting them to take public action. This role requires a deep commitment to the life of the mind—a perennial attempt to clear our minds of cant—which serves to shape the public destiny of a people. Intellectual and political leadership is neither elitist nor populist; rather it is democratic, in that each of us stands in public space, without humiliation, to put forward our best visions and views for the sake of the public interest. And these arguments are present in an atmosphere of mutual respect and civic trust.[43]

Implicit in West's insight is the assumption that the disappearance of political intellectuals in higher education corresponds to the passing of critical politics in public life. The effacement of progressive politics from public life is demonstrated forcefully in the response of many liberals and conservatives to the rise of a group of black public intellectuals who have challenged the notion such that dominant public spheres as the university can be called race-neutral or race-transcendent.[44] Many black academics have raised the volume of the debate on the public intellectual by re-inserting the notion of racial justice into public discourse while simultaneously redefining notions of social commitment, politics and equality. In what follows, I want to analyze the racial politics underlying this debate and address the implications it has for expanding the meaning and role of public intellectuals in and out of the academy.

BLACK, BRUISED, AND READ ALL OVER

"Public intellectual" is by and large an excuse, the marker of a sterile, hybrid variant of "bearing witness" that, when all is said and done, is a justification for an aversion to intellectual or political heavy lifting—a pretentious name for highfalutin babble about the movie you just saw or the rhyme you just heard on the radio.

—Adolph Reed[45]

Reading Jacoby's earlier attack on academics in higher education, it is clear that the lament over the decline of public intellectuals excluded black intellectuals, who appeared at the time to occupy the margins of scholarly and popular discourse. While specific individuals like Toni Morrison, Alice Walker, and Maya Angelou received attention in the national media (as artists and not intellectuals), the scholarly and popular press focused primarily on whites when it addressed the general malaise in intellectual life in America. Such writers as Robert Bellah and Benjamin Barber bemoaned the university's fall from public grace into "the quintessential institution of bureaucratic individualism"[46] and urged various public foundations to support a new generation of public intellectuals. Yet, they virtually ignored race as a crucial category within the larger context. In recent years, observations on race and democracy among a number of relatively young black intellectuals have helped to fill the lacunae, though not without prompting a great deal of criticism among both conservative and liberal intellectuals.

The discovery of the black public intellectual has nevertheless become the new American fashion—a hot topic in both scholarly publications and the popular press.[47] Expressing an historically conditioned anxiety and near manic fascination, journalists and academics seem obsessed with probing the mystique of the "new" black public intellectual, giving particular attention to such African American writers as Michael Eric Dyson, Cornel West, Henry Louis Gates, Jr., Gloria Watkins (bell hooks), Patricia Williams, Robin Kelley, Toni Morrison, Michele Wallace, Stanley Crouch, and Glenn Loury.

But what began as a series of press releases heralding the ascendancy of black intellectuals has turned into a tirade of damning indictments, as indicated in the earlier "insights" by Adolph Reed, Jr. Heartening gestures toward the revitalization of a black public discourse now appear to be marked by cautious and grudging and sometimes indiscriminate criticism, mostly from white intellectuals, suggesting that African American intellectuals are unqualified to assume the role of public intellectuals by virtue of their shoddy scholarship, their narrow focus on racial issues, and their willingness to pander to mainstream audiences. The rest of this article analyzes some of these criticisms and their applicability to a thoughtful discussion of the role that black intellectuals might play in keeping alive the spirit of public criticism while reviving both the moral and pedagogical traditions of inquiry within and beyond the university.

In 1995 a series of articles appeared in the American popular press that framed the reception of the work produced by "new" black intellectuals. These articles legitimated a particular theoretical intervention in the debate about black public intellectuals that set the stage for the counterattack to follow. In the first instance, Michael Berube argued in *The New Yorker* that the advent of a group of black intellectuals commanding significant media attention was an appropriate and welcome phenomenon given the central place of racial issues in American politics and the eruption of creative work by blacks in the realm of culture.[48] Berube saw the unexpected prominence of such a group of intellectuals particularly welcome "at a time when the idea of 'the public' has become nearly unthinkable in national politics."[49] For Berube the new black intellectuals not only disprove the claim that "the academy has been the death of the public intellectuals . . . [but also] have the ability and the resources to represent themselves in public on their own terms."[50]

Claiming that the arrival of the black intellectual was as important as the emergence of the New York intellectuals after the Second World War, Berube compared these groups less in terms of political and ideological considerations and more in terms of personalities. ("Whereas Daniel Bell was criticized for buying nice furniture in his forties, bell hooks now draws stares for driving a BMW."[51]) In the end, Berube said little about the substantive issues that inform the work of the black intellectuals he addressed, and especially notable was his refusal to engage bell hooks's feminist politics.

But Berube did bring up a series of criticisms that would be taken up more stridently by others in the popular press. For instance, he argued that the rising chorus of enthusiasm from young admirers who are taken with the black intellectuals' fluency with popular culture may divert such intellectuals as Michael Eric Dyson from listening more attentively to "the deliberations of Senate subcommittees."[52] Implicit in this criticism is the assumption that theoretical work that critically addresses popular culture is too far removed from the "real world" of politics. This is not simply a facile attack on black intellectuals who choose to write about popular culture; Berube's criticism can be read as a one-dimensional dismissal of cultural politics as a politics of bad faith serving mainly as a "compensation for practical politics."[53]

Appearing in the *Atlantic Monthly* shortly thereafter, Robert Boynton addressed a number of similar issues. Mingling his discussion of the new black intellectuals with a celebration of such earlier public intellectuals as Philip Rahv, Edmund Wilson, and Lionel Trilling, Boynton highlighted the theoretical and ideological differences between the two groups. Eulogizing the New York intellectuals, Boynton paid homage to their belief in the transformative power of high culture, their retreat from the mainstream, and their stalwart anticommunism. Measured against the history of these renowned white intellectuals, Boynton found little in the new black intellectuals to suggest the two groups had much in common.

Damning with faint praise, Boynton granted the new black intellectuals importance because "they provide a viable, if radically different, image of what a public intellectual can be."[54] But Boynton's sustained criticisms of the new black intellectuals more than canceled out any enthusiasm for their public role. Moreover, Boynton strongly implied that the stature of the new public intellectuals shrinks considerably seen next to the likes of Edmund Wilson and Alfred Kazin and those who hung around the *Partisan Review* and the New York City bohemia after World War II. For instance, Boynton's highbrow modernism caused him some discomfort when he addressed the writing styles of the new black intellectuals. The admixture of autobiography with social criticism, along with the amalgamation of black speech, history, and experience with academic discourse found in the work (for example) of Derrick Bell and Patricia Williams signaled for Boynton the centrality of racial identity in the work of such writers, a feature that Boynton concluded "would have made the young Jewish New Yorkers squirm."[55] Such writing represents, for Boynton, an aesthetic limited by a fixation on racial identities and experiences and is "more admirable in a belleslettrist than in a wide-ranging public intellectual."[56]

But more than race fixation haunts the credibility of the new black intellectuals. For Boynton, the new black intellectuals who slide easily between academia and the op-ed pages risk substituting theoretically rigorous social criticism for celebrity punditry. Barely veiled in this criticism is Boynton's displeasure with the forms of border-crossing and social negotiations that mark the discourse of many black public intellectuals. It seems inconceivable to critics like Boynton that popular cultural forms can become serious objects of social analysis.[57]

Both of these essays omit the history of black intellectuals as well as the complicated historical narratives through which emergent black public spheres arose in this century.[58] For both Berube and Boynton, white intellectuals provide the legitimating trope for understanding the strengths and weaknesses of black intellectuals. This is not to suggest that either author indulges in a form of racism. But it does imply that the politics of whiteness provides a fundamental context for understanding how the discourse on black intellectuals is framed and addressed in the popular press. In this case, whiteness, as Toni Morrison reminds us, becomes invisible to itself and hence the all-pervasive referent for judging public intellectuals who speak and write in an effort to engage a broader public.[59]

The politics of whiteness provides an often ignored theoretical framework for understanding why black intellectuals receive routine condemnation for speaking in a language labeled either simplistic or "too public." One cannot but wonder why white public intellectuals like Jonathan Kozol or Barbara Ehrenreich who write in accessible prose and speak "plainly" are not subjected to the same criticism that Michael Eric Dyson or bell hooks receive. Eric Lott, for example, refers to Dyson's more general writings as a "troglodyte's delight." When not drawing overt parallels to cavemen, he charges Dyson with "a leftism of good manners" designed to "furnish cautious analyses of the Other half for the unknowing."[60]

Lott's commentary represents more than a mean-spirited mis-representation of the complexity of Dyson's work; more often than not, it appears to be symptomatic of the elitist posturing of a white academic unaware of (or unconcerned about) his own racial privileges who exhibits a disdain for minority intellectuals who gain public recognition as they address a variety of public cultures. For Lott, Michael Eric Dyson's diasporic writings and public recognition suggest that he has sold out, but for lesser-known black intellectuals like cultural critic Armond White, similar forms of border-crossing become oppositional.

Fame often breeds jealousy among academics, and Lott appears to have succumbed to petty sniping. But his analysis also suggests a one-dimensional response to black public intellectuals whose diasporic politics serve as a powerful critique of the white academic's often romanticized celebration of resistance as a practice confined to the margins of social and political life.[61]

One also finds a strong tendency, especially in the work of such writers as Robert Boynton and Sean Wilentz, to argue that the racialist story line of the black intellectuals represents a form of ghettoization, an overemphasis on the connectedness of black history, experience, and culture to their discourse. The notion that the history, intellectual legacies, and struggles of African Americans—along with their damning indictment of white supremacy and racial oppression—are more than mere flotsam "on capitalism's undulating surface" seems lost on many white intellectuals.[62]

More appears in this critique of black intellectuals than just an impoverished version of political and social history. One also finds a notion of the public intellectual that disregards the enduring formation and influence of racial injustice in national public discourse.[63] In addition, those scholars who reject the constitutive role that black intellectuals play in grounding their scholarship in African American history and discourse arrogantly assume that the moral, aesthetic, political, and social lessons of such work apply only to the interests of the black community, hence the charge that such work constitutes a "veritable ghettoization."[64]

Moreover, theorists such as Boynton, Wilentz, and Wieseltier assume that when black intellectuals focus on race they ignore not only broader issues but also a range of questions relevant to democracy. This appears to be a catch-22 argument. If black intellectuals move beyond race as a central discourse in their work, they both lose their "authenticity," as some of their critics claim, and invalidate the very notion of the black public intellectual. But, if black intellectuals focus on racial issues, they risk accusations of either pandering to the perils of celebrity writing or ghettoizing themselves along the borders of racial politics. Each position cancels out the other and conveniently disavows the complexities, struggles, and value of the hybridized discourses black intellectuals contribute to the national debate about racism, education, politics and popular culture.

Equally important, neither position addresses the difficulties black intellectuals face engaging in social criticism within dominant cultural formations. The main casualty of such reasoning, however, appears to be a notion of democracy attentive to the legacy and contributions of black intellectuals and the vital role they play in their struggles to deepen the critical faculties of public memory and expand the imperatives of freedom and racial justice.[65]

Toni Morrison forcefully challenges the claim that black intellectuals are fixated on racial reasoning, defending racial politics by describing it as a pedagogy and practice for democracy and social responsibility rather than a position limited to the narrow confines of identity politics:

> [T]he questions black intellectuals put to themselves, and to
> African American students, are not limited and confined to
> our own community. For the major crises in politics, in

government, in practically any social issue in this country, the axis turns on the issue of race. Is this country willing to sabotage its cities and school systems if they're occupied mostly by black people? It seems so. When we take on these issues and problems as black intellectuals, what we are doing is not merely the primary work of enlightening and producing a generation of young black intellectuals. Whatever the flash points are, they frequently have to do with amelioration, enhancement, or identification of the problems of the entire country. So this is not parochial; it is not marginal; it is not even primarily self-interest.[66]

Morrison's comments unmask the racist logic that often invokes "the racial story line" as a critique of black intellectuals, and she also affirms the critical capacities of black public intellectuals who as border-crossers address diverse and multiple audiences, publics, racial formations, and discourses.

The assumption that intellectuals who speak to multiple audiences become ipso facto sellouts has gained considerable currency in the broader discussion of public intellectuals and black intellectuals in particular. While the dangers of celebrity are real, cautious voices like David Theo Goldberg's argue that when intellectuals intervene at the level of civic debate and speak to large audiences, they face enormous constraints regarding what they can say and how they represent themselves. Paraded as media stars, such intellectuals risk speaking in sound bites, substituting glibness for analysis, and compromising their role as critical intellectuals. Of course, black intellectuals are no less immune to aligning themselves with the ideology of professionalization or the cult of expertise than are their white counterparts in the academy. For instance, Henry Louis Gates, Jr.'s emergence as a preeminent black public intellectual dispensing his expertise on rap music, black literature, and famous personalities suggests less the demise of what Edward Said calls the dominant discourse of professionalism than new indices to measure the shifting breadth and scope of academic professionalization.

Goldberg's position also implies that, as Cornel West demanded in the early 1980s, black intellectuals need to be vigorously engaged rather than simply dismissed or uncritically celebrated. For West, black public intellectuals must exercise a critical "self-inventory," manifest as a "sense of critique and resistance applicable to the black community, American society and Western civilization as a whole,"[67] a sentiment that resonates with Karl Marx's call for a practical politics that he described enigmatically as the "poetry of the future."[68]

Given the recognition of Henry Louis Gates, Jr., and Cornel West in the popular press as the most prominent black public intellectuals in the United States, it becomes all the more imperative to measure their role as intellectuals against their own critical standards. Both exemplify the dangers that public intellectuals face when they take on the responsibility of speaking for an entire generation of black intellectuals. In the current work of both West and Gates there are indications that the spirit of oppositional discourse that keeps alive the radical thrust of being a public intellectual is being compromised. For example, while it might be too much to expect Gates to act like a democratic socialist, it is disheartening to witness his increasing allegiance to a centrist politics made manifest in numerous media appearances, hastily written publications, and op-ed commentaries in which he seems little concerned with social justice and the dwindling state of democracy.

Cornel West's newest work does little to provide a more oppositional discourse.[69] West's recent *Race Matters* appears smug and insensitive in places. While claiming that black public intellectuals need to pay attention to the younger generation, West barely acknowledges the struggles of young people in the urban centers (except, of course, through the pejorative claim that they embody a culture of nihilism). Withholding strong support for a younger generation of black public intellectuals, West berates them for wearing sloppy attire. Unlike W.E.B. Du Bois, whom he models himself after, West ignores the centrality of public education as a site of political struggle and, according to Goldberg, harshly dismisses the important work waged by black cultural critics "independent of the academy—journalists, artists, writers, feminist groups—as 'mediocre,' thereby offering no independent support to sustain black intellectual culture."[70]

What appears missing in the current work of both Gates and West is a model of leadership embraced by Du Bois later in his life. Positing a principle of self-critique and strategy for practical politics, Du Bois recognized that the best educated people are not necessarily those who are most enlightened ethically or politically. We can extrapolate two assertions from Du Bois's insight. First, public intellectuals, especially those whose pedagogical journeys are fashioned largely in elite Ivy League institutions, must use their scholarship as a tool in order to address the most pressing social issues of the time; but they also must be attentive to those ideas, values, and practices that they need to unlearn given their formative sojourns among the rich and the powerful. Second, intellectuals must do more than cross those borders that separate the university from the commanding heights of the dominant media; they also must cross those boundaries that separate academically based public intellectuals from the politics of "hopeful hope"[71] often exhibited among cultural workers struggling in the public schools, community arts programs, social service centers, shelters for battered women, and other spheres where such intellectuals toil without the fanfare of media hype or celebrity status.

Joy James provides an insightful caution to cultural critics who make intellectualism synonymous with black intellectuals. She writes:

When one renders black intellectualism synonymous with black academics, the intelligentsia increasingly distances [itself] from past and present material, democratic struggles for social justice. Given the poverty, crime, and social denigration many blacks face, as they are caught between being commodified, ignored, or scapegoated by the dominant culture, one would think that analyses and strategies aimed at combating repressive state practices/social inequalities would preoccupy the most prominent contemporary black intellectuals. But do they? . . . Thinking and writing about activists can produce progressive perspectives. However, both educators who study activists and those who ignore them may be influenced by a spectator's view of politics, and such a ken can limit a scholar's ability to comprehend the complexities of risk-taking resistance to oppression.[72]

Pedagogies of self-formation are always at work in presenting and representing ourselves as public intellectuals engaged in the struggle for social justice. Public intellectuals such as Gates and West both need to be attentive to what they have learned, and need to unlearn in light of their close association with centers of power and authority. Clearly, West and Gates are decent human beings who see themselves as grandchildren of Du Bois's Talented Tenth and have taken on the burden of pedagogical sages and political activists. This is a difficult task and while both of these figures have exhibited how challenging and potentially transformative the role is, they have also, in part, indicated how slippery success and public celebrity can be when attempting to hold on to an oppositional politic or egalitarian vision.

The contradictions that attend various appearances of both white and black intellectuals do not automatically suggest that public intellectuals are sellouts. On the contrary, such contradictions register the challenges that public intellectuals must face to avoid co-option either within or outside the university while assuming the challenge of addressing multiple and often broad audiences. It means that public intellectuals, especially those in higher education, must avoid an uncritical romance with American culture. For public intellectuals, critical independence and strategic autonomy must include a willingness to contest the cult of professional expertise and specialization with its emphases on hierarchy, competitiveness, and objective, dispassionate research. This suggests demystifying the dominant politics of professionalism while simultaneously creating institutional spaces for hybridized zones of intellectual work in which faculty can create the conditions for new forms of solidarity consistent with defending the university as a public sphere, what Jeffrey Williams calls "one of the few to remain in the post-Fordist moment, in which many citizens can address and debate public issues."[73]

This position, along with Goldberg's, may be far too dialectical for many theorists who air their views on black public intellectuals in the popular media. For example, Adolph Reed, Jr. argues that black public intellectuals who speak to diverse white and black audiences are little more than a modern-day version of Booker T. Washington, rewriting or explaining the mysteries of black America to please white audiences. According to Reed, such intellectuals turn their backs on a black constituency by refusing to address the collective capabilities of African Americans. Moreover, they gush over each other's fame and produce second-rate scholarly work. In the end, Reed dismisses black public intellectuals because they "are able to skirt the practical requirements of . . . avoiding both rigorous, careful intellectual work and protracted committed political action."[74] Reed is not alone in heaping scorn on black public intellectuals, especially those who are progressive. Lewis Gordon reproduces a similar argument by claiming that the impact of new "black pseudo-intelligentsia" has less to do with any viable form of political organizing than it does with filling the "linings of [the] pockets" of those intellectuals willing to mediate between powerful white communities and "economically comfortable but alienated segments of the black community."[75] Not only does such criticism lack nuance, it wallows in a reductionism that completely misses the complexity and range of black women and men who have emerged as significant black public intellectuals in this country.

Whereas David Goldberg supports the notion of the black public intellectual but rightly notes the dangers attendant upon any role that requires one to engage a massive public audience, Adolph Reed, Jr., simply dismisses many public intellectuals as sellouts. Reed echoes the sentiments of many liberal critics who fail to grasp the political and pedagogical value of black and white intellectuals who locate themselves in the border zones that connect diverse groups, contexts, and public spheres. Cut loose from the ideological moorings of separatism and assimilation, black critical intellectuals, in particular, must renegotiate their place from the experience of "uprooting, disjuncture, and metamorphosis . . . that is, a migrant condition . . . from which can be derived a metaphor for all humanity."[76]

As a dynamic discourse between scattered hegemonies and diverse social struggles, the hybrid rhetoric of the new black public intellectual is one that opens up new forms of enunciation, asks new questions, and incites new forms of shared antagonisms on either side of the racial divide. Post-colonial theorist Homi Bhabha correctly argues that writers like Boynton, Reed, and Wieseltier fail to

> grasp the provocation of cultural hybridity, rhetorical and
> political. Boynton's account doesn't quite get a hold on the
> scandal generated by occupying the hybrid position as a form
> of engaged intellectual and political address—a space of

identity that Reed describes as "flimflam" and Wieseltier dismisses as, in [Cornel] West's case, artful dodging.[77]

For Bhabha, living on the boundary promises more than self-serving, celebratory posturing. Far more importantly, it offers a rhetorical and political borderline space from which to refuse the inside/outside duality, the binaristic reductionism of pure or contaminated, and the static divide between margin and center. Bhabha captures the progressive political and pedagogical possibilities of the black intellectual as a border subject critically negotiating overlapping, contradictory, and diverse public spaces while opening possibilities for new forms of solidarity:

> Communities negotiate "difference" through a borderline process that reveals the hybridity of cultural identity: they create a sense of themselves to and through an other. Reed's metaphoric boundary between black and white communities cannot then be assumed as a binary division. And black or minority intellectuals committed to an antiseparatist politics of community have no option but to place themselves in that dangerous and incomplete position where the racial divide is forced to recognize—on either side of the color line—a shared antagonistic or abject terrain. It has become a common ground, not because it is consensual or "just," but because it is infused and inscribed with the sheer contingency of everyday coming and going, struggle and survival.[78]

Bhabha offers his challenge to minority intellectuals, but its larger significance expands the very meaning of the public intellectual whose work cuts across the divide of race, gender, and class. In this hybridized border area the processes of negotiation, indeterminacy, struggle, and politics provide a new set of registers for developing the conditions for transformative social engagement.

The debate over the public intellectual cannot be abstracted from a broader discourse regarding the centrality of racial justice within democratic public life. Nor can such a debate ignore how public intellectuals address the primacy of the pedagogical in providing the conditions for audiences to reconceptualize their role as active and critical citizens in shaping history and mapping the political dimensions of their economic, social, and cultural lives. The role of the public intellectual is related inextricably with mechanisms of power, politics, and ethics. Recognizing this connection offers no relief for those who deny the relevance of politics in the university just as it demands more from those academics who reduce their role to that of the apolitical technician or neutral guardian of Western high culture. The importance of the concept of the public intellectual is that it provides a referent for rethinking the university as one of a number of crucial public spheres that lend "reality to what were fundamentally moral visions."[79] Public intellectuals can articulate a new vision of what education might be, who can have access to it, and what opportunities it can help to produce for those individuals and groups who recognize and try to shape themselves in the dynamic of citizenship and public accountability.

PLAYING THE RACE CARD
MEDIA POLITICS AND THE
O. J. SIMPSON VERDICT

> Race is a means of knowing and organizing the social
> world; it is subject to continual contestation and reinter-
> pretation, but is no more likely to disappear than other
> forms of human inequality and difference. . . . As Du Bois
> knew it, [race] is also a history of hybridity, of multiplic-
> ity, of reciprocity, and, ultimately, of the struggle for
> democracy. To rethink race is not only to recognize its
> permanence, but also to understand the essential test it
> poses for any diverse society seeking to achieve a modi-
> cum of freedom.
>
> —Howard Winant[1]

The insight of W. E. B. Du Bois that questions of race cannot be separated from the construction of a substantive democracy takes on a new urgency at a time when dominant media culture increasingly frames the national discourse about race. Largely supporting the right-wing agenda toward race relations, the dominant media generally have ignored the underlying historical, economic, and political causes of racism while simultaneously reinforcing the fashionable assumption that whites do not bear any responsibility for exacerbating the country's racial divisions. In both producing and legitimating such a discourse, the dominant media abstract the language of racial justice from public discourse while simultaneously blaming blacks for promoting racial discord.

How the politics and pedagogy of representation work in the media to reproduce America's growing racial divide is illustrated amply in the media coverage of the O. J. Simpson verdict. In the aftermath of the verdict, the dominant electronic and print media consistently provoked the anger many whites felt over O. J. Simpson's acquittal and condemned the black community's longstanding call for racial justice as a form of race-baiting that increasingly served to victimize whites and legitimate their suspicion and fears of blacks. I want to argue that the media response to the O. J. Simpson verdict reveals more than the enduring hold that racism has on this country; it also betrays the complicitous role of the dominant media with right-wing conservatives who are intent on mobilizing white anxiety and racial panic as part of a broader assault on democratic public life. What is at stake in analyzing the media's response to the O. J. Simpson verdict is not only the issue of who has control of the means of representation or how such representations generate certain ways of seeing the relationship between the blacks and whites; equally important is the need for progressives and other cultural workers to address how diverse spaces of representation can be theorized and used as part of a broader struggle against racial bigotry, on the one hand, and for promoting racial justice and the possibilities for deepening and expanding the quality of democracy itself, on the other. The media treatment of the O. J. Simpson verdict must be analyzed and addressed by progressive cultural workers as part of a politics of representation that both undermines racial justice and grossly violates the principle that without a democratic politics of representation there will be neither racial justice nor truly representative democracy in America.

There can be little doubt that the O. J. Simpson trial became a metaphor for America's fixation with celebrity justice, lurid violence, interracial sexuality, and tabloid psychobabble. A public obsession promoted by national media coverage, the trial reduced the painful reality of a horrible human tragedy to an overly dramatized spectacle. Whether or not Judge Lance Ito should have allowed the media to turn the trial into a made-for-television drama will be debated for some time to come. However, it seems to me that the public debates that have followed in the wake of O. J. Simpson's acquittal and his subsequent civil-suit trial raise a number of troubling issues that are far more significant than the spectacle of the criminal trial itself, a spectacle that downplayed the gross injustices inherent in a judicial system in which vast numbers of poor and minority defendants do not have the wealth to defend themselves with high-powered lawyers.

Most troubling is the way in which the national media framed the response to the verdict. Near the end of closing arguments in the trial, *Time* featured as the cover of its October 9th issue a picture of O. J. Simpson and the caption "O. J. and Race: Will the Verdict Split America?" Gearing up for a not-guilty verdict, *Time* helped to sow the seeds of racial discord that were seized upon once the verdict was announced. Across the country the media read the verdict in polarizing racial terms. Prominent magazines and newspapers inflamed racial tensions with blaring headlines such as "Acquittal is Said to Stir Voices of Racial Discord,"[2] "Spellbound Nation Divides on Verdict,"[3] and "Simpson Verdict Drives Wedge Between Blacks and Whites."[4] Daily newspapers across the country tapped into the mounting white racial frenzy, reinforcing the notion that the trial verdict had deepened the racial chasm afflicting the collective psyche of the country. Public emotions ran high as the media provided a post-verdict spin to the division between blacks and whites by juxtaposing contrasting pictures of jubilant blacks against stark images of grieving whites. *Time* skillfully intermingled text and image by juxtaposing a close-up of frenzied black youths, fists in air, ecstatic over the verdict with images of white employees in an Orange County shopping mall crying, stunned, or covering their eyes or mouths in disbelief over the jury's decision.[5] *Time's* caption read: "Most Americans know very well that hatred destroys the one who hates."[6]

At least for the media, the outcome of the verdict was clear. Black Americans were unequivocally and monolithically happy about Simpson's acquittal while nearly all whites were aghast and angered over the verdict.[7] Race had become the defining feature of the public reception of the verdict. Not only had a predominantly black jury legitimated what one commentator called the "triumph of race-baiting over justice," but also they had confirmed the "right-wing article of faith that the most virulent racism in America today is not white but black."[8]

Shock quickly turned to moral panic as the media rounded up experts who confirmed what whites were saying about blacks on talk radio programs and in the popular press. Will Marshall, a senior analyst for the centrist Democratic Leadership Council, told the *Boston Globe* that "A lot of people were perplexed by the celebratory reaction [of blacks] which suggests the trial was a battle between the races." Marshall could not understand why some people (the jury) could not "check their ethnic identities at the door and assess the evidence."[9] White reaction reached a shrill crescendo as enraged whites spread their voices and views through newspapers, talk radio shows, and television programs. In short, the message insisted that blacks had acquitted O. J. because they "wanted to put one over."[10]

The Cable News Network (CNN) is a case in point. CNN fanned the racial fires through its post-verdict coverage. When prosecutor

Marcia Clark announced after the trial that liberals were afraid to admit that it was virtually impossible for a black person to be convicted in this country by a jury composed largely of African Americans, CNN gave the story prime-time coverage, while providing minor time to spokespersons who criticized her statement. CNN hosted a *Talk Back Live* program titled "The Color of Justice" and played up the sensationalism attached to the racial divide over the verdict by baiting the audience with questions such as "If you are white and believe that O. J. Simpson is guilty does that make you a racist?" Race-baiting appeared to win as Ben Stein and Dinesh D'Souza repeatedly indicated that blacks were not fit to serve on juries in America. One angry young man calling into CNN's *Talk Back Live* seemed to capture the sentiments of many white callers flooding the talk show lines with the comment, "Of course it's [the verdict] about race, the blacks have been screaming about everything that does not put them in first place." CNN also provided high visibility to a statement by Andy Rooney, who was once reprimanded by CBS for making racist remarks, in which he offered a million-dollar reward for the killers of Nicole Simpson and Ron Goldman. Convinced that O. J. Simpson was guilty, Rooney remarked that he was not overly concerned about having to pay the reward.

Talk radio pumped up the volume on white racist invective. Hosts such as Bob Grant echoed a sentiment that Ku Klux Klan members have been repeating for decades. Enraged at seeing an image of black female law students cheering the verdict, Grant began a racist tirade that took on an ominous tone: "Who knows, maybe in the future they will be beaten and battered and maybe even murdered."[11] Similarly, all of the major television networks interviewed in talk show format battered women, small-town audiences, and individual middle-class whites on the street, capitalizing on the corrosive bitterness many whites felt over the verdict arrived at by a majority black jury.

Buttressed by the onslaught of divisive racial coverage the trial received in the popular media, a series of policy proposals soon appeared in a number of editorials across the country, many coinciding with mounting publicity that preceded the Million Man March in Washington, D. C. In a shameless editorial in the *Boston Globe*, Dinesh D'Souza argued that only blacks validate racial thinking and in doing so they are not only alienating whites but also are responsible for pushing whites to "rally with increased fervor to support the California Civil Rights Initiative and other anti-affirmative action measures."[12] In a debased twist of logic, blacks were to be blamed for the racist voting patterns and policy initiatives promoted on state and national levels. Legitimated by the national media, D'Souza preached his "rational racism" sentiments on numerous prime-time talk shows. Appearing on CNN, he demonstrated what rational racism meant by asserting that a "black person could not be convicted by a predominantly black jury in this country." On radio and television, right-wing pundits ruminated over whether the Simpson verdict had hurt Colin Powell's presidential aspirations and seemed to delight in the conclusion that the new policy legislation aimed largely at poor minorities and blacks would, in light of the Simpson verdict, receive much stronger support from disgruntled whites. It seems that the qualities of rationality, truthfulness, and trustworthiness had once again become the exclusive preserve of whites.

At the core of white dissatisfaction and media hype was the assumption that O. J. Simpson was acquitted because of the "race card," which served to remind white America that blacks in a position of power were likely to seek racial revenge in light of the legacy of slavery, segregation, urban ghettoization, and poverty rather than render fair judgment. According to such reasoning, O. J. Simpson was set free not because the state failed to convince the jury that he committed murder beyond a reasonable doubt but because he was a black man tried by a largely black jury. Rewriting racial justice as a form of racial privilege, the dominant media's use of the "race card" arguments provided the trope to reinvent racism as a practice that victimized whites.

The public debate about the O. J. Simpson verdict is an exemplary indication of how the "race card" argument is used by whites when it appears that a black person is benefiting from a race-specific rather than a race-neutral decision. From this perspective, race serves to unfairly privilege blacks in relation to a notion of justice that refers to itself as "color-blind." The contradiction that undermines this argument for race neutrality or "color-blind" justice is haunted by more than bad faith; it is politically reactionary and theoretically confused, resting on the false premise that the judicial system is color-blind when administered by whites. It is worth noting that after O. J. Simpson's conviction in his civil trial the popular media said little about the racial makeup of the jury, which was largely white, while consistently referring to the decision as an instance of integrity, responsibility, and rationality. If we are to believe the popular media, race has little to do with securing justice when the racial makeup of the jury is primarily white.

Missing from this perspective is the reality of a judicial system that cannot be disassociated from a history of systemic racism. Currently in the United States, one out of three black men between the ages of eighteen and twenty-four are either imprisoned, on probation, or on parole. Race then becomes the defining principle of how crime is designated and how justice is administered to those who are largely young, poor, and black.[13] At a time in history when a large majority of white citizens associate black urban youth with the erosion of civil society and view criminal behavior and black culture interchangeably, it is both an act of bad faith and an expression of racism to suggest that blacks have no right to be suspicious of the kind of "protection" law enforcement or the criminal-justice system might offer. In some cases, right-wing conservatives have used such statistics to legitimate white fear of blacks as a reasonable and rational response to the alleged increasing criminalization of black culture. In a shameful editorial, the internationally renowned journal *The Economist* recently echoed this sentiment. Arguing that the old racism was based on bigotry, *The Economist* assured its readers that the new racism based on fear was not only acceptable but grounded in an accurate perception of black culture.

> The general nature of racial prejudice has changed. Once the problem was simple bigotry, virulent and widespread. . . . Prejudice then was driven by hate or disdain; now it is driven by fear. White families fear for their security and property values when blacks move in next door—and so most continue to live in all-white neighborhoods. A white woman shivers when she turns in the street at night and sees a young black man walking behind. She crosses the street; and the young man knows why. For him, to be shunned in this way stings as much as the old racism did, and is every bit as unfair. Yet this new racism of fear differs from the old racism of bigotry in a crucial way: it is grounded, alas, in reality [of black crime].[14]

It is commonplace for many whites to point to the Rodney King affair as an egregious manifestation of police brutality and judicial racism that was censured with the federal prosecution of the Los Angeles Police Department (L.A.P.D.) officers involved in the beating. While such an analysis is meant to vindicate the criminal-justice system against charges of racism, the argument often does not focus on King's brutal encounter with the police within a context that would render it continuous with how blacks are mistreated—and have been abused historically—by police in many urban areas. Blacks already knew what their daily encounters with the police were like; moreover, the Rodney King affair, along with the hiring of a black L.A.P.D. police chief, did not prevent Mark Fuhrman from continuing his job on the police force. The Rodney King affair was as much a wake-up call for whites who have continually ignored reports like that of the Kerner Commission and endless examples of police brutality against blacks as it was an occasion for black anger and rage. If many blacks and other subordinated groups are suspicious of how the justice system operates in the United States, it is a measure of the longstanding, systematic racism that undermines the commanding institutions of civil society rather than an expression of how blacks invoke the "race card" via Rodney King to merely act out of a narrowly defined notion of self-interest.

The reaction by many whites and the dominant media to the O. J. Simpson verdict suggests that the resurgence of racism in this country is evident in more than pseudoscientific tracts of the new eugenicists such as Charles Murray and Richard Herrnstein. One can only define as racist a national media that slants its coverage of the response to the O. J. Simpson verdict so as to largely legitimate the assumption that Simpson's acquittal was a debased act of racial revenge. In this perspective, the figure of Mark Fuhrman serves less as a reminder that racism is alive and well in white America than as an excuse for defense lawyer Johnnie Cochran to pander to a mostly black jury's distrust of the L.A.P.D. Central to this argument is the assumption that Cochran was simply a messenger of malice who provided a predominantly black jury with an opportunity to retaliate against a racist criminal-justice system and a widespread culture of racist brutality. This racist assumption further buttresses the claims repeatedly made by whites on call-in shows and in the dominant press that black jurors go easy on black defendants because of race. Of course, such claims are at odds with numerous statements made by the Simpson jurors, who have argued repeatedly that the prosecution simply failed to prove its case.[15]

Thus, playing the "race card" is not simply the prerogative of black Americans. In fact, it has been used by many liberal and conservative whites who have found recourse in a new growing self-consciousness about what it means to be white in America. Moreover, as whites express their anger through the rhetoric of a besieged minority whose rights and privileges are being eroded because of black racial privilege, the notion of racial justice is almost completely excised from the media debate, or used as a trope to portray whites as victims of racial discrimination. When white anxiety—rather than the democratic notions of justice and civic virtue—becomes the motivation for passing judgment on the competence of blacks to exercise power and due process, there is more at work than a concern on the part of whites for justice and impartiality. White anxiety is not the basis for social change; on the contrary, it largely serves to put blacks on the defensive through the invocation of the "race card" argument while substantially excluding them from the political debate.[16]

The "race card" also has been used in this case by many feminists who rightfully seized upon the trial and subsequent verdict to highlight the horrible tragedy of battered women in this country and the failure of the criminal-justice system to take them seriously. But in many cases, such criticisms were waged within a polarizing discourse that pitted black women against white women and race against gender and in doing so reproduced the racist presumption that black women are incapable of thinking rationally about human injustices and how they should be addressed. The national newspaper columnist Ellen Goodman registered her dissatisfaction by claiming that "The jury traded Nicole Simpson for Mark Fuhrman."[17] Eileen McNamara, writing in the *Boston Globe,* flatly declared that the Simpson verdict proved that the "'race card' trumps the gender card every time. . . . The jury chose not to see, not to hear."[18] Ellen Willis used the "race card" in a more provocative sense. For Willis, the defense team won the case by "shifting the focus to a classic black-man-versus-racist-police scenario" and in doing so made the real victims irrelevant. Moreover, race became a metaphor for black men. Not only were black women excluded in this narrative, they were "offered no way to affirm their connection with the black community other than standing by their man."[19] So much for the complexity of views, histories, and possibili-ties open to black women and the forces they bring to bear on making reasonable decisions in exercising their own sense of agency. In these examples, the "race card" assumes black privilege, a homogeneous black population, poor judgment, and disruption and signifies a definition of racial justice that makes whites the victims.

One wonders why the same cries of injustice were not taken up in full force by white female pundits after the acquittal of William Kennedy Smith, who was charged with raping a young woman at his Florida beach compound. To conclude that because a predomi-nantly black female jury found O. J. Simpson not guilty they in turn condoned the battering of women represents a zero-sum logic that is both racist and politically reactionary.[20] Moving beyond the polarizing language of the "race card" is not meant to underestimate the impact the verdict may have had on men who read it as a legitimation to beat women and get away with it. On the contrary, the verdict must be taken up as a political and pedagogical challenge that demands new strategies that seek a common ground that blacks and whites, women and men alike, might share in seeing patriarchy and racism as mutually reinforcing in their disregard for human life, democracy, and social justice.

But there is more at work in the debate over the O. J. Simpson verdict than an assertion of ethnic identity founded on whites as a besieged minority; there is also the racist contradiction implicit in the charge that blacks are incapable of thinking through issues in a critical and intelligent manner. In this position, expressed quite forcefully by prosecutor Marcia Clark, whites are the only ones capable of dispens-ing justice through the court system since blacks cannot subordinate identity politics to the interests of social justice and public safety. Adolph Reed, Jr., is on target in arguing that this position comes "frighteningly close to resuscitating 19th-century demands to prohibit blacks from jury service, reflecting the racist presumption that whites alone are capable of impartiality."[21] White ridicule of the verdict also fuels a racist logic that denies the possibility that the jury may have focused seriously on the evidence—or lack thereof—presented to them over a nine-month period and that they may have had ample grounds for concluding that the prosecution had not proved its case. After the verdict, jurors indicated that they thought the prosecution's case was weak and repeatedly denied that they let Simpson off because he was black. Sloppy lab work, tainted evidence, ill-fitting gloves, lying detectives, questionable claims about DNA tests, and a host of other factors that undermined the prosecution's case did little to appease a media culture intent on legitimizing the conclusion of L.A. District Attorney Gil Garcetti, who announced on the day of the verdict to a prime-time television audience on CNN that "Apparently their [the jury's] decision was based on emotion that overcame reason."[22] Of course, Garcetti saw no reason to publicly retract his statement after Mark Furhman, a key witness for the defense and the detective who directly implicated Simpson by finding a bloody glove, was later found guilty of lying in the O. J. Simpson trial.

The white media played the "race card" in spreading the message that race is the lens through which black people view the world and that the influence of race-consciousness as such can only be pejorative. Such a position is not only self-serving to whites, but also exposes a thinly veiled paternalism that denies black agency while condemning blacks for reverse racism. The "race card" argument used by whites demonstrates a double standard at work. According to this logic, whiteness bestows no specific privileges and powers and has no bearing on how culture and power intersect along racial lines to undermine economic and social justice and legitimate racial inequality.[23] Missing from this refusal to know is an awareness of the long history of dominant social relations in which white identity references "modernity, reason, order, stability and black stand[s] for backwardness, irrationality, chaos, and violence."[24] Historical amnesia and studied indifference aside, the invocation of a race-transcending politics by whites sabotages ethical responsibility and rings hollow against a national politics organized in the shadow of Willie Horton, the aggressive promotion of anti-immigration legislation by Republican presidential candidates, and the spearheading of policy legislation by a right-wing Congress that refuses to acknowledge that the most negative effects of their legislation will be on African Americans, in particular their children. Conservative columnist Barbara Amiel, writing in the October 8, 1995 issue of the London *Sunday Telegraph* responded insightfully to the charge by the white media of reverse racism on the part of the O. J. Simpson jury:

> Perhaps what disturbs me most about the reaction to the Simpson acquittal is what I think can only be described as racism among the white community. For years I have been denying that there is such a thing as systematic racism in our society. But in this case, scratch a white liberal and you may find an attitude towards blacks that is truly horrific . . . thinking people should be able to separate a perfectly sustainable decision by a jury from a more complex question of the relationship between blacks and whites in American society. Black juries convict black defendants all over America. I believe they would have acquitted a white defendant if the police had behaved as they did in this case and the untainted evidence had been as weak. . . . The contempt in which commentators hold this jury is beyond reason.[25]

The justice system itself is not race-neutral. Nor is it a system immune to the workings of power and privilege. Whether one is black or white, poor or rich, male or female influences how the justice system operates. It would not be difficult to argue that white juries are far more prejudicial and racially protective than predominantly black juries are. The first Rodney King trial is only the most visible example in which this point could be made. Moreover, despite the harassment of blacks by police and the mistrust felt by the black community toward them, "black juries vote to convict most black defendants."[26] Jack White sets the record straight in claiming that "In heavily black jurisdictions such as Washington, mostly black juries routinely send African American defendants to prison when the evidence merits it. History shows that from Mississippi during the civil rights era to Simi Valley in the '90s, it is all-white juries that tend to exonerate defendants of their own race despite the evidence."[27]

Examples abound of white juries acquitting whites when the victim is black. For example, after Bernhard Goetz exercised his vigilante-like justice against a group of black youth who allegedly threatened him in a crowded subway car, a white jury let him off with a slap on the wrist. Richard Goldstein rightly remarks that "when the verdict came down, the glee in Whitethnica was every bit as stunning as the cheers for Simpson in the ghettos are today. But no one took that as a sign of social collapse."[28]

The "race card" theory promoted by the media plays upon the current right-wing lament that the country is going to the dogs because of affirmative action and other entitlements demanded by blacks. But what is ignored in such pronouncements is the reality of a country that not only leads the world in the number of citizens it puts in prison, but also incarcerates a high proportion of black men. Even though black men constitute only 8 percent of the population, they account for more than half of the prison population. Social amnesia may be comforting to the white-supremacist mind, but it cannot continue to ignore the racial and social policies responsible for spending more money to send black youth to prison than to college. Nor can whites bank the future of democracy on policies that invest heavily in a prison-industrial-complex that has mushroomed since the 1980s into a multimillion dollar business. Certainly for many black youth entering the criminal-justice system, race is the defining principle shaping their lives. In the aftermath of the exposé of the Philadelphia police force—a force so corrupt that it routinely planted evidence to convict blacks (resulting in hundreds of convictions that may be overturned)—it once again should come as no surprise that poor, urban blacks may be distrustful of the criminal-justice system. And yet, racism is not invoked in the media when talking about the criminal-justice system in general nor is it invoked when analyzing how white juries make their decisions regarding black defendants. There is rarely a public outcry when whites convict African Americans in disproportionate numbers on a daily basis. Whites seemed shocked when Johnnie Cochran highlighted the racism at work in American society, especially in the criminal-justice system. Moreover, they are outraged when blacks fail to convict a high-profile black man and assume that the "race card" was responsible for the acquittal. The cynicism and anger of whites become vehicles for them to conjure up the notion that they are the real victims of racial injustice.

Rather than reinforcing the currently fashionable right wing premise that it is the genetic capacities of blacks that prevent them from being as intelligent as whites and by implication not as qualified for jury duty as whites, it would be more ethical and responsible for the media to suggest that blacks are far more attentive to the ways in which racism works against the implementation of justice and hence might be much more cautious as well as thoughtful in making sure that race is not the deciding factor in establishing convictions. Of course, blacks serve on juries every day in this country, and the ways in which they vote are as diverse as are their histories, experiences, ideologies, political beliefs, and values. What they share, though always under specific and varied conditions, is the scorn, discrimination, and effects of institutional and ideological white racism. In general, the "race card" argument is used largely by whites either to avoid how racism works in this country or to downplay its toxic effects. But at the same time, it would be wrong, as Eric Foner has argued, to "paint all whites with the brush of unyielding racism."[29] It is simply vulgar racial reasoning to assume that either blacks or whites are unified under an absolute set of values, ideologies, and values, or that contradictory communities don't exist among them. Associating racial groups with a counterfeit notion of unity speaks to more than strategic acts of exclusion and inclusion; it points to the formation of new publics of difference rooted in an appeal to whiteness as an organizing principle of separateness and exclusion. The crisis of cultural identity in this instance is exemplary of the crisis of democracy itself.

Following the response to the O. J. Simpson verdict, the "race card" argument was replayed by national media in the attention given to the Million Man March. Focusing most of their attention on Minister Louis Farrakhan, the press largely ignored the Million Man March as a collective expression of both solidarity and urgency in calling upon the leadership of this country to address the problem of rebuilding the nation's schools, health care system, economy, and cities. By concentrating almost exclusively on Farrakhan, the press presented blackness as a metaphor for racial extremism, discord, and separatism. The media coverage of both the O. J. Simpson verdict and the Million Man March exemplified how such events could be framed so as to not call into question the racial politics at work in such reporting. The ideological leap from the reality of black urban life—with its increasing poverty and the dismantling of welfare programs, summer job programs for needy kids, Head Start, assistance for the homeless, and financial aid for poor kids—to the claim that whites are the real victims of racism is more than mendacious; it makes the racism of the L.A.P.D and Mark Fuhrman look tame.

The "race card" argument when used by whites almost always translates into scapegoating people of color. When invoked by black nationalists or by conservatives such as Clarence Thomas it more often than not is used at the expense of black women. In either case, vulgar racial reasoning replaces a broader concern with how racist degradation undermines coalition-building and democratic public life. Moreover, the "race card" argument does little to expand the politics of identity beyond the narrow concerns of specific groups to broader strategies aimed at developing genuine solidarity with those deeply committed to economic and social justice.

The O. J. Simpson verdict says far less about how some black jurors refused to transcend the alleged limitations of race than it does about the refusal of the national media and the general public to make racial justice and racial equality central to reinvigorating the struggle for democracy in a time of resurgent racism and a diminishing respect for ethical and public life. As a defining principle of this country, racism points to histories, experiences, and cultural differences forged in relations of hierarchy, inequality, and abuse. But race is not simply a political and ethical metaphor for domination. It also provides a discursive, representational, and pedagogical space for imagining differences without hierarchies, analyzing contemporary identity politics as a site of historical contestation, rewriting borders of difference as part of a project of reinvigorating public space, making dialogue possible over the shifting historical constructions of whiteness, and fighting for progressive social policies.[30]

As sites of contestation, racial and cultural differences should not become a rationale for constructing collective identities rooted in separatism. On the contrary, notions of identity, difference, and community must be reclaimed within a democratic discourse that signals the importance of educating artists, teachers, and other cultural workers to act with compassion and civic courageousness in a world of turbulent and fractured public spheres. Cultural workers need to reclaim and reinvigorate those public spheres crucial to the construction of critical citizens, the formation of democratic coalitions, and the building of a multiracial and multicultural society. The response to the O. J. Simpson trial should be seized upon by educators as a political and pedagogical lesson for examining and challenging how racialized discourse is produced and legitimated in the media and a wide range of other institutional and pedagogical sites.[31] Such a task means reimagining the space of media culture within a political discourse and set of pedagogical practices that foreground the connection between racial justice and the responsibility of citizens to struggle for a vibrant democracy.

SEVEN

RACE TALK AND THE CRISIS OF DEMOCRATIC VISION
(WITH SUSAN SEARLS)

> Ever since the birth of our nation, white America has had a schizophrenic personality on the question of race. She has been torn between selves—a self in which she proudly professed the great principles of democracy and a self in which she sadly practiced the antithesis of democracy. . . . The white backlash of today is rooted in the same problem that has characterized America ever since the black man landed in chains on the shores of this nation. The white backlash is an expression of the same vacillations, the same search for rationalizations, the same lack of commitment that have always characterized white America on the question of race.
>
> —Martin Luther King, Jr.[1]

INTRODUCTION

Writing a year before he was assassinated, Martin Luther King, Jr. was keenly aware that the reality of racism was at odds with the principles of democracy. King recognized that the most explosive issue facing white America was its refusal to address its role in a history steeped in racial oppression—a history of the Middle Passage, slavery, Southern Reconstruction, segregation, and urban ghettoization—that has crippled the nation since its inception. Bearing witness to centuries of oppression, King consistently sought to reveal the ways in which racism invariably was reproduced through a crisis of leadership in which white America could neither confront the legacy of its white-supremacist doctrines nor, when individual conscience burned, take a firm and unequivocal moral stand against racial injustice. Sustained by a moral vision of a world without racism, King articulated a notion of politics that might challenge and overcome injustices themselves. We want to argue with John Brenkman and others that since the death of Martin Luther King the moral dimension of the public sphere has been neglected by critics and intellectuals who have disregarded "the absence of racial justice in the national political discourse."[2] As a result, the language of public criticism and protest, of politics and public life have been transformed by a shift in discourse about racial justice to what Toni Morrison has described as "race talk." Her definition is worth repeating: Race talk is "the explicit insertion into everyday life of racial signs and symbols that have no meaning other than pressing African Americans to the lowest level of the racial hierarchy. In race talk the move into mainstream America always means buying into the notion of American blacks as the real aliens. . . . Stability is white. Disorder is black."[3]

As America moves toward the close of the century, its citizens have experienced the further erosion of democracy—and the possibilities for democratization—that has resulted from the unchecked reign of the market. Cornel West succinctly sums up the contemporary cultural and economic scene:

> Deindustrialization and deregulation have resulted in relative economic decline; downward mobility for the majority of Americans, cultural decay, and unregulated markets now create market cultures, market moralities, market mentalities, shattering community, eroding civil society, undermining the nurturing system for children.[4]

All of this reinforces the breakdown of democratic public life and the fragmentation of communities. And of course, race remains one of the most explosive issues. The increasing visibility of whiteness as a racial category and subject of scrutiny, coupled with the successful attempts of people of color to write themselves into the history of the United States, has generated a conservative backlash among many whites who define themselves as under siege as public discourse and space becomes more pluralized and racially diverse. In light of what we see as a current crisis of leadership and democracy, Martin Luther King's insights about racism take on a new urgency as race becomes one of the defining principles of a new conservative backlash that has emerged in the nineties.

While the old racism unabashedly employed racist arguments in its endless quest for rationalizations and scapegoats, the new racism offers a two-pronged argumentation that, on the one hand, refuses to acknowledge that the issue of race is at the heart of its policymaking (as in welfare cutbacks, tougher crime bills and anti-immigration legislation) and, on the other hand, offers rationales for policy changes that claim to be color blind (as in the call to end affirmative action and racial gerrymandering). In the first instance, the new racism articulates and legitimates a range of ideologies and practices that deeply affect both the privileges at the heart of the construction of whiteness and the racist practices that bear down heavily on the lives of people of color—while denying that race matters. For instance, conservative politicians such as Newt Gingrich have denied that race has anything to do with the slash-and-cut polices at the heart of their Contract with America, and yet the policies produced by such legislation affected most drastically poor blacks and the urban poor.

Similarly, in his defense of *The Bell Curve,* Charles Murray consistently has denied that the book is primarily about race since only one of its twenty-one chapters centers on arguments about black intellectual inferiority. However, *The Bell Curve* restricts the eight chapters of Part II to a discussion of whites alone, demonstrating that over half the book is organized around questions of race—unless one is willing to make the argument that whiteness is not a racial category. Further, the denial that race is central to *The Bell Curve* is contradictory coming from an author who has legitimated his work by arguing that it provides a language for "a huge number of well-meaning whites [who] fear that they are closet racists . . . [and] tells them they are not. [This book] is going to make them feel better about things they already think but do not know how to say."[5] Clearly, Murray's defense of white America is an argument for privileging whiteness as a racial construction. The authors of *The Bell Curve* make no apologies for arguing "that society is and must be stratified by intelligence, which is distributed unequally among individuals and racial groups and cannot be changed in either."[6]

In the second instance, national leaders propose changes in public policy that disproportionately affect African Americans and other minority groups in efforts to end the alleged reign of special-interest groups and reverse discrimination. As critics have argued, social policies that have a far greater negative impact on the lives of blacks than whites can not be seen as "race-transcending."[7] Such gross distortions reveal not only the failure of conservatives and liberals alike to recognize that there are fundamental institutional obstacles to racial integration in contemporary American society but also the disappearance of racial justice and equality from public discourse. According to Newt Gingrich, criticisms of societal injustices such as racism, what he calls "our newfound sense of entitlement and victimization," are "exactly wrong—and so corrosive to the American spirit."[8] Appealing to a racially coded sense of nationalism and patriotism, Gingrich offers this pedagogical lesson from his book *To Renew America:* "But when confronted with a problem, a true American doesn't ask 'Who can I blame this on?' A true American asks, 'What can I do about it today?'" For Gingrich, civic leadership has nothing to do with social responsibility and social justice since these demand some notion of social criticism and ongoing struggle. Actually, for Gingrich social criticism represents a whining and pessimism that "celebrates soreheads and losers jealous of others' successes."[9] Of course, the soreheads are feminists, critical multiculturalists, environmentalists, civil rights activists, critical educators, and all those others who believe that dissent is central to any reputable notion of citizenship. Former presidential candidate Bob Dole appeals to a similar kind of numbing logic when he attacks affirmative action. Dole argues that "The race counting game has gone too far" and that it is time for the federal government to "get out of the race-preference business."[10] Nor, it appears, can President Bill Clinton support the conditions that foster equality and fair treatment. Ignoring the "glass ceiling" report issued by the United States Labor Department in 1994, which found massive racial and gender disparities in the workplace, Clinton panders to the right stating "First of all, our administration is against quotas and guaranteed results."[11]

As we will later demonstrate, the new racism works through the power of the judicial and legislative process and legitimates and rationalizes its policies through the use of public intellectuals who make racism respectable in their talk radio programs and through wide-circulation magazines, national newspapers, television, and other forms of media culture. Housed and financed in right-wing foundations, the new conservative public intellectuals are enormously skillful in mobilizing racial fears and class resentment and undermining the basic principles of democracy and equality.

We want to argue that any analysis of *The Bell Curve* by Richard J. Herrnstein and Charles Murray has to be addressed within the crisis of democratic vision, ethical leadership, and moral conviction that has been spawned by the rise of the new racism and its growing defense by a number of conservative public intellectuals. In part, the popularity of *The Bell Curve* and the debate it has engendered needs to be placed within a context that signals its continuity with a line of pseudoscientific reasoning, ahistorical confirmation, and quasi-scholarly documentation that has typified white America's response to race. Such appeals to "natural law" and empirical "truth" reflect the need to alleviate moral ambivalence by negating the possibility of social justice.

RACIST SCIENCE AND THE DENIAL OF HISTORY

That Murray and Herrnstein have acute political timing is evinced by the ocean of publicity spurred by the publication of *The Bell Curve.* Capitalizing on the resurgence of racism and racist exclusions in contemporary U.S. culture while at the same time fanning the flames of, and providing "scientific" and philosophic justification for, racist expression, *The Bell Curve* was heralded as an "important" and "brave" book. Indeed, *The Bell Curve* and its pseudoscientific claims set the agenda for discussions on welfare, crime, affirmative action, and civil rights on public-affairs programs such as *Larry King Live, Nightline, The MacNeil/Lehrer News Hour, The McLaughlin Group, Charlie Rose, Think Tank, Primetime Live,* and *All Things Considered.*[12] The "controversy" made the covers of *Newsweek* and the *New York Times Magazine* and was reviewed in such prominent and respectful newspapers as the *Wall Street Journal,* the *New York Review of Books,* and the *New York Times Book Review.* In addition, journals such as *The New Republic* and *Discover* devoted almost entire issues to the debate.

The publication of *The Bell Curve* and the wide-ranging publicity it has received in the dominant media raises questions about the range of cultural, pedagogical, and social conditions that contributed to the book's widespread success and its relevance in the current political conjuncture. Of course, the diverse set of factors contributing to the book's success cannot be abstracted from the particular ideological interests that it legitimates. A few brave reviewers of *The Bell Curve* have exposed the contorted statistics, contradictory data buried in appendices, unsupported and illogical claims, research funding by a neo-Nazi organization, and "scholarly sources" including eugenicists, racists, and advocates of far-right agendas. In spite of the evidence mounting against *The Bell Curve,* the alleged "fact" of genetically encoded racial differences and their correlation with large "behavioral" disparities between blacks and white in the areas of crime, welfare dependency, and teenage pregnancy undergird the call for social change.[13]

Bearing these exceptional critiques in mind, we want to examine the popular reception of *The Bell Curve* in order to understand how racist culture is both produced and legitimated by public intellectuals in the United States. Against the popularity of *The Bell Curve,* it seems reasonable to ask how mainstream commentators would have treated a book that relied upon statistics drawn from neo-Nazi sources to support the claim that the Holocaust never happened. In fact, when such books do get published, they are often denounced as anti-Semitic and dangerous in their whitewashing of the genocidal crimes of the Nazis. Yet, when *The Bell Curve* appeared in 1994, few reviewers in the mainstream media denounced the text as a racist tract or, for that matter, even questioned its basic propositions regarding the measurability of intelligence, the causal relationship between intellectual ability and race, or the hereditarian justification of inequality. Pseudoscientific babble as an argument for black intellectual inferiority along with the advocacy of policies designed to justify the existence of an "inferior" black underclass seemed to warrant little, if any, critical attention as an attack on the very nature of democracy itself. It is clear that Herrnstein and Murray anticipated an outcry against their antidemocratic rhetoric by providing a lengthy discussion of the limits, indeed the dangers, of egalitarianism in their concluding chapters. While Herrnstein and Murray provide an opportunity for educators and others to address pedagogically and politically the question of how racist cultural divisions are being legitimated through this book and its widespread popular support, this provides neither a rationale for the publication of the book by The Free Press nor an explanation for the fact that the book has sold over 400,000 copies. *The Bell Curve* is a popular expression of "race talk," and it resonates powerfully with a broader public discourse that increasingly finds expression in talk radio, film, theater, television, advertising, the press, and other channels of mass culture. We believe that underlying *The Bell Curve* is a racist agenda that is fundamentally at odds with any viable notion of democracy and demands that educators respond to it by engaging its implications for political and ethical leadership. We are not arguing that the book be censored; we are suggesting that educators and other cultural workers attempt to understand and confront the economic, political, and social conditions that provide the pedagogical and political contexts for the book's success.

In many ways, *The Bell Curve* not only suggests what cultural critic Edward S. Herman has called "the renewed acceptability and/or tolerance of straightforward racist doctrine,"[14] but also points to the refusal of the dominant liberal and conservative press, the White House, and numerous academics and public intellectuals to denounce the ever-increasing popularity of racist discourse as dangerous to the very precepts and principles of democracy in the United States. This is not to suggest that *The Bell Curve* has not been denounced by many critical commentators. On the contrary, the book has been treated as a racist tract by many reviewers in the academic press. But very few commentators have gone further and linked the racist assumptions that fuel the book with an attack on the most fundamental principles of democratic public life. In this instance, racist ideology can be denounced while supporting policy recommendations that are equally undemocratic but do not employ the discourse of race to legitimate themselves. Conservative and liberal commentators such as Mickey Kaus, Rush Limbaugh, and Nathan Glazer separate them-selves from the racism of *The Bell Curve,* but support policies that are similar in their effects on the black underclass and urban poor.

The editors of *The New Republic* announced unapologetically in the issue devoted entirely to discussing *The Bell Curve* that scientific research designed to investigate racial differences in intelligence should not be dismissed as racist.[15] The *New York Times Magazine* ran a review of *The Bell Curve* and two other books on heredity and race in which the reviewer, Malcolm Browne, argued that Herrnstein and Murray's basic premises were really important to society, especially to a democratic society. With no wrong intended, Browne argued that the authors under review, all of whom offered a hereditarian justifica-tion for racial inequality, were actually exercising a healthy form of truth-seeking in their plea for "freedom of debate and an end to the shroud of censorship imposed upon scientists and scholars by pressure groups and an acquiescing society."[16] The liberal-oriented *Chronicle of Higher Education* gave Charles Murray major coverage as a reputable scholar and argued that whatever evidence exists on race and intelligence "is open to widely varying interpretation, and how researchers read the data often suggest as much about their politics as anything."[17] In spite of the falsifications and misrepresentations of scholarship, the use of neo-Nazi research, and the racist implications of his writings, the liberal establishment praised Murray as a serious, albeit conservative, scholar rather than denouncing him for reproducing a legacy of racist science that supports a racially anti-egalitarian society. Herrnstein and Murray helped make racism respectable and even chic and paved the way for the popular reception of *The End of Racism* by Dinesh D'Souza, another Free Press book full of racial invective and packed with over 150 pages of endnotes as verification for its "rigorous and scientific" scholarship.[18] Marketing racist tracts under the guise of rigorous and scientific scholarship—in other words, as "race talk"—appears to enhance their marketability. And if a "racist tract is impressively footnoted and aggressively marketed, it can launch its author into the heady world of flashy cover stories, obsequious television interviews, and lucrative lectures."[19]

The popularity of *The Bell Curve* points, in part, to a number of important considerations at work in American society that must be acknowledged by critical educators who wish to fight against the perpetuation of a racist culture and its deeply anti-democratic practices. First, it must be recognized that *The Bell Curve* represents a significant manifesto in what appears to be a developing and dangerous antidemocratic movement that uses pseudoscience and racial fear as a rationalization for white supremacy. Critical agency is reserved for those who are white and privileged and the "valued places" of mindless work, dead-end jobs, and grueling labor are allotted for those who happen to be black and of less intelligence. Low IQ in this scenario is linked causally with social pathology, suggesting that societal intervention is unproductive because inherited intelligence fixes one's level of accomplishment and agency.[20]

Hence, the new counterculture rationalizes racist thought and practice without having to evoke the critical language of ethics, democracy, or justice. In fact, these categories are irrelevant in the new beehive state imagined by Herrnstein and Murray. The force of such an argument and its interconnecting links to elitism, the market economy, and the emerging discourses of mean-spiritedness are well captured by Lee Siegel:

> Murray and Herrnstein's fantasy of a beehive society, in which mobility is frozen and stations assured, crops up across the political spectrum. So does their notion of aristocracy. At a time of collapsing boundaries—social, cultural, psychological—accompanied by new fragmentations, a pseudo-aristocracy based on genetic transmission simulates a sense of real aristocratic birthright and stability. And a pseudo-science nicely fits the modern, rationalist habit of mind, while also answering the need for comfort beyond reason's sterile categories. At the same time, the genetic "edge," the Darwinian struggle to survive, and the fiction of biologically inevitable social strata all mesh neatly with the dominant market ethos of untrammeled competition, no less than they did in Dickens's day.[21]

Second, the massive public attention that conferred upon *The Bell Curve* a halo of academic respectability suggests a crisis of moral leadership within American society that is as pedagogical as it is political. Civic leadership appears to have lost its ethical referents for sustaining, defending, and struggling over the principles of social justice, equality, and freedom. It comes as a surprise to no one that American political opinion has shifted to the right since the Reagan-Bush era. But what has been undertheorized is the retreat from racial justice that has accompanied the Republican revolution. As John Brenkman insightfully observes:

> What has been insufficiently observed and what is perhaps crucial to understanding the dynamics of this moment in American political history is how Reaganism succeeded in dislocating a value painstakingly established in the years following the Second World War. Reaganism excised racial justice from public discourse, transforming this powerful, tenuously shared expression of a common good into a tabooed slogan.[22]

In the current seats of power, both in the nation's capital and in the major cultural apparatuses of our society, intellectuals casually reject democracy as unworkable and embrace the laws of the marketplace as the most relevant principles driving society. Within such a context, there is no language to reinvigorate a sense of community, strengthen the bonds between various progressive movements, articulate a broader vision of power and passion, or educate the young in the discourse and practice of critical citizenship. Against the democratic imperative that grounds citizenship in social responsibility, the new conservative public intellectuals speak in a language that shuns human compassion, legitimates excessive individualism and greed, and encourages racial conflict. We can see echoes of such a discourse in the attack on welfare mothers, anti-immigration legislation, calls to dismantle public schooling, and in Herrnstein and Murray's claim that "there is nothing [people with low cognitive ability] can learn that will repay the cost of teaching."[23] This is more than self-serving cynicism; it is an emerging world view that considers mass democracy dangerous and racism acceptable.

Third, the popularity of *The Bell Curve* signals the rewriting of history through an omission of the legacy of slavery and racism in the

United States. In this case, the history of the eugenics movement and its disparaging attempts to fashion a theory of scientific racism appears to have been lost in the mainstream discussions of *The Bell Curve*. Neither Arthur Jensen's nor Cyril Burt's discredited research have been called into question in popular discussions of *The Bell Curve*. With the exception of mostly academic reviews of the book, few theorists have revealed the bogus research relied upon by Murray and Herrnstein in their claims. Although much of the research used by Murray and Herrnstein was provided by the Pioneer Fund, described by the London *Sunday Telegraph* as a "neo-Nazi organization closely integrated with the far right in American politics," the authors were consistently labeled as "serious scholars" by the American press.[24] Conservative academic Richard Lynn, heavily quoted in *The Bell Curve,* has been less than subtle about his own scientific insights on race. In a 1991 article, "Race Differences in Intelligence: A Global Perspective," he concluded, forsaking all scholarly integrity, "Who can doubt that Caucasoids and the Mongoloids are the only two races that have made any significant contribution to civilization?"[25] Another pillar of research for Herrnstein and Murray's hereditarian defense of inequality and racism can be found in the work of J. Philippe Rushton. Rushton, whom many liberals have defended as a worthy scholar, was censured by his university for conducting a survey in a local mall (using Pioneer Fund money) in which he asked 150 participants—a third were black, a third were white, and a third were Asian—questions regarding the size of their penis and how far they could ejaculate. But Rushton has done more than try to correlate the size and use of sex organs with racial groups; he also has suggested that "'Negroids' are genetically programmed for sexual behavior that spreads the deadly AIDS virus."[26]

Racist and bogus research aside, Charles Murray is a fellow at the American Enterprise Institute and exemplifies the rise of a new breed of conservative intellectuals in this country who are heavily financed and educated within public spheres that are aggressively ideological, right-wing, and primed to develop and shape public policy in the United States. However, as we have suggested, it would be disingenuous to view *The Bell Curve*'s attack on democratic principles such as egalitarianism and social justice as an isolated event in the American landscape or as a brief lapse of consciousness in a nation that has fought consistently for racial justice. Neither is the case. In what follows, we would like to explore the current social and political contexts that have created the conditions for a favorable reception of *The Bell Curve* as an accurate depiction of the phenomenon of intelligence and legitimate commentary on race relations in America.

AMERICA'S TURN TO THE RIGHT

The 1994 and 1996 elections that ushered in Republican majority rule in Congress do not represent the beginning of a political and cultural revolution as much as they signal that one already has taken place. The shift to the ideological right and the circulation and affirmation of its particular constructions of (racialized) Otherness are everywhere apparent on the national landscape. Rising conservatism is visible not only in the nation's capital, but on the airwaves, in the media, in the judicial system, in education, in the workplace, and in the home. Moreover, the right has won new allegiances among youth and minority communities.

One of the most disturbing signs of the times is the entrenched nature of right-wing talk radio across the country. Rush Limbaugh is estimated to reach 20 million people a week for a daily monologue of welfare-trashing punctuated by the angry cry of the white male. As a talk-show radio host at New York City's WABC, Bob Grant emerged as an important figure in regional politics in spite of the fact that he often spewed out racist remarks over the airwaves. Grant was fired when the Walt Disney empire took over WABC, because of remarks he made about the death of Secretary of Commerce Ronald H. Brown, but he was quickly hired by another New York City radio station, WOR-AM, allowing him to continue to vent his racist diatribes on the radio. According to Jim Naureckas, a reporter for *Extra!,* Grant repeatedly has described African Americans as "savages," arguing that the United States has "millions of sub-humanoids, savages, who really would feel more at home careening along the sands of the Kalahari or the dry deserts of eastern Kenya—people who, for whatever reason, have not become civilized."[27] His solution to the problem, frequently promoted on air, is the "Bob Grant Mandatory Sterilization Program." Yet, while at WABC, Grant received call-ins on his program from Senator Alfonse D'Amato, New Jersey governor Christine Todd Whitman, New York City Mayor Rudolph Giuliani and New York governor George Pataki to thank him for his support in their 1994 successful election bids.

In San Francisco former liberal talk radio KSFO went conservative virtually overnight. The station's hosts and callers have described themselves as "beleaguered revolutionaries" in the new right-wing countercultural movement.[28] Jack Swanson, the operations director at KSFO, compares the station's new format to the first "Gay Talk" show fifteen years earlier, stating: "We're letting the last group [conservatives] out of the closet."[29] Attesting to the increasing influence talk radio wields, Jonathan Freedland reports that according to one poll "44 per cent of Americans regard talk radio as their prime source of political information."[30] Further, polls indicate that audiences are not drawn to talk radio because it shocks; on the contrary, "attitude surveys suggest that the firebreathers of AM radio are merely saying what everyone else already thinks."[31]

The national proliferation of overtly racist sentiment is repeated by "reputable scholars" such as Herrnstein and Murray who quip that the white elite's "fear of the black underclass has been softened by the complicated mixture of white guilt and paternalism that has often led white elites to excuse behavior in blacks that they would not excuse in whites." Herrnstein and Murray make good on their media reputation as "serious scholars" producing scientific truths by reassuring the white underclass in the next breath that "This does not mean that white elites will abandon the white underclass, but it does suggest that the means of dealing with their needs are likely to be brusque."[32] It appears that promoting racial fears and divisiveness in *The Bell Curve* can be overlooked as long as such a claim appeals to the dictates of scientific "truth."

On issues related to criminal justice, politicians meet the public outcry to "get tough on crime" with such policies as the "Three Strikes and You're Out!" plan that demands life imprisonment for the three-time offending criminal. Some politicians are backing a "Two Strikes" policy while others are willing to throw away the key with one violent felony conviction.[33] Doing his share to promote punishment-driven policies, Bob Dole relentlessly promised in his 1996 presidential bid to build more prisons and lower the age at which children can be tried as adults for violent crimes. Meanwhile, the media relentlessly hammered away at the legacy of the O. J. Simpson murder trial as well as the civil-suit trial, bent on forging the link between black men and criminality.[34]

One of the most important issues of the political campaigns of 1994 and 1996 was immigration and how America's changing racial and ethnic demography affected the "core values of the country."[35] In efforts to exclude the racial Other, the passing of California's Proposition 187 effectively barred illegal immigrants from going to public school and prevented them from receiving nonemergency care in hospitals. With the passage of Proposition 209, California's governor, Pete Wilson, dealt a blow to affirmative action and outlawed positive discrimination policies at the state level, while President Clinton agreed to review affirmative action policies to see if they in fact work. More recently, the Supreme Court has declared that certain affirmative action programs are unconstitutional.

The Supreme Court considered right-wing allegations that enough is enough when it comes to forcing schools to desegregate. Supreme Court Justice Antonin Scalia argued that "societal discrimination" is discrimination that courts have no power to remedy. He insisted that it is not fair "to impose on a school district the obligation to remedy discrimination not of its own making."[36] Demonstrating not only its refusal to "remedy" discrimination but its capacity to perpetuate its legacy, the Supreme Court moved to invalidate a black-majority congressional district in Georgia, a decision the *Boston Globe* termed "a landmark ruling that could slash the number of minorities in Congress and local governments."[37] Other rulings include a decision to allow the Ku Klux Klan to erect a wooden cross in a public square in front of the state capital in Columbus, Ohio on the grounds that the display constituted private religious speech fully protected by the First Amendment.

Public schools also have come under fire in the Republican-controlled Congress. The GOP 1996 budget proposal not only attempted to eliminate funding for President Clinton's Goals 2000 education program, but also attempted to reduce or eliminate federal monies for more politically popular programs. Fortunately, a last-minute compromise saved a number of federal programs from being cut. These included Head Start, a program designed to prepare young children, predominantly poor and nonwhite, for school; low-income college prep programs such as Upward Bound; and Pell Grants, which help low-income families pay college tuition.

Attempts to cut such programs, which disproportionately affect the poor and children of color, reflect not only a complicity with the racist logic of social scientists such as Herrnstein and Murray who make similar proposals on the grounds that federal aid can do little to help the cognitively disenfranchised who also happen to be poor and often black, but also demonstrate how the logic of the market overwhelms the imperatives of a democratic society. Other issues facing the nation's educational system concern prayer in schools and the relative "waste" of the school lunch program. Advocates of school "choice" also see victory on the horizon in their quest to turn public schools over to the free market, encouraging parents to become consumers of education. Absent from national agendas are concerns with improving the conditions or quality of education per se. Little if anything is said regarding overcrowded classrooms, inadequate resources, deteriorating buildings, underpaid teachers, school violence, lack of employment opportunities for young people, poverty, and health and child care inadequacies.

The conservative backlash is also visible at the cultural level. Increasingly, there is a growing culture of violence in the United States that exhibits an indiscriminate rage, if not outright violence, against those deemed as the racial other, especially African Americans. This is obvious not only in the rise of police brutality against urban black youth, the high levels of incarceration among young black men, or the violent attacks on black college students across the United States, but also in the popular reception of racist films such as *Pulp Fiction,* hate talk radio programs, and the demonization of black youth in media culture.[38] The culture of racist violence is also evident in the discourse of right-wing public intellectuals who have become apologists for a form of racism that parades as a legitimate voice for a universal white culture that defines itself as both under siege and willing to fight back in defense of its power and privileges.

Needless to say, Herrnstein and Murray's *The Bell Curve* fits well with current political agendas. Worried about the "cognitive capital" of the country, they suggest that Latino and black immigrants are putting downward pressure on the distribution of intelligence and spurring the need to rethink current immigration policy. Abstracting equity and issues of racial justice from the discourse of educational excellence, Herrnstein and Murray further argue against funding for educational programs such as Head Start, since they allege that special programs to improve intelligence have had negligible and short-lived effects. In reality, the effects of Head Start have been positive and far from negligible, especially for poor and working-class children of color—an irrelevant concern for Herrnstein and Murray. In the name of excellence, they argue that public schools simply waste their resources on those subordinate groups, especially blacks, who are too dumb to be educated when, in reality, they can only be expected to perform simple tasks.

In this scenario, public schools become training centers warehousing poor and black urban youth while voucher programs funded by the federal government offer besieged whites a range of choices that will enable "all parents, not just affluent ones" to choose the school that their children attend. Here, free-market choice becomes an attribute of inherited intellectual capital and provides an opportunity for intelligence to work in the service of quality education. Not only does choice form an unholy alliance with racial injustice in this discourse, it also serves as an ideological marker for ignoring how choice becomes a luxury for the rich in the face of massive economic, racial, and social inequality. Of course, since civil rights laws regulate both employers—from businesses to cultural institutions to the government—regarding whom they hire and the state's allocation of public assistance, Herrnstein and Murray argue for the dismantling of affirmative action and for draconian cuts in public assistance programs. Arguing that intellectual inequality is genetically deter-mined, they set out to disprove the underlying assumption of affirmative action—that ethnic groups do not differ in abilities that contribute to their success academically or professionally—and to challenge egalitarianism as a fundamental principle of democratic society.

While few politicians and pundits sought to embrace Herrnstein and Murray's genetic determinism, many found the concluding chapters of *The Bell Curve* useful in justifying newly proposed cutbacks to federal programs. Patrick Buchanan, of course, did not miss a beat: "I think a lot of data are indisputable. . . . It does shoot a hole straight through the heart of egalitarian socialism which tried to create equality of result by coercive government programs."[39] Indeed, Herrnstein and Murray not only offer a kind of neo-Darwinian social theory to legitimate the pursuits of the state, but also provide a potent, if skewed, critique of egalitarianism in order to redefine state interests.

While Herrnstein and Murray support the notion that people are equal in terms of the rights afforded them, they contend that people are different in all other aspects. For them, the egalitarian ideal of contemporary political theory "underestimates the importance of differences that separate human beings" as it simultaneously "overes-timates the ability of political interventions to shape human character and capacities."[40] According to their logic, the discourse of egalitarian-ism is at odds with a discourse of rights that grants people the freedom to "behave differently" and would naturally lead to social and economic inequalities—inequalities that egalitarianism in turn at-tempts to suppress. What lies ahead of the nation if it continues to accept the main tenets of the welfare state? In short, the "coming of the custodial state." Murray and Herrnstein explain, "by *custodial state,* we have in mind a high-tech and more lavish version of the Indian reservation for some substantial minority of the nation's population, while the rest of America tries to go about its business."[41] Such insipid rationalizations and fear-mongering recall Harlem Renaissance poet Jean Toomer's assertion: "white minds, with indolent assumptions, juggle justice and a nigger."[42]

Offering a form of resistance to the uniformity that the state imposes in the interests of so-called social justice, Herrnstein and Murray condemn "egalitarian tyrannies" with the charge that they are "worse than inhumane. They are inhuman."[43] Their solution to this social-democratic nightmare is a society in which all members occupy "a valued place"—whether IQ has destined them to manage a UniMart or head a multinational corporation—and presumably know their place and stay there. The rigidity of the proposed caste-like system in many ways masks as it reconfigures the centuries-old dream of much of white America for a racially homogenous society. And of course, members of such a society would not be expected to value other members' positions in quite the same way; that wouldn't be *discriminatory,* "a once useful word with a praiseworthy meaning."[44] The irony of Herrnstein and Murray's modest proposal, as David Theo Goldberg insightfully argues, is that people "assume value . . . only in so far as they are bearers of rights, and they are properly vested with rights only in so far as they are imbued with value."[45]

It would seem logical to assume that the resurgence of racism at a time when conservatives and liberals alike have insisted upon the urgency of moral reform and the return of "values" would appear deeply contradictory and troubling to most minds. Herrnstein and Murray, however, have a different worry, one that pits the principles of equality and social justice against the discourse of "truth":

> The ideology of equality has stunted the range of moral dialogue to triviality. In daily life—conservation, the lessons taught in public schools, the kinds of screenplays or newspaper feature

stories that people choose to write—the moral ascendancy of equality has made it difficult to use concepts such as virtue, excellence, beauty, and—above all—truth.[46]

THE CRISIS OF MORAL LEADERSHIP AND DEMOCRACY

The rhetoric for truth and value were the mainstays of Nathan Glazer's commentary on *The Bell Curve*. As a prominent neoconservative, Glazer questions whether we should be talking about a book that claims to prove the genetically encoded intellectual inferiority of black people at all.[47] In light of the ocean of publicity the book has received, he acknowledges that of course "we must" and so ponders the question of the viability of racial improvement. Glazer notes that Herrnstein and Murray do not argue specifically against efforts to improve the education of blacks; however, in his view, closing the gap between blacks and whites remains a vexing possibility:

> In a few cases, in our large cities in particular, greater resources are put into the education of blacks than whites. But the kind of difference that might help close the gap is hardly imaginable. And politically, it would be impossible. How could one argue that the holding back of improvement of white intelligence so that blacks could catch up is morally legitimate, or would improve society?[48]

Read as a kind of zero-sum game, Glazer's words invoke the discourse of rights to argue that black improvement necessarily impinges on the possibility of white improvement insofar as disparities in intelligence foster unequal allocation of resources in education. (We are left to imagine which inner cities provide greater resources for black youth.) For Glazer, the scientific weight of Herrnstein and Murray's analysis, coupled with the moral imperatives of truth and the political philosophy of rights, sanctions a departure from the principle of equal division and social justice. The necessary end of egalitarianism, as morally and rationally as it has been argued, is nonetheless a bittersweet moment for this alleged lover of the truth and the common good:

> Our society, our polity, our elites, according to Herrnstein and Murray, live with an untruth: that there is no good reason for this inequality, and therefore society is at fault and we must try harder. I ask myself whether the untruth is not better for American society than the truth.[49]

There is more at stake here than Glazer's efforts to ground his racist and antidemocratic arguments in the acceptable sociopolitical discourses of science and philosophy; there is also a failure of moral leadership and an arrogance characteristic of a new breed of right-wing public intellectuals who turn their backs on the poor and offer no language for challenging racism, discrimination, and social injustice.

As we have argued, the lack of vision and mean-spiritedness that informs the conservative notion of leadership is not limited to *The Bell Curve* and its defenders but can be found among those who occupy honored positions in government, higher education, and other important public spheres. In an essay appearing in *Newsweek,* Newt Gingrich argued that the most important elements of being an American are to be found in personal responsibility and individual ability. But these are not merely elements in a larger ethic of responsibility; they are the only elements and as such are transfigured into a notion of citizenship that eschews a moral focus on suffering and abstracts individual agency from social responsibility. What is one to make of Gingrich's claim that entitlement is just another form of victimization, that social criticism is an escape from personal responsibility, or that "Captain John Smith's 1607 statement 'If you don't work you won't eat' [serves as] a guiding principle of social life?"[50] In Gingrich's model of leadership, nonmarket values such as community, generosity, and trust get sacrificed in the name of entrepreneurial spirit. Conservatives such as Gingrich seem unable to comprehend that it is "precisely unfettered markets which are now most responsible for the breakdown of community and traditional values. Walmart, not big government, is responsible for the demise of Main Street across America."[51] A similar political ignorance and moral indifference fuels the conservative's assumption that school reform offers an opportunity to "comb through our educational system and laws to clean out the barriers to starting businesses and creating new wealth."[52] The notion that community, generosity, and trust might be employed effectively to check market culture and immorality or that schools might be important in creating a critical citizenry rather than merely a work force for the global economy is lost in this model of leadership.

From Martin Luther King, Jr. to Czechoslovakia's leading playwright and president, Vaclav Havel, we have alternative models of leadership that embrace the necessity for substantive democracy. King and Havel, living in different times, point to a notion of leadership and a responsibility for public intellectuals that allow them to "identify with humanity, its dignity, and its prospects."[53] For Havel, public intellectuals represent the conscience of society and in doing so, they

> build people-to-people solidarity. They foster tolerance, struggle against evil and violence, promote human rights, and argue for their indivisibility. . . . They care about the fate of virgin

forests in faraway places, about whether or not humankind will soon destroy all its nonrenewable resources, or whether a global dictatorship of advertisement, consumerism, and blood-and-thunder stories on TV will ultimately lead the human race to a state of complete idiocy.[54]

We began this chapter with an allusion to the legacy of Martin Luther King, Jr. and we want to conclude with his passionate reminder that "We are now faced with the fact that tomorrow is today. We are confronted with the fierce urgency of *now*."[55] This urgency is signaled in the current threat to democracy posed by the rise of racist discourse, the attacks on equality and social justice, and the growing indifference to human suffering and misery. *The Bell Curve* is not *the* problem, it is symptomatic of a larger and more dangerous crisis of democracy in the United States—a crisis made increasingly visible as the intellectual storm troopers spread their messages of hate, greed, and racism through the airwaves, newspapers, halls of government, and other public forums across the nation.

NOTES

PREFACE

1. Lawrence Grossberg, "The Political Status of Youth and Youth Culture," in *Adolescents and Their Music,* ed. Jonathan S. Epstein (New York: Garland, 1994), 34.
2. Robert Bork, "Multiculturalism Is Bringing Us to a Barbarous Epoch," *The Chronicle of Higher Education,* October 11, 1996, B7.
3. Hal Foster, *The Return of the Real* (Cambridge: MIT Press, 1996), x.
4. Grossberg, 27.
5. Jacques Derrida, *Specters of Marx* (New York: Routledge, 1994), 51.
6. Cary Nelson and Dilip Gaonkar, "Cultural Studies and the Politics of Disciplinarity: An Introduction," in *Disciplinarity and Dissent in Cultural Studies* (New York: Routledge, 1996), 7.

CHAPTER 1

1. Okwui Enwezor, "The Body in Question," *Third Text* 31 (summer 1995): 67.
2. Ibid.
3. Lee Quinby, *Anti-Apocalypse: Exercises in Genealogical Criticism* (Minneapolis: University of Minnesota Press, 1994), 6.
4. Stuart Elliott, "Will Calvin Klein's Retreat Redraw the Lines of Taste?," *New York Times,* August 29, 1995, D1, D8.
5. James Kaplan, "Triumph of Calvinism," *New York,* September 18, 1995, 50.
6. See the figures offered by Barbara Reynolds, "Now We've Learned Who Clinton Is Not," *USA Today,* November 17, 1995, 15A. For an insightful

critique of such cuts, see Susan Mayer and Christopher Jencks, "War on Poverty: No Apologies, Please," *New York Times,* Thursday, November 9, 1995, Op-Ed, A3. Once President Clinton passed the dreadful welfare legislation in 1996 just before the election even conservative-leaning liberals such as Senator Daniel Patrick Moynihan claimed it would be a disaster for kids in this country and would sink large numbers of children into poverty-level existences.

7. Ruth Sidel, "Giving Voice to the Vulnerable," *Tikkun* 10, no. 6 (November/December, 1995): 76.

8. Camille Paglia, "Kids for Sale," *The Advocate,* October 31, 1995, 80.

9. For some excellent analysis of industry's abuse of child labor laws and the exploitation of children in sweatshops, see Laurie Udesky, "Sweatshops Behind the Labels," *The Nation,* May 16, 1994, 665-68; Mark Clifford, "Levi's Law," *Far Eastern Economic Review* (April 14, 1994), 60-61; Pradeep S. Mehta, "Cashing in on Child Labor," *Multinational Monitor,* 15 (April 1994), 24-25; Jonathan Silvers, "Child Labor in Pakistan," *The Atlantic Monthly,* 277 (February 1996), 79-92.

10. For an interesting analysis of the Kathie Lee Gifford debacle, see Eyal Press, "Kathie Lee's Slip," *The Nation,* June 17, 1996, 6-7; Eyal Press, "No Sweat: The Fashion Industry Patches Its Image," *The Progressive* (September 1996), 30-31.

11. Cited in Cyndee Miller, "Sexy Sizzle Backfires," *The American Marketing Association Marketing News,* September 25, 1995, 1.

12. Michael Musto, "Teenage Lust," *Artforum* 34 (December 1995), 73.

13. Herman Gray, *Watching Race: Television and the Struggle for "Blackness,"* (Minneapolis: University of Minnesota Press, 1995), 158.

14. Cited in Maureen Dowd, "What Calvin Means," *New York Times* August 31, 1995, A25. The advertisement appeared in the *New York Times* on August 28, 1995, A5.

15. Cited in Kaplan.

16. Andrew Ross, "Culture Vultures," *Artforum* 34 (December 1995), 36.

17. I am drawing on the productive notion of desire from Gilles Deleuze and Felix Guattari, *Anti-Oedipus: Capitalism and Schizophrenia* (Minneapolis: University of Minnesota Press, 1983); Bryan S. Turner, *The Body and Society* (London: Basil Blackwell, 1984). On the relationship between meaning

maps and mattering maps, see Lawrence Grossberg, *We Gotta Get Outta Here* (New York: Routledge, 1992), especially pages 201-32.

18. Eurydice, "Topspin," *Spin* (January 1996), 16.

19. Stanley Aronowitz and Henry A. Giroux, *Postmodern Education* (Minneapolis: University of Minnesota Press, 1992); Henry A. Giroux, *Disturbing Pleasures* (New York: Routledge, 1996); Henry A. Giroux, *Fugitive Cultures: Race, Violence, and Youth* (New York: Routledge, 1996).

20. Suzanne Lacy, "Introduction: Cultural Pilgrimages and Metaphoric Journeys," in *Mapping the Terrain: New Genre Public Art,* ed. Suzanne Lacy (Seattle: Bay State Press, 1995), 42-43.

CHAPTER 2

1. Cornel West, "America's Three-Fold Crisis," *Tikkun* 9, no. 2 (March 1994): 42.

2. Deena Weinstein, "Expendable Youth: The Rise and Fall of Youth Culture," in *Adolescents and Their Music,* ed. Jonathon S. Epstein, (New York: Garland, 1994), 67-83.

3. Donna Gaines, "Border Crossing in the U.S.A.," in *Microphone Fiends: Youth Music and Youth Culture,* eds. Andrew Ross and Tricia Rose, (New York: Routledge, 1994), 227. For a more specific indication of how black youth are faring in the age of Bill Clinton and Newt Gingrich, see Andrew Hacker, "The Crackdown on African-Americans," *The Nation,* July 10, 1995, 45-49.

4. George Lipsitz, "We Know What Time It Is: Race, Class and Youth Culture in the Nineties," in *Microphone Friends.*

5. Camille Sweeney, "Portrait of the American Child," *The New York Times Magazine,* October 8, 1995, 52-53.

6. Cited in Robert Kuttner, "The Overclass Is Waging Class Warfare With a Vengeance," *Boston Globe,* July 24, 1995, 11.

7. Cited in Associated Press, "Global Study: U.S. Has Widest Gap Between Rich and Poor," *Chicago Tribune,* October 28, 1995, Section 1, 21.

8. See the figures offered by Barbara Reynolds, "Now We've Learned Who Clinton Is Not," *USA Today,* November 17, 1995, 15A. For an insightful critique of such cuts, see Susan Mayer and Christopher Jencks, "War on

Poverty: No Apologies, Please," *New York Times,* November 9, 1995, Op-Ed, A3.

9. Holly Sklar, "Young and Guilty by Stereotype," *Z Magazine* (July/August 1993), 54.

10. "Tagging is the police practice of picking up all Black men at least once and entering their names into police records." In Denver, it has been reported that tagging was so successful that an "estimated two-thirds of all Black men between the ages of 12 and 24, were on the list. Whites made up only 7 percent of the list in a city that is 80 percent Caucasian." Cited in Christian Parenti, "Urban Militarism," *Z Magazine* (June 1994), 49.

11. Cited in Fox Butterfield, "More Blacks in Their 20's Have Trouble With the Law," *New York Times,* October 5, 1995, A18.

12. Paul Gilroy argues, and rightly so, that the bodies of black youth, in particular, are no longer the privileged space of agency; instead, they have become the location of violence, crime, and social pathology. In this discourse, the body is the principal mark of identity. See Paul Gilroy, "'After the Love Has Gone': Bio Politics and Etho-poetics in the Black Public Sphere," *Public Culture* 7, no. 1 (1994): 49-76.

13. Some interesting sources documenting the moral panics around the emergence of youth and rock 'n' roll include: Simon Frith, *Sound Effects* (New York: Pantheon, 1987); Jonathan S. Epstein, ed. *Adolescents and Their Music* (New York: Garland, 1994); Simon Frith and Andrew Goodwin, eds., *On Record: Rock, Pop, & the Written Word* (New York: Pantheon, 1990); and Lawrence Grossberg, *We Gotta Get Outta Here* (New York: Routledge, 1992).

14. Lawrence Grossberg, "The Media Economy of Rock Culture: Cinema, Post-Modernity and Authenticity," in *Sound and Vision,* eds. Simon Frith, Lawrence Grossberg (New York: Routledge, 1993), 196-97.

15. Saul Friedlander, *Memory, History, and the Extermination of the Jews of Europe* (Bloomington, Indiana: Indiana University Press, 1993), 47.

16. Grossberg, 197.

17. Tricia Rose, "A Style Nobody Can Deal With: Politics, Style and the Postindustrial City in Hip Hop," in Ross and Rose, 78.

18. For an excellent analysis of the racial coding that goes on in the electronic and mass-mediated culture, see Herman Gray, *Watching Race: Television and*

the Struggle for "Blackness" (Minneapolis: University of Minnesota Press, 1995), 165.

19. Marilyn Ivy, "Memory, Silence and Satan," *The Nation,* December 25, 1995, 834-35.

20. Ibid.

21. Lee Quinby, *Anti-Apocalypse: Exercises in Genealogical Criticism* (Minneapolis: University of Minnesota Press, 1994), 6.

22. Gray, 160.

23. John Berger, *Ways of Seeing* (London: BBC, 1972), 7.

24. Trip Gabriel, "Think You Had a Bad Adolescence?" *New York Times,* July 31, 1995, C1.

25. Cited in Michael Warner, "Negative Attitude," *Voice Literary Supplement,* September 6, 1995, 25.

26. In response to a interviewer who suggests that one message of the film is that boys are bad news and girls should beware, Clark responded, maybe ironically, that "the girls come off as the most honest, the strongest." One can't help but wonder how Clark defines these terms and in comparison to what references both within and outside of the film. Cited in Jack Womack, "Teenage Lust," *Spin* (September 1995), 70.

27. Michael Atkinson, cited in Ed Morales, et. al., "Skateboard Jungle," *Village Voice,* September 12, 1995, 66.

28. Teresa de Lauretis, *Technologies of Gender* (Bloomington: Indiana University Press, 1987), 13.

29. David Denby, "School's Out Forever," *New York,* July 31, 1995, 44.

30. Sklar, 11.

31. Cited in Stanley Aronowitz, *Dead Artists, Live Theories and Other Cultural Problems* (New York: Routledge, 1994), 42.

32. West, 42. For two books that deal specifically with the complex forces that poor kids negotiate while retaining a sense of dignity and agency, see Sharon Thompson, *Going All the Way: Teenage Girls' Tales of Sex, Romance & Pregnancy* (New York: Hill and Wang, 1995); Jane Pratt and Kelli Pryor, *For Real: The Uncensored Truth about America's Teenagers* (New York: Hyperion, 1995).

33. On Clark's documentary realism, see James Crump, "Quasi-Documentary: Evolution of a Photographic Style," *The New Art Examiner* 23 (March 1996), 22-28.

34. On the issue of how public memory is constructed, see Geoffrey Hartman, "Public Memory and Its Discontents," *Raritan* 8, no. 4 (spring 1994): 28.

35. Amy Taubin, "Chilling and Very Hot," *Sight and Sound* 5 (November 1995), 17.

36. Ibid.

37. Marcus Reeves, cited in Ed Morales, et. al., "Skateboard Jungle."

38. Toni Morrison, "On the Backs of Blacks," *Time* 142, no. 21 (fall 1993): 57.

39. Some interesting interviews and comments on Clark's life can be found in Jim Lewis, "Larry Clark's First Feature Film, 'Kids'," *Harper's Bazaar* (August 1995), 144-45, 190-91; Gabriel, C1, C7; Jack Womack, "Teenage Lust," *Spin* (September 1995), 65-70; Terrence Rafferty, "Growing Pains," *The New Yorker,* July 31, 1995, 80-82.

40. Rafferty, 80, 82.

41. John Fiske, *Power Plays, Power Works* (London: Verso Press, 1994), 15.

42. Ibid.

43. David Smith Allyn, "Sex With a Heart," *Tikkun* 10, no. 6 (November/December 1995): 92.

44. Eve Kosofsky Sedgwick, *Epistemology of the Closet* (Stanford: University of California Press, 1990), 7.

45. Gray, 160.

CHAPTER 3

1. Ruth Sidel, *Keeping Women and Children Last* (New York: Penguin, 1996), 140.

2. Luis J. Rodriguez, "Turning Youth Gangs Around," *The Nation,* November 21, 1994, 607.

3. Ruth Sidel, "Giving Voice to the Vulnerable," *Tikkun* 10, no. 6 (1995): 76.

4. For an excellent analysis of the failure of such proposals and what they miss in dealing with the problems facing poor white and black youth, see Luis J. Rodriguez, "Turning Youth Gangs Around," *The Nation* November 21, 1994, 605-9.

5. Donna Gaines, *Teenage Wasteland: Suburbia's Dead End Kids* (New York: Harper Collins, 1991), 158-59.

6. James Q. Wilson cited in Mike Males and Faye Docuyanan, "Crackdown on Kids: Giving up on the Young," *The Progressive,* February 24, 1996, 25.

7. Males and Docuyanan, 24.

8. Cited in John M. Hagedorn, "War on Drugs Steeped in Discriminatory Practices," *The Milwaukee Journal Sentinel,* September 10, 1995, 51.

9. Derrick Z. Jackson, "The Double Standard On Drug Crimes," *Boston Globe,* September 23, 1996, A19.

10. For a brilliant analysis of this issue, see Sidel.

11. In a recent report published in the *New York Times* it was noted that the United States "rather than being an egalitarian society...has become the most economically stratified of industrial nations....The most recent [statistics] available show that the wealthiest 1 percent of American households—with net worth of at least 2.3 million each—owns nearly 40 percent of the nation's wealth." Cited in Keith Bradsher, "Gap in Wealth in U.S. Called Widest in West," *New York Times* April 17, 1995, A1, C4.

12. I address this issue in Henry A. Giroux, *Disturbing Pleasures: Learning Popular Culture* (New York: Routledge, 1995). See also Stephen Kline, *Out of the Garden: Toys and Children's Culture in the Age of TV Marketing* (London: Verso, 1993); Ellen Seiter, *Sold Separately: Parents and Children in Consumer Culture* (New York: Rutgers, 1993); and Michael F. Jacobson and Laurie Ann Mazur, *Marketing Madness* (Boulder: Westview, 1995).

13. The idea of the hollow state drained of its compassionate services is in Stanley Aronowitz, *The Death and Rebirth of American Radicalism* (New York: Routledge, 1997).

14. Lisa Robinson, "Magic and Loss," *Spin* (July 1996), 105.

15. James Carroll, "The Rebels of 1968—Wronged Then and Now, But Ultimately Right," *Boston Globe,* August 20, 1996, A23. The critical literature on the history of the sixties is too vast to cite, but for some representative samples, see James Miller, *Democracy Is in the Streets* (New York: Simon and Schuster, 1987); Maurice Isserman, *If I Had a Hammer: The Death of the Old Left and the Birth of the New Left* (New York: Basic, 1987); Todd Gitlin, *The Sixties: Years of Hope, Days of Rage* (New York: Bantam Books, 1993), revised edition; and Aronowitz. For an analysis of the conflicting interpretations of the meaning and legacy of the sixties, see Rick Perlstein, "Who Owns the Sixties?" *Lingua Franca* 6 (May/June, 1996), 30-37.

16. Gary Webb, "CIA Linked to Bay Area Cocaine Ring," *The Denver Post*, September 13, 1996, 1; Jesse L. Jackson, "CIA-Cocaine Link Must be Probed," *Chicago Sun-Times* (September 16, 1996), 1.

17. Newt Gingrich, *To Renew America* (New York: Harper Collins, 1995), 3.

18. Ibid., 30.

19. Ibid., 31.

20. Sidel, 55.

21. Edward Morgan, "Nixon and the Sixties: Mass Media and the Sanitized Past," *Tikkun* 9, no. 5 (September/October 1994): 69.

22. Bruce James Smith, *Politics and Remembrance* (Princeton: Princeton University Press, 1985), 16.

23. Nicholas Bromell, "Both Sides of Bob Dylan: Public Memory, the Sixties, and the Politics of Meaning," *Tikkun* 10, no. 4 (July/August 1995): 14.

24. For an historical analysis of how the dominant media misrepresented the sixties, see Edward Morgan, 66-72.

25. For an excellent theoretical and empirical analysis of the changing nature of social protest and values among students in the 1980s and 1990s, see Paul Rogat Loeb, *Generations at the Crossroads* (New Brunswick: Rutgers University Press, 1994).

26. Liza Featherstone, "Young, Hip and Loud: Youth Papers Give the 411," *The Nation*, February 26, 1996, 17. Featherstone mentions newspapers such as *La Youth,* with 300,000 readers; Chicago's *New Expression,* with 60,000; San Francisco's *Yo!,* with 50,000; and *United Youth of Boston,* with 30,000.

27. For an insightful analysis of the French strike, see Katha Pollitt, "French Lessons," *The Nation*, February 19, 1996, 9.

28. I take this issue up in great detail in Henry A. Giroux, *Fugitive Cultures: Race, Violence, and Youth* (New York: Routledge, 1996).

29. Paul Rogat Loeb, *Generation at the Crossroads: Apathy and Action on the American Campus* (New Brunswick, NJ: Rutgers, 1994), pp.3-4.

30. For a discussion of the "symbolical" centrality of youth and the historically and politically constructed nature of the crisis of youth, see Charles R. Acland, *Youth, Murder, Spectacle: The Cultural Politics of "Youth in Crisis"* (Boulder: Westview Press, 1995).

CHAPTER 4

1. James Baldwin, "On Being . . . And Other Lies," *Essence* (April 1994), 90.

2. For an excellent analysis of the new work on whiteness, especially the historical approaches, see Peter Erickson, "Seeing White," *Transition* 5, no. 3 (fall 1995): 166-85. For more general treatments, see Liz Macmillan, "Lifting the Veil From Whiteness: Growing Body of Scholarship Challenges a Racial 'Norm,'" *The Chronicle of Higher Education,* September 8, 1995, A23; David W. Stowe, "Uncolored People: The Rise of Whiteness Studies," *Lingua Franca* 6, no. 6 (September/October 1996): 68-77.

3. David Roediger, *Toward the Abolition of Whiteness* (London: Verso Press, 1994), 13.

4. Eric Lott cited in Stowe, 76. Stowe's piece also serves as an overview and critical interrogation of the recent scholarship on whiteness. See 68-77.

5. This distinction is taken up in Ruth Frankenberg, *The Social Construction of Whiteness* (Minneapolis: University of Minnesota Press, 1993), 7.

6. For example, see James Joseph Scheurich, "Toward a White Discourse on white Racism," *Educational Researcher* 22, no. 8 (November 1993): 5-15; Christine Sleeter, "Advancing a White Discourse," *Educational Researcher* 22, no. 8 (November 1993): 13-15.

7. In this context, Hall is not talking about whites but blacks. It seems to me that his point is just as relevant for rearticulating whiteness as it is for debunking the essentialized black subject, though this should not suggest that such an appropriation take place outside of the discourse of power, history, inequality, and conflict. See Stuart Hall, "Ethnicity: Identity and Difference," *Radical America* 13, no. 4 (winter 1991): 57. Fred Pfeil raises a similar set of issues about white masculinity in his book *White Guys* (London: Verso Press, 1995), 3-4.

8. One exception worth noting is AnnLouise Keating, "Interrogating 'Whiteness,' (De)Constructing 'Race,'" *College English* 57, no. 8 (December 1995): 901-18.

9. Howard Winant, "Amazing Grace," *Socialist Review* 75, no. 19 (fall 1992): 166.

10. For an excellent analysis of this issue, see Thomas Byrne Edsall and Mary D. Edsall, *Chain Reaction: The Impact of Race, Rights, and Taxes on American Politics* (New York: W.W. Norton, 1992).

11. On the meaning of the new racism and its diverse expressions, see Howard Winant, *Racial Conditions* (Minneapolis: University of Minnesota Press, 1994). See also, Henry A. Giroux, *Border Crossing* (New York: Routledge, 1992).

12. George Yudice, "Neither Impugning Nor Disavowing Whiteness Does a Viable Politics Make: The Limits of Identity Politics," in Christopher Newfield and Ronald Strickland, eds., *After Political Correctness* (Boulder: Westview, 1995), 255-81.

13. John Brenkman, "Race Publics: Civic Illiberalism, or Race After Reagan," *Transition* 5, no. 2 (summer 1995): 14.

14. I take up this issue in extensive detail in Henry A. Giroux, *Fugitive Cultures: Race, Violence, and Youth* (New York: Routledge, 1996).

15. Kaus cited Brenkman, 34.

16. On the rise of right-wing groups in the United States, see Sara Diamond, *Roads to Domination: Right-Wing Movements and Political Power in the United States* (New York: Guilford Press, 1995) and Sara Diamond, *Facing the Wrath* (Monroe, Maine: Common Courage Press, 1996). On racism and right-wing movements, see Michael Novick, *White Lies, White Power* (Monroe, Maine: Common Courage Press, 1995). For a number of articles on the right-wing backlash, see Chip Berlet, ed., *Eyes Right!: Challenging the Right Wing Backlash* (Boston: South End Press, 1995).

17. Both Richard Dyer and bell hooks have argued that whites see themselves as racially transparent and reinscribe whiteness as invisible. While this argument may have been true in the 1980s, it no longer makes sense as white youth, in particular, have become increasingly sensitive to their status as whites because of the racial politics and media exposure of race in the last few years. See Richard Dyer, "White," *Screen* 29, no. 4 (autumn 1988): 44-64; bell hooks, *Black Looks: Race and Representation* (Boston: South End Press, 1992).

18. Aaron D. Gresson III, "Postmodern America and the Multicultural Crisis: Reading Forrest Gump as the 'Call Back to Whiteness,'" *Taboo,* 1 (spring 1996), 11-33.

19. Richard J. Herrnstein and Charles Murray, *The Bell Curve: Intelligence and Class Structure in American Life* (New York: The Free Press, 1994); Dinesh D'Douza, *The End of Racism: Principles for a Multiracial Society* (New York: The Free Press, 1995).

20. The sources documenting the growing racism in the dominant media and popular culture are too extensive to cite. Some important examples include Jimmie L. Reeves and Richard Campbell, *Cracked Coverage: Television News, the Anti-Cocaine Crusade, and the Reagan Legacy* (Durham: Duke University Press, 1994); John Fiske, *Media Matters* (Minneapolis: University of Minnesota Press, 1994); Jeff Ferrell and Clinton R. Sanders, eds., *Cultural Criminology* (Boston: Northeastern University Press, 1995); Herman Gray, *Watching Race* (Minneapolis: University of Minnesota Press, 1995); Michael Dyson, *Between God and Gangsta Rap* (New York: Oxford University Press, 1996); and Henry A. Giroux, *Fugitive Cultures: Race, Violence and Youth* (New York: Routledge, 1996). For a summary of the double standard at work in the press coverage of rap music, see Art Jones and Kim Deterline, "Fear of a Rap Planet: Rappers Face Media Double Standard," *Extra* 7, no. 2 (March/April 1994): 20-21.

21. "The Issue," *The New Republic,* October 31, 1994, editorial, 9.

22. For a brilliant analysis of the racial politics of *The Atlantic Monthly,* see Charles Augnet, "For Polite Reactionaries," *Transition,* 6, no. 1 (spring 1966): 14-34.

23. Stuart Hall, "Race, Culture, and Communications: Looking Backward and Forward at Cultural Studies," *Rethinking Marxism* 5, no. 1 (spring 1992): 13.

24. William A. Henry III, "Upside Down in the Groves of Academe," *Time,* April 1, 1991, 66-69.

25. David Gates, "White Male Paranoia," *Newsweek,* March 29, 1993, 48.

26. Ibid., 51.

27. Ibid., 49.

28. Shirley Fisher Fishkin, "Interrogating 'Whiteness,' Complicating 'Blackness': Remapping American Culture," *American Quarterly* 47, no. 3 (September 1995): 430. Fisher provides an excellent analysis of the historical and contemporary work interrogating whiteness; see 428-66.

29. Some representative examples of recent scholarship on whiteness include: David Roediger, *The Wages of Whiteness* (London: Verso Press, 1991);

Alexander Saxton, *The Rise and Fall of the White Republic* (London, Verso Press, 1991); bell hooks, *Black Looks: Race and Representation* (Boston: South End Press, 1992); Vron Ware, *Beyond the Pale: White Women, Racism, and History* (London: Verso Press, 1992); Ruth Frankenberg, *White Women, Race Matters* (Minneapolis: University of Minnesota Press, 1993); Toni Morrison, *Playing in the Dark* (New York: Vintage, 1993); Howard Winant, *Racial Conditions* (Minneapolis: University of Minnesota Press, 1994); Theodore Allen, *The Invention of the White Race* (London: Verso Press, 1994); Michael Omi and Howard Winant, *Racial Formations in the United States from the 1960s to 1990s* (New York: Routledge, 1994); David Roediger, *Towards the Abolition of Whiteness* (London: Verso Press, 1994); Noel Ignatiev, *How the Irish Became White* (New York: Routledge, 1995); Fred Pfeil, *White Boys* (London: Verso Press, 1995); and Noel Ignatiev and John Garvey, eds., *Race Traitor* (New York: Routledge, 1996).

30. David Roediger, *Toward the Abolition of Whiteness*, 75.

31. Ibid., 75.

32. Ibid., 12.

33. Toni Morrison, *Playing in the Dark: Whiteness and the Literary Imagination* (Cambridge: Harvard University Press, 1992), xii, 9.

34. Ruth Frankenberg, *The Social Construction of Whiteness*.

35. Dyer, 45.

36. bell hooks, *Yearning* (Boston: South End Press, 1990), 55.

37. hooks, 54. See also hooks's critique of Wim Wenders's film, *Wings of Desire* (1988), 165-71.

38. bell hooks, "Representations of Whiteness in the Black Imagination," in *Black Looks: Race and Representation* (Boston: South End Press, 1992), 165-78.

39. Ibid., 13.

40. Cone cited in Ibid., 14.

41. Thomas K. Nakayama and Robert L. Krizek, "Whiteness: A Strategic Rhetoric," *Quarterly Journal of Speech* 81 (1995), 291-309.

42. Roediger, *Toward the Abolition of Whiteness*, 13.

43. Noel Ignatiev, "Editorial" in *Race Traitor*, eds. Noel Ignatiev and John Garvey (New York: Routledge, 1996), 10.

44. Derrick Bell, *Faces at the Bottom of the Well: The Permanence of Racism* (New York: Basic Books, 1992); Andrew Hacker, *Two Nations, Black and White, Separate, Hostile, Unequal* (New York: Charles Scribners Sons, 1992).

45. James Joseph Scheurich, "Toward A White Discourse on White Racism," *Educational Researcher* (November 1993), 6.

46. Two excellent articles addressing the possibilities for rearticulating whiteness in oppositional terms are: Diana Jester, "Roast Beef and Reggae Music: The Passing of Whiteness," *New Formations,* no. 118 (winter 1992), 106-21; George Yudice, "Neither Impugning Nor Disavowing Whiteness Does a Viable Politics Make: The Limits of Identity Politics," in *After Political Correctness,* eds. Christopher Newfield and Ronald Strickland (Boulder: Westview, 1995), 255-81. I have relied heavily on both of these pieces in developing my analysis of white youth.

47. hooks, *Black Looks,* 168.

48. Charles A. Gallagher, "White Reconstruction in the University," *Socialist Review* 94, nos. 1 & 2 (1995): 166.

49. Jester, 111.

50. Ibid., 115.

51. For an insightful analysis of how an appeal to white racial identity is used by extremists to appropriate white youth into extremist organizations, see Mark Schone, "Redneck Nation," *Spin* (February 1992), 69-75, 98.

52. Jester, 107.

53. Gallagher, 170.

54. Ibid., 182, 185.

55. I want to thank my colleague at Penn State University, Bernard Bell, for this insight (personal communication).

56. Howard Winant, *Racial Conditions* (Minneapolis: University of Minnesota Press, 1994), xiii.

57. I think Houston Baker is instructive on this issue in arguing that race, for all of its destructive tendencies and implications, also has been used by blacks and other people of color to gain a sense of personal and historical agency. This is not a matter of a positive image of race canceling out its negative underside. On the contrary, Baker makes a compelling case for the dialectical nature of race and its possibilities for engaging and overcoming its worse dimensions while extending in the interest of a transformative and democratic polis. See Houston Baker, "Caliban's Triple Play," in Henry

Louis Gates, Jr., *Loose Canons: Notes on the Culture Wars* (New York: Oxford University Press, 1992), 381-95.

58. James Snead, *White Screens, Black Images* (New York: Routledge, 194), especially chapter 10, "Mass Visual Productions," 131-49. For an analysis of the importance of race in the broader area of popular culture, two representative sources include: Michael Dyson, *Reflecting Black* (Minneapolis: University of Minnesota Press, 1993); Henry A. Giroux, *Fugitive Cultures: Race, Violence, and Youth* (New York: Routledge, 1996).

59. Frankenberg, *The Social Construction of Whiteness*, 49.

60. On the localization of crime as a racial text, see David Theo Goldberg, "Polluting the Body Politic: Racist Discourse and the Urban Location," in *Racism, the City and the State,* eds. Malcolm Cross and Michael Keith (New York: Routledge, 1993), 45-60.

61. Robin D. G. Kelley, "Notes on Deconstructing 'the Folk'," *The American Historical Review* 97, no. 5 (December 1992): 1406.

62. Roy Grundmann, "Identity Politics at Face Value: An Interview with Scott McGehee and David Siegel," *Cineaste* 20, no. 3 (winter 1994): 24.

63. David Theo Goldberg, *Racist Culture: Philosophy and the Politics of Meaning* (Cambridge: Blackwell, 1993), 69.

64. For instance, see Jon Glass, "'Dangerous Minds' Inspires Teachers," *The Virginian-Pilot* (September 2, 1995), B1; Catherine Saillant, "School of Soft Knocks," *Los Angeles Times* (October 11, 1995), B1; Sue Chastain, "Dangerous Minds No Threat to This Tough Teacher," *The Times Union* (August 13, 1995), G1.

65. For example, in Ruth Frankenberg's study of white women, radical positions on race were in the minority, and in Gallagher's study of white college students, liberal and conservative positions largely predominated. See Frankenberg's *The Social Construction of Whiteness* and Gallagher.

66. Gayatri Chakravorty Spivak, *Post-Colonial Critic: Interviews, Strategies, Dialogues,* Sarah Harasym, ed. (New York: Routledge, 1990), 137.

67. Ibid, 67.

68. Frankenberg, *The Social Construction of Whiteness*, 234.

69. Keating, 907.

70. Ibid., 915.

71. See Yudice, 276-77.

72. David Roediger, "White Ethnics in the United States," in *Towards the Abolition of Whiteness*, 181-98.

73. Stuart Hall takes up the rewriting of ethnicity in a variety of articles, see especially Stuart Hall, "New Ethnicities" in *Stuart Hall: Critical Dialogues in Cultural Studies*, David Morley and Kuan-Hsing Chen, eds. (New York: Routledge, 1996), pp.441-49; Stuart Hall, "Cultural Identity and Diaspora" in *Identity, Community, Culture, Difference*, ed. Jonathan Rutherford (London: Lawrence and Wishart, 1990), 222-37; Stuart Hall, "Ethnicity: Identity and Difference," *Radical America* 13, no. 4 (June 1991): 9-20; Stuart Hall, "Old and New Identities, Old and New Ethnicities," in *Culture, Globalization and the World System*, ed. Anthony D. King (Binghamton: State University of New York Press, 1991), 41-68.

74. Hall, "New Ethnicities," 29.

75. Ibid.

76. Hall, "Cultural Identity and Diaspora," 235.

77. Ien Ang, "On Not Speaking Chinese: Postmodern Ethnicity and the Politics of Diaspora," *Social Formations* no. 24 (winter 1995): 110.

78. Chantal Mouffe, "Feminism, Citizenship, and Radical Democratic Politics," in *Feminists Theorize the Political*, eds. Judith Butler and Joan Scott (New York: Routledge, 1992), 380.

79. Erickson, 185.

80. Yudice, 276.

81. Howard Winant, *Racial Formations* (Minneapolis, MN: University of Minnesota Press, 1994), 169.

CHAPTER 5

1. Vaclav Havel, "The Responsibility of Intellectuals," *New York Review of Books*, June 22, 1995, 37.

2. Russell Jacoby, *The Last Intellectuals: American Culture in the Age of Academe* (New York: Basic Books, 1987).

3. I think Michael Denning is right to argue that "the demand that all leftist intellectuals be literary journalists, writing plain English for plain people,

is no less objectionable than the Old Left demand that playwrights write agitprop and novelists stick to a comprehensible social realism." Cited in Michael Denning, "The Academic Left and the Rise of Cultural Studies," *Radical History Review* No. 54 (1992), 36. For sustained critical commentary on the politics of clarity, see Henry A. Giroux, "Language, Difference, and Curriculum Theory: Beyond the Politics of Clarity," *Theory into Practice* 31, no. 3 (summer 1992), 219-27.

4. According to Jacoby, the academy undermines the oppositional role that academics might play as public intellectuals. This is especially important in light of Jacoby's belief that "Today's nonacademic intellectuals are an endangered species" coupled with his claim that "universities virtually monopolize . . . intellectual work." Cited in Jacoby, 7, 8.

5. Cornel West, "The Dilemma of the Black Intellectual," *Cultural Critique* No. 1 (fall 1985), 109-25.

6. This charge can be found in Roger Kimball, *Tenured Radicals* (New York: Simon and Schuster, 1989).

7. A number of books provide a far more thoughtful and optimistic view of both intellectuals and the academy as a viable public sphere. Some important examples include Bruce Robbins, ed., *Intellectuals: Aesthetics, Politics, Academics* (Minneapolis: University of Minnesota Press, 1990); Andrew Ross, *No Respect: Intellectuals and Popular Culture* (New York: Routledge, 1989); Stanley Aronowitz and Henry A. Giroux, *Education Still under Siege* (Westport, CT.: Bergin and Garvey, 1993); Bruce Robbins, *Secular Vocations: Intellectuals, Professionalism, Culture* (London: Verso Press, 1993); and Michael Berube, *Public Access: Literary Theory and American Cultural Politics* (London: Verso Press,1994).

8. Conservative books on this issue are too numerous to mention, but representative examples include Allan Bloom, *The Closing of the American Mind* (New York: Simon & Schuster, 1987); Charles J. Sykes, *Profscam: Professors and the Demise of Higher Education* (Washington, D.C.: Regnery Gateway, 1988); Roger Kimball, *Tenured Radicals: How Politics Has Corrupted Our Higher Education* (New York: Harper Perennial, 1991); Dinesh D'Souza, *Illiberal Education: The Politics of Race and Sex on Campus* (New York: Free Press, 1991).

9. This issue is examined in great detail in Stanley Aronowitz and Henry A. Giroux, *Education Still under Siege* and Stanley Aronowitz and Henry

Giroux, *Postmodern Education* (Minneapolis: University of Minnesota Press, 1991).

10. John Dewey, *The Public and Its Problems* (New York: Holt, 1927), 31-32.

11. My referent to the public sphere draws primarily from the following: Various papers collected in Craig Calhoun, ed. *Habermas and the Public Sphere* (Cambridge, MA: MIT Press, 1992), especially Nancy Fraser, "Rethinking the Public Sphere: A Contribution to the Critique of Actually Existing Democracy," 99-108; Oscar Negt and Alexander Kluge, *Public Sphere and Experience: Toward an Analysis of the Bourgeois and Proletarian Public Sphere* (Minneapolis: University of Minnesota Press, 1993); Chantal Mouffe, *The Return of the Political* (London: Verso Press, 1993); Bruce Robbins, ed., *The Phantom Public Sphere* (Minneapolis: University of Minnesota Press, 1993).

12. For example, see Ellen W. Schrecker, *No Ivory Tower: McCarthyism and the Universities* (New York: Oxford University Press, 1986).

13. On the legacy of anti-intellectualism in the United States, see Richard Hofstadter, *Anti-Intellectualism in American Life* (New York: Alfred A. Knopf, 1970).

14. It is important to note that the "end of ideology" thesis advocated by Daniel Bell in the fifties and the more recent "end of history" position put forth by Francis Fukuyama legitimizes the assumption that with the death of ideology and the victory of capitalism and liberalism, public intellectuals— especially those who proclaim themselves as social critics—can be dismissed as either hopelessly ideological or simply unpatriotic.

15. Janny Scott, "Thinking Out Loud: The Public Intellectual Is Reborn," *New York Times,* August 9, 1994, B1, B4.

16. Three excellent sources documenting the assault on public cultures in the United States include: Kevin Phillips, *The Politics of Rich and Poor* (New York: Harper Perennial, 1990); and Donald L. Barlett and James B. Steele, *America: What Went Wrong?* (Kansas City: Andrews and McMeel, 1992); Ruth Sidel, *Keeping Women and Children Last* (New York: Penguin, 1996).

17. One social critic who makes this point in order to interrogate the complexity, limits, and possibilities of what it means to be a public intellectual is Jeffrey Williams. See Jeffrey Williams, "Spin Doctorates: From Public Intellectuals to Publicist Intellectuals," *Voice Literary Supplement,* November 1995, 28-29; "Edward Said's Romance of the Amateur Intellec-

tual," *The Review of Education/Pedagogy/Cultural Studies* 17, no. 4 (1995): 385-95.

18. This argument is taken up and brilliantly developed in Stanley Aronowitz and William Di Fazio, *The Jobless Future* (Minneapolis: University of Minnesota Press, 1994), especially chapter 8, "A Taxonomy of Teacher Work," 226-63. See also Jeffrey Williams, "Spin Doctorates: From Public Intellectuals to Publish Intellectuals."

19. Cited in the *Boston University Faculty Council Bulletin*, February 19, 1996, 35.

20. Carol Becker, "The Artist as Intellectual," *The Review of Education/Pedagogy/Cultural Studies* 17, no. 4 (1995): 386.

21. Lewis Menand, "Lost Faculties," *The New Republic* July 9 and 16, 1990, 39.

22. One example of this can be found in the abundant critiques on critical pedagogy by Gerald Graff. Graff consistently cites work by critical-pedagogy theorists that is either outdated or grossly misrepresented. If one were to rely on Graff's analysis of Paulo Freire's work, it would appear that the only book Freire wrote was *Pedagogy of the Oppressed*. Needless to say, Freire has written over 15 books since that publication and consistently has revised his pedagogical theories. Graff ignores the later work. See Gerald Graff, *Beyond the Culture Wars* (New York: Norton, 1992); *Teaching the Conflicts* (New York: Garland Publishing, 1994).

23. Mariam Hansen, "Early Cinema, Late Cinema: Permutations of the Public Sphere," *Screen* 34, no. 3 (autumn 1993): 206.

24. Fish is indifferent to the connection between the dynamics of professionalism and the forms of petty careerism and academic jealousy it often legitimates. William S. Sullivan captures an element of this connection in the following commentary:

> Shorn of the shared loyalty to public purposes that characterizes genuine professionalism, there can be no secure recognition for individual achievement, leaving individuals anxious, having to validate their self-worth through comparative ranking along an infinite scale of cleverness, wealth, and power.

In William S. Sullivan, "Experts and Citizens: Rethinking Professionalism," *Tikkun* 11, no. 1 (1996): 17.

25. Stuart Hall, "Race, Culture, and Communications: Looking Backward and Forward at Cultural Studies," *Rethinking Marxism* 5, no. 1 (1992): 11.

26. Ibid., 11, 18.

27. I examine this issue in detail in Henry A. Giroux, *Disturbing Pleasures* (New York: Routledge, 1994), especially the chapter "Schools for Scandal: Whittling Away at Public Education," 47-66.

28. Stanley Fish, *Professional Correctness: Literary Studies and Political Change* (New York: Oxford University Press, 1995), 118.

29. Ibid., 119.

30. Ibid.

31. The real irony is that the most public of all politicians, Ronald Reagan, made institutional education one of the primary battle sites for extending the political culture of the right. See Evan Watkins, *Throwaways: Work Culture and Consumer Education* (Stanford: Stanford University Press, 1993).

32. Fish, 125.

33. Leon Wieseltier, "All and Nothing at All," *The New Republic*, March 6, 1995, 36.

34. I take up this issue in Henry A. Giroux, *Schooling and the Struggle for Public Life* (Minneapolis: University of Minnesota Press, 1988); Henry A. Giroux, *Fugitive Cultures: Race, Youth, and Violence* (New York: Routledge, 1996).

35. Edward Said, *Representations of the Intellectual* (New York: Pantheon, 1994).

36. Becker, 388. Another crucial issue raised by Becker, one that haunts most of the writing on public intellectuals, is the question of why only writers are considered in the pantheon of what it means to be a public intellectual. Clearly, this is a modernist hangover that refuses to legitimate other forms of cultural production such as painting, dance, video production, etc. and the significance the cultural workers who engage in these different forms of re-presentation of images and other performative practices might have for shaping public life.

37. Paul Bove, "The Function of the Literary Critic in the Postmodern World," in *Criticism Without Boundaries*, ed. Joseph A. Buttigieg (Notre Dame: University of Notre Dame Press, 1987), 38.

38. Howard Zinn, *The Politics of History* (Boston: Beacon Press, 1970), 14-15.

39. Said.

40. John Brenkman, "Race Publics: Civic Illiberalism, or Race After Reagan," *Transition* 5, no. 2 (summer 1995): 8.

41. Ibid.

42. William M. Sullivan, "Experts and Citizens: Rethinking Professionalism," *Tikkun* 11, no. 1 (1996): 16. For a more radical view of linking critical work to professionalism, see Williams, 397-410.

43. Cornel West cited in Henry Louis Gates, Jr., and Cornel West, *The Future of the Race* (New York: Knopf, 1996), 71.

44. For a critique of this issue, see Patricia Williams, *The Alchemy of Race and Rights* (Cambridge: Harvard University Press, 1991), especially "The Death of the Profane," 44-51.

45. Adolph Reed, "What are the Drums Saying, Booker? The Current Crisis of the Black Intellectual," *Village Voice,* April 11, 1995, 35.

46. Paul Desruisseaux, "Foundations are Asked to Help Train and Encourage New Leaders," *The Chronicle of Higher Education,* April 30, 1996, 19.

47. The "discovery" corresponds with a reality more complex than the media suggest. The category, black public intellectual, should not suggest an ideologically specific group of black intellectuals, as is generally the case in media coverage. In fact, those black intellectuals who have received the most recognition are characterized by a wide range of ideological and political positions extending from left-progressive and liberal to conservative and nationalist. Moreover, the distinctiveness of the group is taken up around the signifiers of class, race, and numbers. As Gerald Early points out, "Indeed, for the first time in African-American history there is a powerful, thoroughly credentialed and completely professionalized black intellectual class. . . . [Moreover] today's generation of black intellectuals has been well publicized; in fact, it has access to the entire machinery of intellectual self-promotion." Gerald Early, "Black Like Them," *New York Times Book Review,* April 24, 1996, 7.

48. See, for example, Gina Dent, ed., *Black Popular Culture* (Seattle: Bay Press, 1992).

49. Michael Berube, "Public Academy," *The New Yorker,* January 9, 1995, 80.

50. Ibid., 75.

51. Ibid.

52. Ibid., 79.

53. Ibid. Joy James makes a similar point in her work *Transcending the Talented Tenth: Black Leaders and American Intellectuals* (New York: Routledge, 1970).

54. Robert S. Boynton, "The New Intellectuals," *The Atlantic Monthly* (March 1995), 56.

55. Ibid., 70.

56. Ibid.

57. Boynton's modernist hangover and dislike of critical work that addresses "popular" issues is made more visible in a theoretically incompetent and politically conservative critique of cultural studies that soon followed his piece on black intellectuals. See Robert S. Boynton, "The Routledge Revolution," *Lingua Franca* 5, no. 3 (April 1995): 24-32.

58. On the black public sphere, see the wide-ranging essays in "The Black Public Sphere Collective," *The Black Public Sphere* (Chicago: University of Chicago Press, 1995).

59. Toni Morrison, *Playing in the Dark: Whiteness and the Literary Imagination* (Cambridge: Harvard University Press, 1992).

60. Eric Lott, "Public Image Limited," *Transition* 5, no. 4 (winter 1996): 68, 54.

61. One of the worst examples of this type of critique can be found in Leon Wieseltier, "All and Nothing at All," *The New Republic,* March 6, 1995, 31-36. In a highly selective and grossly simplified reading, Wieseltier concludes that after reading all of Cornel West's works, he finds that "They are almost completely worthless." 31. One can only assume that West's popularity rests solely with the hype of the media culture and the cult of celebrity.

62. Cited in Michael Hanchard, "Intellectual Pursuit," *The Nation,* February 19, 1996, 22.

63. For an excellent analysis of this issue, see Brenkman, 4-36; see also the excellent history of black intellectuals in William M. Banks, *Black Intellectuals: Race and Responsibility in American Life* (New York: Norton, 1996).

64. This position is addressed and criticized in Michael Kilson, "Wilentz, West, and the Black Intellectuals," *Dissent* 43 (winter 1996): 93-94. Two of the most famous critiques of this position can be found in Harold Cruse, *The Crisis of the Negro Intellectual* (New York: Morrow, 1967) and Richard Wright, *Native Son* (New York: Grosset and Dunlap, 1940).

65. On the issue of the black public sphere, see Houston A. Baker, "Critical Memory and the Black Public Sphere," *Public Culture* 7, no. 1 (1994): 3-33; Banks; and Jerry Gafio Gates, *Heroism and the Black Intellectual* (Chapel Hill: University of North Carolina Press, 1994).

66. Toni Morrison cited in Joy James, "Politicizing the Spirit," *Cultural Studies* 9, no. 2 (1995): 220.

67. Cornel West, "The Dilemma of the Black Intellectual," in *Keeping Faith* (New York: Routledge, 1993), 85. Originally published in *Cultural Critique* no. 1 (fall 1985), 1-13.

68. Karl Marx, *The Eighteenth Brumaire of Louis Bonaparte* (New York: International Publishers, 1963), 18.

69. I think that Stanley Aronowitz is on target in arguing that while black public intellectuals such as Gates and West have been able to open up a new public space, this space also is severely limited. Aronowitz writes: "For example, intellectuals such as Henry Louis Gates, Jr. and Cornel West may be feted, celebrated, and made visible in white liberal circles. However, they are still racially coded; their pronouncements have weight only as information about the other America. And their intellectual work, however compelling, must not only maintain race as a frame of reference, but must be tacitly aware of the limits of discourse. When, and if, African American intellectuals step out of the identity codes to speak of class issues like the recent General Motors strike, international relations, or, heaven forbid, the viability of current political arrangements they, like Martin Luther King who publicly opposed the Vietnam War, risk marginalization, let alone excoriation." Stanley Aronowitz, "Race and Racism: A Symposium," *Social Text* no. 42 (September 1995): 38.

70. David Theo Goldberg, "Whither West? The Making of a Public Intellectual," *The Review of Education/Pedagogy/Cultural Studies* 16, no. 1 (1994): 5.

71. I take the phrase "hopeful hope" from the insightful article by Nell Irvin Painter. See Nell Irvin Painter, "A Different Sense of Time," *The Nation*, May 6, 1996, 38-43.

72. Joy James, *Transcending the Talented Tenth*, 156-57.

73. Williams.

74. Reed, 35. Reed attempts to backtrack on this attack in a more recent response to criticisms of his piece on black intellectuals. The latter commentary simply dismisses a number of black intellectuals for not

taking a critical stand on Louis Farrakhan's role in the Million Man March and his recent global tour to a number of dictatorships in Africa. Reed says little about his role as a public intellectual speaking for a newspaper and readership that is largely white. He simply assumes that because other black scholars differ with him on the significance of Farrakhan's role in national politics, they do not hold themselves accountable for the positions they take as public intellectuals. Hence, Reed implicitly proclaims himself as the only black public intellectual with integrity. See Adolph Reed, "Defending the Indefensible," *Village Voice*, April 23, 1996, 26.

75. Lewis Gordon, "Race and Racism: A Symposium," *Social Text* no. 42 (September 1995): 44.

76. Salman Rushdie, "In Good Faith," in *Imaginary Homelands: Essays and Criticism 1981-1991* (London: Penguin Books, 1991), 394.

77. Homi Bhabha, "Black and White and Read All Over," *Artforum* 34 (October 1995): 17.

78. Ibid., 114.

79. Brenkman, 8.

CHAPTER 6

1. Howard Winant, *Racial Conditions* (Minneapolis: University of Minnesota Press, 1994), xii-xiii.

2. *Boston Globe,* October 5, 1995, 1.

3. Headline appeared in the *New York Times,* October 4, 1995, A, 1, 6.

4. Headline from *Atlanta Journal,* October 4, 1995, 1.

5. Of course, there were many blacks who did not celebrate the O. J. Simpson acquittal. But this seemed to be lost even on some of the trial's most astute critics. For example, Adolph Reed, Jr. in commenting on the highly publicized response by blacks who cheered the verdict suggested that all blacks unequivocally supported the decision. His comments in this regard come off as arrogant and harsh. He writes: "Black celebration of the verdict reflects the desperation and lack of credible options that currently define black politics. This is a pathetic travesty of racial independence and autonomy, betraying the celebrants' naive blindness to the fact that they, far

more than O.J., have been set up to act out a part that at best mistakes empty symbolism for political victory and at worst is a pretext for declaring black people unworthy as citizens." Is it possible that not all blacks cheered or that some applauded because they thought that justice had come their way from a system that generally turned its back on blacks? Adolph Reed, Jr., "We Were Framed," *Village Voice,* October 24, 1995, 24.

6. *Time,* October 16, 1995, 42, 44.

7. For an excellent analysis of the imbalance in the media, see Frederic M. Biddle, "After Verdict, TV Coverage Largely Goes With the Winners," *Boston Globe,* October 4, 1995, 24. For one of the few analyses of the white racism informing the reaction to the Simpson verdict, see Alexander Cockburn, "Beat The Devil," *The Nation,* October 30, 1995, 491.

8. "Verdict on America," *The Nation,* October 23, 1995, editorial, 450.

9. Marshall cited in Peter S. Canellos, "Acquittal is Said to Stir Voices of Racial Discord," *Boston Globe,* October 5, 1995, 1, 30.

10. Cited in Richard Goldstein, "O.J. Can You See?," *Village Voice,* October 17, 1995, 18.

11. Bob Grant cited in Ibid., 19.

12. Dinesh D'Souza, "The Racialization of America," *Boston Globe,* October 5, 1995, 12.

13. These figures have just been released by the Justice Department in a study conducted by the Sentencing Project. Cited in Fox Butterfield, "More Blacks in the 20's Have Trouble with the Law," *New York Times,* October 5, 1995, A18.

14. *The Economist,* October 21, 1995, editorial, 19.

15. For a powerful defense of the jury's verdict, see Barbara Amiel, "L.A. Law a Triumph for Justice," *Sunday Telegraph,* London, October 8, 1995, 38; see also various comments by the jurors themselves in Wire Services, "Juror Confident About Decision," *Boston Globe,* October 4, 1995, 21, 26; Adam Pertman, "Simpson Jurors Saw Police Plot," *Boston Globe,* October 5, 1995, 1, 30. In the latter article, Pertman's headline appears to be completely at odds with statements made by the individual jury members.

16. For an insightful analysis of this issue, Brenkman. On the issue of the race card, see A. Leon Higginbotham, Jr., Anderson B. Francois, and Linda Y. Yueh, "The O.J. Simpson Trial: Who Was Improperly 'Playing the Race

Card'?" in *Birth of a Nationhood,* eds. Toni Morrison and Claudia B. Lacour (New York: Pantheon, 1997), 31-56.

17. Ellen Goodman, "An Apartheid of Perceptions," *Boston Globe,* October 5, 1995, 19.

18. Eileen McNamara, "The Jury Chose Not to See, Not to Listen," *Boston Globe,* October 4, 1995, 24.

19. Ellen Willis, "Rodney King's Revenge," *Village Voice,* October 17, 1995, 29.

20. This is not to deny the important connection between spousal abuse and homicide but to argue that the charge that the predominantly black jury ignored such a connection often is expressed at the expense of examining the broader issue of how the prosecution failed to establish the credibility of a police department that seem to bungle and taint everything it touched in this case.

21. Reed; see also Nikol G. Alexander and Prucilla Cornell, "Dismissed or Banished? A Testament to the Reasonableness of the Simpson Jury," in Morrison and Lacour, 57-96.

22. Cited in Cockburn, 491.

23. On the issue of race and whiteness, see Morrison; Ruth Frankenberg, *The Social Construction of Whiteness* (Minneapolis: University of Minnesota Press, 1993); David Theo Goldberg, *Racist Culture: Philosophy and the Politics of Meaning* (Cambridge: Basil Blackwell, 1993); Ella Shohat and Robert Stam, *Unthinking Eurocentrism* (New York: Routledge, 1994); and David Roediger, *Towards the Abolition of Whiteness* (London: Verso Press, 1994).

24. Richard Dyer, "White," *Screen* 29, no. 4 (autumn 1988): 49.

25. Amiel, 39.

26. Goldstein, 20.

27. Jack E. White, "A Double Strand of Paranoia," *Time,* October 9, 1995, 39.

28. Goldstein, 18.

29. Eric Foner, "The Great Divide," *The Nation,* October 30, 1995, 488.

30. For an excellent analysis of race, politics, the media, and the O.J. Simpson trials, see the various articles in Morrison and Lacour.

31. For a theoretically rigorous and brilliant analysis of this issue, see David Theo Goldberg, *Racist Culture* (Cambridge: Basil Blackwell, 1993).

CHAPTER 7

1. Martin Luther King, Jr. "Racism and the White Backlash," *Where Do We Go From Here: Chaos or Community?* (Boston: Beacon Press, 1968), 68.

2. John Brenkman, "Race Publics: Civic Illiberalism, or Race After Reagan," *Transition* 5, no. 2 (summer 1995): 11-12.

3. Toni Morrison, "On the Backs of Blacks," *Time* 142, no. 21 (fall 1993): 57.

4. Cornel West, "America's Three-Fold Crisis," *Tikkun* 9, no. 2 (March 1994): 42.

5. Charles Murray cited in Jason DeParle, "Daring Research or 'Social Science Pornography'?" *New York Times Magazine,* October 9, 1994, 50.

6. Adolph Reed, Jr., "Looking Backward," *The Nation,* November 28, 1994, 660.

7. Brenkman, 19.

8. Newt Gingrich, "Renewing America," *Newsweek,* excerpt, July 10, 1995, 26.

9. Ibid.

10. Dole cited in Derrick Jackson, "The Rhetoric of Job Freeze Out," *Boston Globe,* July 7, 1995, 15.

11. Clinton cited in Ibid.

12. Jim Naureckas, "Racism Resurgent: How Media Let *The Bell Curve's* Pseudo-Science Define the Agenda on Race," *Extra* (January/February, 1995), 12.

13. For a superb analysis of the shoddy scholarship and neo-Nazi sources of scholarship used in *The Bell Curve,* see specific articles in Sections I and II in Russell Jacoby and Naomi Glauberman, eds., *The Bell Curve Debate* (New York: Times Books, 1995), especially Leon J. Kamin, "Lies, Damned Lies, and Statistics," Adam Miller, "Professors of Hate," and John Sedgwick, "Inside the Pioneer Fund." Also, see Jeffrey Rosen and Charles Lane, "Neo-Nazis! Scouring *The Bell Curve's* Footnotes," *The New Republic,* October 31, 1994, 14-15; Michael Lind, "Brave New Right: Conservatism's Lunge Into Its Darker Past," *The New Republic,* October 31, 1994, 24-26. For a superb blasting of the basic assumptions underlying Herrnstein's and Murray's scientific views on measuring and quantifying intelligence, see Stephen Jay Gould, "Curveball," *The New Yorker,* November 28, 1994, 139-49; and Claude S. Fischer, Michael Hout, Martin Sanchez Jankowski, Samuel Lucas, Ann

Swidler, and Kim Voss, *Inequalilty By Design: Cracking the Bell Curve Myth* (Princeton: Princeton University Press, 1996).

14. Edward S. Herman, "The New Racist Onslaught," *Z Magazine* (December 1994), 24.

15. "The Issue," *The New Republic,* October 31, 1994, editorial, 9.

16. Malcolm W. Browne, "What is Intelligence and Who Has It?" *New York Times Book Review,* October 16, 1994, 45.

17. Ellen K. Coughlin, "Class, IQ, and Heredity," *The Chronicle of Higher Education,* October 26, 1994, A12.

18. For a devastating critique of the scholarship that attempts to give legitimacy to *The End of Racism,* see David Theo Goldberg, "Wedded to Dixie: Dinesh D'Souza and the New Segregationism," *The Review of Education/Pedagogy/Cultural Studies* 18, no. 3 (1996), 231-65.

19. Cited in Joseph Barnes, "The Right & Racist Chic," *Z Magazine* (December 1995), 55.

20. For an excellent critique of the data used by Richard Herrnstein and Charles Murray to connect inherited differences in intelligence with inequality, see Claude S. Fischer, Michael Hout, Martin Sanchez Jankowski, Samuel R. Lucas, Ann Swidler, and Kim Voss, *Inequality by Design: Cracking the Bell Curve Myth* (Princeton: Princeton University Press, 1996).

21. Lee Siegel, "For Whom the Bell Curves," *Tikkun* 10, no. 1 (January/February 1994): 28.

22. Brenkman, 4.

23. Richard J. Herrnstein and Charles Murray, *The Bell Curve* (New York: The Free Press, 1994), 520.

24. Cited in Naureckas, 13.

25. Cited in Jeffrey Rosen and Charles Lane, "Neo-Nazis," *The New Republic,* October 31, 1994, 14.

26. Cited in Adam Miller, "Professors of Hate," in Jacoby and Glauberman, 169.

27. Naureckas, 20.

28. John Tierney, "A San Francisco Talk Show Takes Right-Wing Radio to a New Dimension," *New York Times,* February 14, 1995, A10.

29. Ibid., A10.

30. Jonathan Freedland, "The Right Stuff," *Guardian* London, January 31, 1995, T2.

31. Ibid.

32. Both citations are from Herrnstein and Murray, 521.

33. Freedland, T2.

34. For a critical discussion of this issue, see Henry A. Giroux, "Playing the Race Card: Media Politics and the O. J. Simpson Verdict," *Art Papers* 6 (November/December, 1995): 14-19.

35. Farai Chideya, "Letters," *New York Times Book Review*, November 13, 1994, 75.

36. David Cole, "'Hoop-Dreams' and Colorblindness," *Legal Times*, January 23, 1995, 43.

37. Ana Puga and Michael Kranish, "Supreme Court Rejects Black-Majority District," *Boston Globe*, June 30, 1995, 1.

38. For an analysis of the racism at work in the immensely popular and critically acclaimed film, *Pulp Fiction*, see Henry A. Giroux, *Fugitive Cultures: Race, Youth, and Violence* (New York: Routledge, 1996).

39. Cited in Naureckas, 15.

40. Herrnstein and Murray, 532.

41. Ibid., 526.

42. Jean Toomer, *Cane* (1923; reprint. New York: Perennial Classics, 1969), 163.

43. Herrnstein and Murray, 533.

44. Ibid.

45. David Theo Goldberg, *Racist Culture* (London: Basil Blackwell, 1993), 37.

46. Herrnstein and Murray, 534.

47. Nathan Glazer, "The Lying Game," *The New Republic*, October 31, 1994, 15-16.

48. Ibid., 16.

49. Ibid.

50. Gingrich, 26, 27.

51. Michael Sandel cited in Thomas L. Friedman, "Buchanan for President," *New York Times*, November 24, 1995, Op-Ed, E9.

52. Gingrich, 27.

53. Vaclav Havel, "The Responsibility of Intellectuals," *New York Review of Books*, January 22, 1995, 37.

54. Ibid.

55. King, Jr., 191.

INDEX